Tri-State

GARDEN GUIDE

TOP 10

Edited by Mike MacCaskey, Lynn Ocone,
and the Editors of Sunset Books

Photography by Susan A. Roth

MENLO PARK · CALIFORNIA

SUNSET BOOKS, INC.

VICE PRESIDENT, GENERAL MANAGER: Richard A. Smeby
VICE PRESIDENT, EDITORIAL DIRECTOR: Bob Doyle
PRODUCTION DIRECTOR: Lory Day
OPERATIONS DIRECTOR: Rosann Sutherland
RETAIL SALES DEVELOPMENT MANAGER: Linda Barker
EXECUTIVE EDITOR: Bridget Biscotti Bradley
ART DIRECTOR: Vasken Guiragossian
SPECIAL SALES: Brad Moses

STAFF FOR THIS BOOK

PROJECT EDITORS: Mike MacCaskey and Lynn Ocone
SUNSET BOOKS SENIOR EDITOR: Marianne Lipanovich
COPY EDITOR: Vicky Congdon
ASSOCIATE EDITOR: Carrie Dodson Davis
RESEARCH: Lynne Steiner
DESIGN & PRODUCTION: Linda M. Bouchard
ILLUSTRATORS: Lois Lovejoy, Erin O'Toole, Jenny Speckels
MAP DESIGN AND CARTOGRAPHY:
Reineck & Reineck, San Francisco
PREPRESS COORDINATOR: Danielle Javier
PROOFREADER: Michelle Pollace
INDEXER: Mary Pelletier-Hunyadi

COVER: Photograph by Susan A. Roth.
Design by Vasken Guiragossian.

10 9 8 7 6 5 4 3 2 1
First printing January 2005
Copyright ©2005 Sunset Publishing Corporation,
Menlo Park, CA 94025.
First edition. All rights reserved, including the right
of reproduction in whole or in part in any form.

Library of Congress Control Number: 2004109880.
ISBN 0-376-03790-3.

Printed in the United States.

For additional copies of *Tri-State Top 10 Garden Guide*
or any other Sunset book, call 1-800-526-5111 or visit
our web site at **www.sunsetbooks.com**.

CONSULTANTS

Wayne Cahilly is a graduate of the New York Botanical Garden School of Professional Horticulture and the Manager of NYBG's Institutional Mapping Department. He is the owner of Cahilly's Horticultural Services, a consulting business, and resides in New Jersey.

David Chinery is a Senior Educator at the Rensselaer County office of Cornell's Cooperative Extension. He lives in Castleton-On-Hudson, New York.

Ruth Rogers Clausen is the co-author of the classic book *Perennials for American Gardens,* and is currently horticulture editor of *Country Living GARDENER* magazine. She lives in Westchester County, New York.

Marcia Eames-Sheavly is a vegetable, fruit, and herb specialist with the Department of Horticulture at Cornell University. Also an avid home gardener, she lives with her family in upstate New York.

Judy Glattstein is a bulb expert, garden consultant, garden writer, and a regular instructor at the New York Botanical Garden. She lives in western New Jersey.

Anne O'Neill, an internationally recognized rose expert, is the curator of the Cranford Rose Garden at the Brooklyn Botanic Garden. She resides in Brooklyn, New York.

Nancy Seaton has worked at the Brooklyn Botanic Garden for 10 years, most recently as Curator of the Warm Temperate Pavilion, but also as a continuing education instructor. She is currently pursuing a Masters degree in Landscape Studies at Bard Graduate Center. She lives in New York City.

PHOTOGRAPHERS

UNLESS OTHERWISE NOTED, ALL PHOTOGRAPHS ARE BY
SUSAN A. ROTH.

LAURA DUNKIN-HUBBY: 240; JERRY PAVIA: 92; NORM PLATE: 230;
SOUTHERN PROGRESS CORPORATION: 208; THOMAS J. STORY: 238;
TOM WOODWARD: 5, 16, 38, 60, 110, 112, 114, 138, 184

GARDEN DESIGN

BEN PAGE ASSOCIATES: 167
DIANE BEDRICK: 230
CONNIE CROSS: 11, 105, 111, 139, 267
RICK DARKE: 133
PETER AND JOAN FRACCALVIERI: 47 (RIGHT)
KRISTIN HORNE: 14, 17, 108, 210, 258
LANDCRAFT ENVIRONMENTS: 7 (BOTTOM), 13, 40, 260
PAULA MANCHESTER: 9, 15
ROBERT WARREN AND BOB LANE: 213 (BOTTOM)

Contents

Gardening in the Tri-State Region

It's like the honk of migrating geese, an infallible sign of the season. Late in November every year my Southern and Californian gardening friends start to call, and sooner or later the conversation turns to sympathy about the weather that I, a Tri-Stater, am enduring. What my friends never seem to grasp is that it's the rich variety—in weather, topography, soils, and vegetation—that makes gardening in our part of the world so rewarding.

Think what the changes bring us. I gardened for several years in Texas, and I remember how my neighbors had to store tulip bulbs in their refrigerator for many weeks so that they would produce flowers when finally planted out in the garden. Many of the most rewarding garden perennials, shrubs, and trees also require a period of cool and dormancy to flourish, which our region provides. What's more, our long, cool springs prolong the blooming season not only of the hardy bulbs but also of the early-flowering perennials and annuals. And though we may curse the summer showers that disturb our picnics, the regularity and abundance of our precipitation means that irrigation, if you choose your plants skillfully, is not a major or constant task.

OPPOSITE PAGE: *A chorus of colorful evergreen and deciduous azaleas framing brick-paved steps is at its spring best in this Long Island garden. The evergreen dwarf Alberta spruce anchors the display, and forget-me-nots provide blue accent color.*

In terms of natural floras, our region lies at a crossroads. We can successfully grow azaleas from the Appalachians, and conifers native to the north woods. Long Island still boasts the remnant of a natural prairie, the Hempstead Plains; meadow gardens thrive here. With some attention to site and drainage, you can grow outdoors alpine plants that even British gardeners can only maintain in the protection of a greenhouse. Woodland gardens are another obvious choice for our naturally forested region.

Having said all of this, it's important to recognize that certain special challenges are also native to the Tri-State region. Gardening success depends on understanding these, and on knowing the plants that can cope with them.

CHALLENGES AND OPPORTUNITIES

My mother was my first gardening teacher, and my classroom was a couple of acres along the western bank of the Hudson River. Over millennia the river had deposited a deep layer of loam on our property, and I took that magnificent soil for granted. I've since found that a heavy clay, often filled with rocks, is more likely to be the Tri-Stater's lot. Perhaps you are as lucky as Mother was and is. If not, remember that clay, though it is sticky, heavy, and poorly drained in its natural state, also tends to be a fertile soil. Dig in several inches of compost or sphagnum peat to break up the clay, and you are well on your way to good gardening soil. The deeper you dig in such amendments, the deeper your plants' roots will be able to penetrate, and the better able they will be to find their own water and nutrients. Old-time gardeners in our region used to "double-dig," digging and mixing in amendments to a depth equal to two lengths of the spade's blade.

If such a transformation seems beyond you, or there's immovable rock or ledge close to the surface, consider building raised beds. This approach will also ensure good drainage. Alternatively, you can follow the example of a very patient but also very successful gardener I know. He begins a new bed by cutting the grass in the designated area very short in early spring. He next covers the bed-to-be with a layer of newspaper several sheets thick and finally covers the paper with a couple of inches of compost.

He keeps the bed moist and lets the earthworms do the soil mixing for him. When the weather has warmed, he plants a crop of annuals, just cutting holes through the newspaper and compost mulch with his trowel. Every fall thereafter, he spreads another inch of compost over the bed, and its soil just gets better and better. I've tried this method myself and found that it not only spared my back, it also produced a bed that was virtually weed free. Within a year of establishing the bed, the soil was adequate for planting perennials.

OPPOSITE PAGE: *Pinkshell azalea, an Appalachian native, thrives throughout our region.* RIGHT: *Creeping phlox spills out of a raised bed under Harry Lauder's walking stick (Corylus).* BELOW: *This stylized meadow features fountain and feather reed grasses. In back is pink 'Turkestanica' salvia and yellow loosestrife (Lysimachia).*

This no-dig method, incidentally, highlights one of the advantages enjoyed by Tri-State gardeners. In southern climates, any humus in the soil rapidly decays in areas that are irrigated or kept naturally moist. In our cooler climate, the effect of any compost or peat we add to the soil is much longer lasting.

WEATHER

Another challenge common to the Tri-State region is summers that combine heat with humidity. These conditions set the stage for many fungal diseases, such as the black spot that plagues hybrid tea roses and crabapples in our region. The best way to deal with this climatic challenge is to select plants that are naturally

disease resistant, and to keep your garden as open and airy as possible so that breezes sweep away excess humidity and fungal spores.

Our winter temperatures help to keep populations of insect pests in check, but they can still spell doom for tender plants. Keep in mind that the winter lows in coastal regions are likely to be, on average, 20 degrees higher than those in the inland hills a few miles away.

Snow cover helps to insulate perennials—as a student at the New York Botanical Garden, I remember spending winter days shoveling snow onto the rock garden to protect the alpine plants. We did that because even though those plants could tolerate the low temperatures, they, like many other hardy perennials, could *not* cope with the changeable nature of our winter weather. Not uncommonly, our winter temperatures rise well above freezing during the day, only to plunge down again toward single digits at night. Any way you can temper these sudden swings will greatly reduce winter damage to your plants.

The most effective way to accomplish that, as I learned as a student, is to insulate the plants so that they stay evenly cool throughout the winter months. Covering dormant perennials with a blanket of evergreen boughs provides excellent protection (when I'm feeling thrifty, I may delay this cover-up until

OPPOSITE PAGE, TOP AND BOTTOM: *One of the classic evergreen shrubs of the Tri-States is mountain laurel* (Kalmia)*, a native. It's hardy in winter, showy in spring.* ABOVE: *Japanese flowering apricot waxes and wanes through the seasons while white-barked Himalayan birch and Japanese cryptomeria stand sentry.*

December 26th, when there are unsold Christmas trees for the taking).

A prolonged winter (one that lasts several days and melts the frost out of the soil) is, however, an opportunity for the gardener with broad-leaved evergreen shrubs like hollies and rhododendrons. The expansive leaves of such plants are more vulnerable to dehydration from dry winter winds than the needles found on most evergreens. Seize the opportunity of a thaw to water those broad-leaved shrubs.

Of course, the very best way of protecting your garden against winter weather is to fill it with reliably hardy plants, ones that are well adapted to the vagaries of the Tri-State climate. This is one of the main criteria by which the plants featured in this book were chosen.

WOODLAND GARDENING

Given that so much of the Tri-State region is or once was forested, it shouldn't surprise you that a woodland garden may be your best landscaping option. If your lot is shaded with big trees, finding enough sunlight for a conventional flower border will be a challenge. But the dappled light such a canopy provides is ideal for many woodland wildflowers and shrubs.

Before planting, though, spend some time exploring your property. You'll want to identify aesthetic assets, such as the best trees or a handsomely rugged rock outcropping. You can then plan your path or paths to provide a voyage of discovery from attraction to attraction. At the same time, while you explore, look for the niches that will suit different kinds of plants. The north side of that rock outcrop, for example, is likely to be ideal for ferns, which typically prefer a spot protected from the sun's heat.

Woodland plants are often quite specific in their cultural needs, which is why it's wise, initially, to experiment with small plantings in the various niches. When you've learned which species do well in a specific area, you can build those populations.

If your lot is wooded, you may have to remove some trees and shrubbery to make passage possible. You may also want to open some gaps in the canopy overhead to allow sunlight to penetrate to the woodland floor. This step will greatly increase the variety of plants your woodland garden can support and can even enhance the growth of such shade-lovers as hostas. Think of this stage of the garden's creation as one of sculpture. You are carefully carving out the spaces. There's an incidental benefit too: the wood chips produced in disposing of your cuttings make an ideal surface for a woodland path.

If your lot is shady but not actually wooded, you can interplant shrubs strategically among the existing trees to create a more authentic woodland look. In placing these additions, try to plan for a succession of bloom—native witch hazel for early spring bloom can be followed by azaleas and mountain laurels. These shrubs make a striking background for the native woodland wildflowers such as bloodroot, trilliums, and trout lilies. Early spring-flowering bulbs like daffodils find a suitable niche along woodland edges; because they complete much of their growth before the trees leaf out, they will persist in spots that would be too shaded for ordinary perennials. Astilbes, however, do thrive in shaded spots, and they can provide the woodland garden with floral color on into summer. The endlessly varied foliages of hostas furnish another source

ABOVE: *A stylized woodland garden includes a variety of cultivated plants to create a woodland feel. Lilacs and weigela shelter cut-leaf Japanese maple, 'Goldmound' spirea, columbine, and hosta.*
OPPOSITE PAGE: *Columbine, Biedermeier strain.*

of summertime interest in the shady woodland garden. Fall, with the coloring of the leaves, will be this area's most spectacular season, though a winter walk to enjoy the outline of the bare branches and the fruits of such native shrubs as the winterberry holly can be, in its own way, just as rewarding.

A word of encouragement, but also of warning, about woodland gardens: They provide ideal habitat for many kinds of wildlife. Various species of birds, for example, will find food in the berries and nesting opportunities among the branches. Deer, however, may also want to take up residence and use this area as a base from which to make raids upon your plantings. Deer find hostas particularly irresistible. If, like many gardeners, you find this prospect unacceptable, you should plan to enclose your woodland area with one of the relatively inexpensive but sturdy plastic nettings sold for deer fencing. If woven through the trees, such a barrier disappears from view at a few yards' distance.

WATER

Having boasted of how well watered our region is, I must also admit that the precipitation doesn't always come as regularly as we gardeners could wish, or in the precise quantities we need at that point in the gardening year. Newly planted trees and shrubs will need weekly watering during rainless periods throughout their first growing season. Flower beds and borders will produce far more blossoms if they receive similar treatment. This is especially important for summertime beds of annuals. Remember that in our climate, the growing season for such plants is relatively short. If annuals are to make a good showing, you must encourage fast growth and that involves supplying ample moisture. In particular, flowers in containers or hanging baskets are likely to need daily irrigation in midsummer, unless you have planted in a container with a built-in water reservoir.

The frequency with which you water will, naturally, depend partly on what you plant. Succulents, such as the sedums, are highly drought resistant and will survive a dry spell that would thoroughly traumatize or even kill an impatiens. Likewise, where you place a plant affects its water needs. Plants that thrive in sun or shade will, typically, need more water when located in a sunny spot than in a shady one. This guideline is especially true of large-leaved plants like hostas because it is through the leaves, for the most part, that a plant loses water.

A factor that also affects your garden's need for irrigation is the quality of the soil, and in the Tri-State region that characteristic can change dramatically over a distance of just a few miles. Garden soil near the shore is likely to be sandy and especially dry, whereas inland a heavy clay soil may have difficulty absorbing water. In either case, digging in a large dose of compost or some other organic material will benefit the garden, helping the sandy soil to retain water and improving the structure of the clay soil so that it absorbs water more readily.

PESTS

Without a doubt, the most devastating garden pest of the Tri-State region these days is the white-tailed deer. An average-sized adult deer may devour up to 15 pounds of greenery daily; this means that a single visit can negate years of your careful cultivation. Many efforts have been made to identify ornamental plants that are unpalatable to deer, but the fact is that if they are truly hungry, these animals will browse almost any plant.

Protect individual shrubs or flower beds by enclosing them in the plastic netting that is sold at garden centers to keep birds off of berry bushes and fruit trees. Commercially available spray-on repellents will also help to discourage deer, but these products must be reapplied conscientiously. However, in areas as densely populated with deer as many of our suburbs are, enclosing the garden with fencing of a type designed to bar deer is the only really effective solution.

The worst insect pests of this region are, typically, those accidentally introduced from abroad, especially from northeastern Asia, which has a climate and flora similar to our own. Japanese beetles and the gypsy moth both came from that region, as did the woolly adelgid that has devastated our native hemlocks. Selecting plants that are naturally resistant to insects, such as marigolds, is the easiest way to cope with such problems. Too much fertilizer or compost can increase your pest problems, as such treatment encourages soft growth that insects find especially attractive. Pests also tend to hone in on plants stressed by drought.

Finally, though the warm days followed by cool nights of our early summer and fall may be ideal for human comfort, the combination encourages the spread of powdery mildew. This fungal disease attacks a wide range of garden plants, spreading what looks like a white or gray powder over leaves, flowers, and fruits. It can be treated with fungicidal sprays, but prevention is better for the environment and less work for you. Avoid crowding your plants; it encourages infection. Read and respect the planting instructions on the nursery labels so that each of your plants has ample space to develop to its mature spread and height without impinging on its neighbors. Finally, set mildew-prone plants out in airy spots where the breeze can sweep away fungal spores.

AVOIDING DISAPPOINTMENT

Most gardeners learn by looking. We like to visit other gardens, grand or modest, to collect ideas about what to do and plant in our own. This tendency can be a great aid but also a pitfall, especially if you like to tour gardens when you travel far from home. It seems an obvious point, but we gardeners are prone to deluding ourselves that the phlox or rose that grows so enthusiastically in, say, an English garden, is going to behave similarly in a New Jersey suburb. This could happen, but it's more likely that if you translate literally to New Jersey from England or some other distant spot, what you create will be a source of frustration, unnecessary work, and constant expense as year after year you must replace the losses among your imported and poorly adapted plants.

OPPOSITE PAGE: *'Globemaster' allium and Allium giganteum rise above blue catmint and giant hyssop (Agastache).* RIGHT: *Soaring 'William Baffin' rose (left) echoes equally robust 'Roseum Elegans' rhododendron at peak flower on the right.*

The reality is that while it's useful to note how plants are cultivated and used in other gardens, when you seek to reproduce these effects, you should do so with plants that you know will perform well in your region and your garden. In other words, begin your self-education by learning what does well locally. When you have identified those plants, use them to assemble your palette, so to speak. Then you can start designing and deciding how you are going to paint them onto the landscape.

Reliability is the special value of the selection of plants offered in this book. All have been chosen as particularly foolproof choices for our region. If you plan a simple garden, this selection may offer every plant you need or want. If your intention is to go on to something more ambitious, these plants can provide a basic framework on which to build. They also offer a guide to what else will do well in your garden. If French marigolds (which actually originated in Mexico) like the sun-drenched flower bed along your front walk, consider expanding that planting to other annuals like zinnias or dwarf dahlias that also favor full sun and a well-drained, open situation. Similarly, if meadow phlox and black-eyed Susans are at home in your yard, you should contemplate building on this beginning with other meadow grasses and flowers. — THOMAS CHRISTOPHER

Perennials

Perennials are plants that live for more than two years, as opposed to annuals, which complete their life cycle in only one season, or biennials, which live no longer than two. In our cold climate most herbaceous (nonwoody) perennials die back to the ground when winter comes, their roots remaining dormant until longer, warmer days nudge them awake.

Perennials reproduce by dropping fertile seeds from spent flowers. Some perennials are vigorous self-sowers, and their progeny rise up every spring for years after the original plants have died. Some also reproduce themselves vegetatively by spreading underground runners, or by gradually expanding in size while the center may or may not die out.

in winter. Growing a perennial garden is a bit like conducting an orchestra; it can take awhile to get all the plants in tune, but it is gratifying when the colors and textures create a pleasing composition.

CHOOSING PLANTS

Before shopping for plants, review the perennials in this chapter and select a palette of early, mid-season, and late-blooming plants that will thrive in your garden's soil and its sun or shade conditions. Also choose plenty of annuals (see pages 38 to 59) to fill in gaps during skimpy flowering periods.

ORCHESTRATING A SHOW

The trick to designing a beautiful perennial garden is timing the different bloom periods so that you have harmonious color, especially in spring, summer, and fall. A garden of just annuals is colorful but static, whereas a well-planned perennial garden is constantly changing, even

To figure out where plants will look best and how many of each kind you need, it's

ABOVE: *Midsummer's exuberance is nowhere more evident than in a perennial border.* OPPOSITE PAGE: *Perennials such as wild sweet William, hostas, and tulips combine in this naturalistic garden.*

helpful to draw a planting plan on paper first. Think about the overall shape of your perennials. Are they tall and skinny? Round? Clumpy? Do they creep, soar, or sprawl? These traits may be more important than bloom color, as the plants themselves will be around long before and after their flowers have faded. Combine plants with contrasting shapes. Do the same with leaf texture and color.

Resist the temptation to grow one of everything. Instead, plant in groups of three or more. Repeat these groupings if you have room; repetition lends a sense of order and calm, whereas too many individual species vying for attention has the opposite effect. While it's generally wise to arrange plants with the shortest in front and the tallest in back, don't hesitate to move them around if the scheme seems boring or out of balance.

DIGGING IN

Perennials generally have long roots and need soil at least 1½ feet deep. Amend the soil with plenty of rotted organic matter such as compost, decayed leaves, aged manure, or peat moss before planting, and apply more as a mulch in spring and fall. Roots, earthworms, and microorganisms will do more soil conditioning.

Over time a plant may lose vigor, flower less, or develop a hole in its center. In that case, it's time to dig it up and split the root mass into two or more chunks before replanting. Dividing plants is a good way to expand your garden—and to make new friends. Who wouldn't be charmed by the offer of a free plant?

Pay attention to these simple tasks and water as needed, and your perennials will be trouble free—at least, my Top 10 perennials will. These plants can make even a novice look like a pro!

—RUTH ROGERS CLAUSEN

Astilbe
Astilbe

Astilbes 'Fanal', 'Deutschland', and 'Peach Blossom' bring color to a shaded bed.

Astilbe's airy flower clusters are invaluable additions to summer borders and woodland gardens. Either upright or gracefully arching, the plumes are borne on stems from 6 inches to 3 feet or taller; they are carried above clumps of handsome, fernlike green to bronze leaves. By selecting cultivars with staggered bloom times, you can enjoy flowers from late spring or early summer right through to summer's end.

Astilbes are valued for the delicate quality of their plumelike flowers and attractive foliage, and for their long bloom times from late spring through summer. Fernlike leaves are typically divided, with toothed or cut leaflets, though in some species they are simply lobed, with cut margins. Tiny white, pink, or red flowers are held in graceful, branching, feathery plumes borne on slender, wiry stems. Most plants grow 2 to 3 feet wide at maturity.

Do not deadhead (remove faded flowers) too early in the season; the spent flowers become rust colored and are attractive for several months into the winter.

Astilbes are a mainstay of shady perennial borders, although in cool-summer climates they can withstand full sun if watered adequately. Some are useful as cut flowers.

PEAK SEASON

Late spring through summer, depending on the chosen cultivar

MY FAVORITES

Astilbe × *arendsii* 'Fanal' blooms early, produces bloodred flowers on 1½- to 2½-foot stems. 'Glow' has bright red flowers and grows 1½ feet tall.

A. chinensis 'Pumila' is a late-blooming cultivar. Its stems of rose-lilac flowers are only 1 foot tall and are held stiffly above its mat of leaves. It makes a dense ground cover.

A. × *japonica* 'Deutschland' also flowers early in the season and bears 1½-foot plumes of white flowers. 'Peach Blossom' has pink flowers.

A. taquettii 'Superba' is a late flowering form that grows 4 to 5 feet tall and has bright pink-purple flowers.

A. × *thunbergii* 'Professor van der Wielan' blooms in midseason and may reach 3 feet tall. Its spikes of white flowers are loose and airy.

GARDEN COMPANIONS

Combine with bergenia, columbine (Aquilegia), hosta, meadow rue (Thalictrum), and blue star (Amsonia) in shady borders; with delphinium, globeflower (Echinops), Siberian iris, monkshood (Aconitum), and peonies in sunnier locations.

When Plant nursery-grown plants from containers in spring or fall.

Where Beds and borders shaded for part of the day, especially by deciduous trees, are ideal spots for astilbes. They mix well with other shade-loving perennials and shrubs. Where summers are cool, astilbes tolerate sunny conditions as long as the soil remains moist.

How Grow astilbes in moist but well-drained soil enriched with plenty of organic matter. Astilbes are greedy feeders and appreciate a spring application of well-rotted manure.

TLC Tall kinds are self-supporting and require no staking. When bloom production declines noticeably (usually after 3 to 5 years), it's time to divide the clumps; do the job in early spring for best results. Survival in the coldest regions depends on good snow cover; where snow cover is unreliable, apply a heavy mulch of shredded leaves.

ABOVE: *Rose-red flowers of 'Glow' shine as the name suggests.* BELOW: *'Peach Blossom' flowers are light pink with just a hint of peach, and the leaves are especially bold and shiny.*

Black-eyed Susan
Rudbeckia

Black-eyed Susan is one of the most familiar and best-loved perennials in the Tri-State landscape. Never heard of it? Think again. It's daisylike, with bright golden yellow petals surrounding a dark brown central cone, on stems that grow to about 2 feet tall. I especially like it planted in masses or with other prairie-type plants and grasses in a big, open landscape, where its dazzling color can be fully appreciated. Bees, butterflies, and American goldfinches all flock to it, so if you like to think of your garden as a habitat for wildlife, you'll love black-eyed Susan. Its sturdy stems and long-lasting flower heads make this mid- to late-summer bloomer a good cut flower as well. A late-summer shearing not only removes fading leaves and flowers but also encourages fresh growth and maybe even some reblooming. In a small garden a little goes a long way, so keep rudbeckia in check.

Rudbeckia fulgida sullivantii 'Goldsturm', named Perennial Plant of the Year in 1999, is descended from the native wild species *R. hirta*. Both are easy to grow even in clay soils and will spread—though not rampantly—and self-sow. The self-seeded off-spring of most cultivars do not maintain the same characteristics and may vary considerably from their parents.

'Goldsturm' black-eyed Susan flowers midsummer until frost.

When Plant nursery-grown plants from containers at any time, but spring is best. If planting in summer, wait for a cool, cloudy day. Water well. Seeds can be started indoors about 8 weeks before the last spring frost date, but plants from seeds do not bloom reliably their first year.

PEAK SEASON

Midsummer to fall; seed heads are interesting in winter and attract seed-eating birds.

MY FAVORITES

Rudbeckia fulgida is longer blooming and takes the heat even better than *R. f. s.* 'Goldsturm'. Its flowers are slightly smaller and the plant is generally more delicate looking.

R. nitida is sometimes called yellow coneflower; 'Herbstonne' grows to 6 feet tall and has yellow rather than gold flowers.

GARDEN COMPANIONS

All the rudbeckias work well in mixed prairie-style or meadow gardens. Try combining them with:

• New England asters
• garden phlox
• ornamental grasses such as fountain grass, feather reed grass, and switch grass

Where Choose a site in full sun with well-drained, average soil. Borders and meadow gardens are ideal; black-eyed Susan can be spectacular massed in drifts in informal areas.

How Amend the soil with organic matter before planting. Plant in groups of three, five, or more, spacing plants 1½ to 2 feet apart, depending on the cultivar. Crowding encourages fungal diseases such as leaf spot and powdery mildew. Water thoroughly and keep the soil moist until plants are established. Avoid wetting the leaves late in the day.

TLC Although sometimes listed as drought tolerant, black-eyed Susans do best with constant moisture. Once the soil has warmed, apply a 1- to 2-inch layer of organic mulch to retain moisture, improve the soil, and reduce weeds. Remove spent flowers to keep plants looking neat until toward the end of the season when you might want to leave some seed heads on for the birds to enjoy. Staking may be necessary for taller types. A winter mulch of evergreen boughs or a 6-inch layer of organic mulch, applied after the ground freezes, is valuable for new plants, and in areas without reliable snow cover, it will discourage root heaving. Be sure to keep the mulch away from the crowns of the plants as it may cause rot. Divide plants every 3 or 4 years in spring, splitting them through the crown and replanting the sections with generous spacing.

ABOVE: *Yellow-flowered R. nitida is combined here with purple Russian sage.* LEFT: *This typical clump of 'Goldsturm' shows the quantity of flowers you can expect.*

Common Sundrops
Oenothera fruticosa

These adaptable, carefree plants produce an abundance of silky, four-petaled flowers in a flattish bowl shape. Some species bloom during the day; others open as sunlight wanes in late afternoon, then close the following morning. Common sundrops, *Oenothera fruticosa* (often listed as *O. tetragona*), grow in zones 32–44. A shrubby plant 1½ to 2 feet high, it has green leaves, reddish brown stems and flower buds, and bright, clear yellow, 1½-inch-wide flowers that open in the daytime. When conditions are just right, this plant may become invasive. Mexican evening primrose, *O. speciosa* (often sold as *O. berlandieri* or *O. speciosa childsii*), succeeds in zone 33. Planted in the right spot, it's a useful garden plant, a good choice as a free-flowering ground cover—especially in difficult locations like the exposed strip of ground between sidewalk and street. Be cautious about locating it where it can advance on other plantings, though; under favorable conditions it spreads briskly by underground stems. The slender, 10- to 15-inch-tall stems bear numerous delicate 1½-inch-wide pink flowers that open in the daytime.

Flowers of 'Rosea' Mexican evening primrose open during the day, covering the ground with a cloud of pink.

When Plant nursery-grown plants from containers in spring or fall.

Where Thrives in full sun or very light shade.

How Poor to average soil is suitable for evening primroses. Avoid rich soil and fertilizer as they tend to promote leafy growth at the expense of flowers.

TLC These carefree plants are tolerant of both drought and poor soil, but they do need reasonably good drainage to do their best. To rejuvenate crowded plantings or obtain new plants, divide in early spring or root stem cuttings in spring.

TOP: Oenothera speciosa 'Rosea'.
BOTTOM: Yellow common sundrops.

PEAK SEASON
Summer

MY FAVORITES
Common sundrops (*Oenothera fruticosa*) has yellow flowers and reddish stems that bear bright green leaves. It grows 2 feet high and spreads vigorously. Look for 'Erica Robin' (1½ feet tall, blooms and foliage emerge golden yellow, then turn reddish).

Mexican evening primrose (*O. speciosa*) grows 10 to 12 inches high and blooms profusely with 1½-inch-wide rose pink flowers in summer. Flowers open in daytime, despite the common name. Stems die back after bloom, but the underground stems spread rapidly. 'Rosea' is similar; 'Siskiyou' bears light pink flowers on 8-inch plants; and 'Woodside White' (to 15 inches tall) has white blooms that fade to pale pink. Zones 32, 33.

Missouri sundrops (*O. macrocarpa*) is low growing; trailing stems reach 10 inches long, bearing soft, velvety, 5-inch leaves and showy, paper-thin, 4- to 5-inch-wide yellow goblet-shaped flowers that open in the afternoon. Large winged seedpods follow the blooms. Zones 32–37, 39, 41.

GARDEN COMPANIONS
Effective with false indigo (*Baptisia*), lychnis, and mullein (*Verbascum*).

Daylily
Hemerocallis

As a child I loved the look of orange daylilies: clusters of flowers on leafless stems (scapes) rising 3 to 5 feet above clumps of strappy leaves. My mother had a different opinion. Certainly those old-fashioned "wildflowers" *(Hemerocallis fulva)* had little in common with the elegant Oriental lilies she loved. They were available only in orange, yellow, or red; they grew from rhizomes, not bulbs; and they were "uncultured"—like the roadsides, yards, and ditches where they sprung up. Daylilies have come a long way since then, thanks to the efforts of hybridizers obsessed with creating ever-frillier petals, more color and fragrance, shorter cultivars, and some that repeat bloom. But as of yet, no one's figured out how to make a daylily flower last longer than a day.

If you're a neatness freak you may find yourself wading into the border three or four times a week with scissors. Always take care to remove the whole flower so the ugly spent bloom won't be replaced by an even uglier seed head, which will sap energy from the plant as it develops its seeds. Also remove yellowing or unsightly leaves. Give daylilies proper care and they'll flower from June to October. Protect plants from browsing deer, which are a serious problem in many areas of the Tri-State region; daylilies are one of their favorites.

'Stella de Oro' daylily adapts to life in a pot as well as in a garden. Compared with older daylilies, it is shorter and neater, and blooms longer.

PEAK SEASON

Early summer to frost

MY FAVORITES

Old but still popular hybrids include 'Hyperion' with fragrant lemon flowers on 40-inch stems, and 3-foot-tall 'Red Magic' with deep red flowers.

The newer dwarf daylilies, which grow 1 to 2 feet tall, are "everblooming" and tidy. 'Cherry Cheeks' flowers are rose red with a yellow throat; 'Happy Returns' and 'Stella de Oro' have yellow flowers. The yellow flowers of 'Black-eyed Stella' are punctuated with a dramatic dark red center.

GARDEN COMPANIONS

Daylilies shine in sunny flower beds alone, or in informal gardens where they hide the dying foliage of spring bulbs and add bright color in lightly shaded areas. They are spectacular with tall ornamental grasses, especially on informal banks where their tough roots hold the soil and reduce erosion. Bright yellow or gold daylilies complement blue-flowered plants such as: 'Bressingham Spire' monkshood (Aconitum); 'Blue Chips' bellflower (Campanula); 'Johnson's Blue' hardy geranium (Geranium); and 'Caesar's Brother' Siberian iris (I. sibirica).

When Although nursery-grown plants, can be set out in spring, summer, or fall, spring is best. If planting in summer, wait for a cool, cloudy day and water well. Plant bare-root plants in spring.

Where Choose a site in full sun or very light shade. Modern hybrids need at least 8 hours of sun for best bloom. The soil should drain well and be average to rich. Daylilies are great for mass planting, and once established they are a beautiful solution for stabilizing a slope and crowding out weeds.

Individual flowers of 'Happy Returns' (TOP) and 'Cherry Cheeks' (BOTTOM) last only one day, but plants continue producing flowers for months.

How Amend the soil with organic matter before planting. Space daylilies 1½ to 3 feet apart, depending on the cultivar. The plants spread, so give them plenty of room. Water thoroughly and keep the soil moist until plants are established.

TLC Young plants need regular watering. Once the soil has warmed, apply a 1- to 2-inch layer of organic mulch, such as compost or shredded leaves, to retain moisture, improve the soil, and reduce weeds. Remove faded flowers regularly to keep plants attractive, and cut off the bloom stalks after the last flower fades. Protect young plants for the winter with a 6-inch layer of organic mulch after the ground has frozen. Every year in early spring, lightly dig in a controlled-release or complete fertilizer or an organic equivalent, such as fish emulsion or compost. Apply it again 4 to 6 weeks later. Divide plants when clumps become crowded or begin to bloom less (typically every 4 to 6 years), either in early spring or right after they finish flowering. Be sure to protect from deer throughout the season.

Hosta

Hosta

Until I took up gardening I called all hostas "funkia," the old common name for the plainest types, which grow like weeds. These days hosta is very near the top of my favorite-plant list. And while breeders have developed cultivars vastly more varied in form and color over the years, all this improving hasn't changed the basic good nature of the genus. Hostas are still the most stoic of garden plants, unfazed by extremes of weather, content to live in the shade, and to serve as a backdrop for more spectacular plants. They can be used as fillers in the border, as edging plants, or massed as a ground cover in semi-shade; several are distinctive enough to serve as bold specimen plants. They grow and multiply without becoming invasive, their foliage remains handsome all season long, and they have but two enemies: slugs and deer.

Hostas flower spikes can be regal or quite unremarkable in appearance depending on the cultivar, but they're seldom the main attraction anyway. Mostly we grow hostas for their magnificent foliage. Leaves may be wide or slender; smooth or puckered; and either solid colored, deeply veined, variegated, or striped.

A hosta shade garden is beautiful if you combine plants with contrasting foliage colors and textures.

In August, lightly scented pale lilac flowers of 'Honeybells' rise 8 inches above the 2-foot-high clump of leaves.

TOP: *'Blue Cadet'*
BOTTOM: *'Gold Standard'*

PEAK SEASON

Late spring to fall

MY FAVORITES

Fragrant plantain lily *(Hosta plantaginea)* has large white flowers and blooms late. Look for 'Aphrodite', 'Grandiflora', or 'Royal Standard'.

H. sieboldiana is the puckered-leaf species. 'Frances Williams' is best known. It has blue-green leaves that are irregularly edged in yellow; flowers are white.

Favorite hosta hybrids

'Blue Angel' has huge, bluish leaves shaped like hearts and white flowers.

'Blue Cadet' develops low mounds of small, heart-shaped, blue-green leaves; flowers are lavender.

'Francee' has green leaves edged in white; lavender flowers.

'Gold Standard' has light green leaves that become golden, with dark green margins; pale lavender flowers.

'Honeybells' produces large light green leaves and late-blooming fragrant, lavender flowers.

GARDEN COMPANIONS

Plant with early-spring bulbs, primroses, forget-me-nots, and lily-of-the-valley, which will provide interest until the hostas emerge. Ferns, meadow rue *(Thalictrum)*, astilbes, and Solomon's seal *(Polygonatum)* are other attractive companions.

When Set out nursery-grown plants preferably in spring, but summer and fall are okay. If planting in summer, wait for a cool, cloudy day and keep moist.

Where Most hostas need partial to full shade and well-drained, rich soil. A spot with morning sun is ideal for variegated and golden-leafed cultivars; too much sun scorches the leaves. Use hostas almost anyplace in the shade garden, especially along the edges of ponds, as ground covers, and as specimen plants.

How Amend soil with organic matter before planting. Recommended spacing varies: give each plant enough room to expand to its mature size, which may take 2 to 4 years. Water thoroughly and keep the soil moist until plants are established.

TLC After the soil has warmed in spring, apply a 1- to 2-inch layer of organic mulch to retain moisture, improve the soil, and reduce weeds. Although established plants are fairly tolerant of drought, hostas prefer even moisture. Protect from slugs and deer. Cut off the bloom stalks if you find the flowers unattractive. Winter hardiness varies by species and cultivar; it is prudent to provide winter protection in colder zones, especially where snow cover is unreliable. Plants emerge rather late in spring; mark locations of plants before winter if necessary. Every year in early spring, apply a light dressing of a controlled-release or complete fertilizer or an organic equivalent, such as fish emulsion or compost. Hostas may self-sow, but they seldom come true from seed so weed out unwanted seedlings. Hostas can go for years unattended, but when they become overcrowded, lift and divide plants in early spring just as new growth emerges. Hostas are notorious for their susceptibility to slug damage; handpick the pests or use pans of beer to trap them. Cultivars with waxy leaves are slightly less susceptible. Deer tear off the emerging young leaves before they have unfurled, leaving a jagged edge; cut back damaged leaves to the ground to encourage new growth to develop.

Lungwort

Pulmonaria

Charming perennials for shady garden spots, lungworts are striking edging a bed or woodland path, or as a ground cover on a small scale. The long-stalked, hairy leaves—often attractively dappled with gray or silver and up to 1 foot long—grow mostly from the base of the plant, though some smaller leaves appear on the flower stalks as well. Drooping clusters of small, funnel-shaped, usually blue flowers are enchanting in spring, opening just before or just as the leaves emerge. After they have bloomed, remove the spent flower stems to allow plenty of room for more young leaves to grow and expand. If plants are well watered, foliage will remain ornamental through the growing season. All have creeping roots and can be used as small-scale ground covers or edgings for beds or woodland paths. Many hybrid lungworts are available, most featuring especially beautiful foliage.

Flowers of blue lungwort (Pulmonaria angustifolia) begin as pink buds but change to a rich, dark blue upon opening.

ABOVE: 'Bertram Anderson'. BELOW, CLOCKWISE FROM TOP LEFT: 'Roy Davidson'; 'Mrs. Moon'; 'Spilled Milk'; and 'Sissinghurst White'.

PEAK SEASON

Spring for flowers; throughout the season for foliage

MY FAVORITES

Bethlehem sage (Pulmonaria saccharata) has blue flowers and silver-spotted leaves. 'Pierre's Pure Pink' has bright pink flowers; 'Mrs. Moon' has large, silver-blotched leaves and light blue flowers.

Blue lungwort (P. angustifolia) has clusters of bright blue flowers that open from pink buds. 'Azurea' has sky blue flowers; 'Blaues Meer' flowers are larger and brighter blue.

P. montana (P. rubra) has light green, unspotted leaves and coral red blossoms. 'David Ward' bears rich coral flowers that enhance its foliage. Plant in shade, as the light margins are easily scorched by hot sun.

Hybrid lungworts include: 'Bertram Anderson' (deep blue flowers; foliage freckled with silver); 'Excalibur'; 'Roy Davidson'; 'Sissinghurst White' (pure white flowers and spotted leaves); and 'Spilled Milk' (solid silver white foliage, lightly flecked with green).

GARDEN COMPANIONS

For a long spring display, interplant with groups of bulbs such as daffodils, summer snowflakes (Leucojum), and grape hyacinths, or with pansies or violas.

When Plant nursery-grown plants from containers in spring or fall.

Where Excellent at the front or in borders or along the edges of paths, especially in light shade. Lungwort is also useful as a ground cover under shrubs, including azaleas, witch hazels, and fothergillas. Avoid full sun, as the large leaves droop during the heat of the day. Well-drained soil amended with plenty of moisture-holding organic matter, such as compost or shredded leaves, is ideal.

How For a ground cover planting, set the individuals about a foot apart so that they knit together quickly. Specimen plants can be spaced more widely. Keep plants well watered; stress caused by drought encourages the growth of mildew, which mars the leaves, especially in humid climates.

TLC Lungworts need soil that drains well but is always moist. Incorporate plenty of organic matter before planting. Choose a spot in partial to full shade; the leaves tend to wilt in full sun even if the soil is moist. Crowded clumps will need dividing after several years. Do the job in early autumn, and be sure to keep the newly planted divisions well watered. Protect from slug damage, especially in rainy spring weather.

Meadow Phlox
Phlox

Mainstays of the summer perennial garden for generations, the tall phloxes display large clusters (trusses) of flowers in a wide range of colors. *Phlox maculata* and *P. carolina* bloom in early summer, with 15-inch-long trusses of blooms that range in color from white through all shades of pink to magenta, often with a contrasting eye. The plants grow 3 to 4 feet high and have shiny green, somewhat mildew-resistant foliage. Nurseries offer named selections (which may be assigned to either species).

Garden phlox *(P. paniculata)* also has flowers in a spectacular range of colors and combinations, but it is more susceptible to mildew.

'Bright Eyes' phlox mixes it up with 'Zebrinus' Japanese silver grass (Miscanthus), red flowering tobacco, and 'Blue Charm' speedwell (Veronica).

When Set out container plants in spring or fall, or anytime during the season.

Where Best where summers are cool to mild; in hot-summer regions, phlox fare better with more shade and a mulch of rotted leaves or compost to help keep their roots cool and moist.

How Plant in well-prepared soil enriched with plenty of organic matter, and water regularly throughout the growing season.

TLC The tall phloxes need regular attention to remain healthy and attractive. They send up numerous stems in each clump, but it is wise to cut out all but the strongest four to six of these to improve air circulation and reduce the likelihood of mildew. Remove spent flower heads routinely; this may encourage a second flush of bloom from side shoots—and, in the case of garden phlox, will prevent seed production and a resultant crop of volunteer seedlings (they generally bloom purplish pink, regardless of the color of the parent plant). To maintain vigor, divide clumps every 2 to 4 years in early spring. Mildew can be a problem, but can be combatted with regular sprays of a fungicide. Protect from browsing deer.

PEAK SEASON
Summer

MY FAVORITES
'Alpha' has rose pink flowers accented with a darker eye.

'Miss Lingard' has large panicles of pure white flowers. It is sometimes known as the "wedding phlox."

'Rosalinde' is dark pink.

Other excellent cultivars

'Bright Eyes' has pale pink flowers accented with a crimson eye.

'David' is pure white, fragrant, and disease resistant.

'Nora Leigh' sports cream-edged foliage and pale pink flowers with a darker eye, late in the season.

Low-growing phloxes that are well worth growing include spring-blooming sweet William phlox *(P. divaricata)* with blue, white, or lavender flowers on 12- to 15-inch stems.

Creeping phlox *(P. subulata)* also produces spring bloom. It has sharp needlelike leaves and small flowers in white, lavender blue, and a range of pinks and reds.

GARDEN COMPANIONS
Tall phloxes are effective with bugbane *(Cimicifuga),* delphinium, beebalm *(Monarda),* obedient plant *(Physostegia virginiana),* and balloon flower *(Platycodon grandiflorus).*

TOP: *Sweet William phlox.*
ABOVE: *'Miss Lingard'.*
BELOW: *Wild sweet William masses as a ground cover.*

Montauk Daisy

Chrysanthemum nipponicum

Come fall this simple daisy—and namesake of the Long Island town where it's essentially wild—blooms, blooms, and then blooms some more. Few perennials are better where salt-laden wind is a fact of life.

While the name "chrysanthemum" is often associated with fall-blooming mums, the genus also includes favorite spring- and summer-flowering daisies, among them the brightly colored painted daisy, marguerite, feverfew, the perennially popular Shasta daisy.

The Montauk daisy, a fall bloomer, looks like a large, rounded, shrubby Shasta daisy, up to 3 feet tall, with a dense mass of shiny, succulent-looking, bright green leaves. The plants are well branched and become woody at the base as the season progresses. When the weather cools, the lower leaves often turn yellow and drop, leaving unsightly "ankles" on the plants; it is prudent to plant lower-growing companions at their feet to camouflage this problem. In late fall, long-stemmed, 2½-inch-diameter white flowers with green centers cover the plants. They are seldom bothered by pests and diseases.

These easy-to-grow perennials deserve a wider audience. Their tolerance of exposed, full-sun positions and salt spray make them first-rate perennials for seaside gardens; their late bloom time takes the garden well into the fall when there is little else to provide fresh flowers.

In mild climates, the plants may not die down naturally; they are best cut back in spring but only when the new growth starts to appear.

When Set out plants in spring or summer.

Where Select a site in full sun with average, well drained soil. Montauk daisy is very tolerant of coastal environments including salt spray and fast-draining sandy soil. (The common name "Montauk" is from the Montauk region of Long Island, where it has naturalized.)

How Plant in well-prepared soil enriched with plenty of organic matter, and water regularly throughout the growing season.

ABOVE: *Tiny daisy flowers of feverfew.*
BELOW: *Red-flowered painted daisy.*

TLC Cut back after bloom through zone 39, but in zones 40 and 41 do not disturb plants until they put on strong new growth in spring; at that time, you may cut back partway to maintain compactness. If the plants are not killed to the ground over the winter, cut them nearly to the ground in early spring to control their height. Where the season is long, encourage bushy growth by pinching off the tips of new stem growth whenever it is 3 to 5 inches long. Continue pinching as needed until July 4th. Where the season is short, excessive pinching may result in the plants not blooming until after the first frost. Divide older plants in the spring every 2 to 3 years.

PEAK SEASON
Fall until frost

RELATED SPECIES
Painted daisy (*Chrysanthemum coccineum*) grows 2 to 3 feet high and in late spring bears long-stemmed single daisies in pink, red, or white.

Marguerite (*C. frutescens*) is a tender perennial and is popular as a summer container plant in our region. Its flowers are yellow, white, or pink.

Feverfew (*C. parthenium*) is smaller (usually 1 to 2 feet tall), and produces many small flowers. Leaves are noted for a peppery scent.

Shasta daisy (*C. × superbum*) is a common and popular perennial; many cultivars are available.

GARDEN COMPANIONS
Montauk daisies are especially attractive with other late perennials such as Russian sage (*Perovskia atriplicifolia*), tender sages including brilliant blue *Salvia guaranitica* and Mexican bush sage (*S. leucantha*). They also make fine companions for ornamental grasses such as fountain grass (*Pennisetum*), blue oat grass (*Helictotrichon sempervirens*), and the taller *Miscanthus* species. Brilliant blue plumbago (*Ceratostigma plumbaginoides*) is effective as a ground cover beneath Montauk daisies. (See page 96 for more about plumbago.)

Sage
Salvia nemerosa

With some 700 species, the sages constitute an enormous—and enormously useful—genus of plants, ranging from the ubiquitous flaming red annual (see page 54) to low, flowering ground covers, to the culinary herbal sage and its many close relatives. Russian sage *(Perovskia atriplicifolia)* is no relation but probably got its common name from the silvery leaves and blue flower spikes that resemble those of some salvias.

While many plants have a brief moment of glory and then fizzle out, *Salvia nemerosa* doesn't need much care to retain its good looks well into fall. It is extremely hardy and disease resistant. It doesn't mind long dry spells and isn't finicky about soil. The whole plant can be sheared back to the new growth at the plant's base if dry weather or high winds damage the older leaves. The flowers attract butterflies and hummingbirds.

I depend on the perennial 'May Night' to keep my very public boulevard garden looking respectable. This narrow strip of earth is subjected to car fumes, pet wastes, road salts, occasional trampling by passersby, and blazing sun.

Bees and butterflies will crowd around 'Blue Hill' and its spikes of pure blue flowers that bloom from June until frost.

When Nursery-grown container plants can be planted in spring, summer, or fall, but spring is optimum. If planting in summer, wait for a cool, cloudy day and water well.

Where This sage requires a site in full sun with average to rich soil. Good soil drainage is important, especially in winter. Avoid windy sites. Use salvias in mixed borders or mass plantings.

How Amend the soil with organic matter before planting. Plant in groups of three, five, or more, spacing plants 1½ to 2 feet apart, depending on the variety. Water thoroughly and keep the soil moist until plants are established.

TLC Once the soil has warmed in spring, apply a 1- to 2-inch layer of organic mulch to retain moisture, improve the soil, and reduce weeds. If you want bushier, more compact plants, pinch off the growing tips when plants are 6 inches tall. Deadheading will extend the bloom time. Apply a 6-inch layer of winter mulch after the ground freezes to protect the crown. Every year in early spring, apply a controlled-release or complete fertilizer or an organic equivalent, such as fish emulsion or compost. When older plants begin to die out in the center, divide them in early spring. Mature plants are drought tolerant, but they do best with a consistent moisture supply. Good air circulation helps prevent mildew, which can be a problem.

TOP: 'May Night'. MIDDLE: 'East Friesland'.
BOTTOM: 'East Friesland' showing a combination of fresh and faded flower spikes.

PEAK SEASON

Summer to fall

MY FAVORITES

'Blue Hill' ('Blauhugel') is noted for its clear blue flowers, though it is not as robust as other cultivars.

'May Night' (also known as 'Mainacht'), named Perennial Plant of the Year in 1997, has spikes of deep blue flowers 1½ to 2 feet tall that fan out from clumps of gray-green leaves and bloom throughout the summer if deadheaded. After the flowers fade, attractive reddish purple bracts are left behind.

'East Friesland' also grows to 1½ feet and has deep purple flowers.

GARDEN COMPANIONS

This salvia's vertical flower spikes are the ideal complement to full, mounding plants. Try combining it with:

- 'Powis Castle' artemisia and 'Silver Mound' angel's hair (*A. schmidtiana*)
- Cheddar pink (*Dianthus gratianopolitanus*)
- hardy geraniums
- lady's-mantle (*Alchemilla*)
- ornamental grasses, especially fountain grass (*Pennisetum*)

The blue-indigo of *S. nemerosa* is the perfect foil for the dwarf, lemon yellow daylily 'Stella de Oro' and the creamier yellow 'Moonshine' yarrow (*Achillea*), which has broad, flat flowers and silvery foliage.

35

Upright Sedum
Sedum

If I had to choose one plant to give a beginning gardener, it would be *Sedum* 'Autumn Joy', a hybrid of *S. spectabile* and *S. telephium*. It teaches two important lessons: that foliage and shape are just as important as flowers, and that a handful of reliable performers planted in groups of three or more makes a garden, whereas one of everything makes a mess.

In late summer, the purple leaves of 'Vera Jameson' sedum contrast with the rose pink flowers.

With their resilient beauty, upright sedums anchor a garden as well as any clipped shrub, bringing out the best in showier plants and keeping the peace among them. 'Autumn Joy' is attractive in spring, when its fleshy leaves poke up through the soil; in midsummer, when its pale green broccoli-like heads slowly age to the color of a fine claret, and even in winter, when its still-intact but now russet-colored seed heads look charming under caps of pure white snow. While in bloom, these "work horse" plants are magnets for nectar-seeking butterflies. Occasionally sedums are bothered by aphids but are otherwise disease free.

Like all sedums, including the creeping ground covers, the upright sedums are succulents. They can get along with little water, and less care.

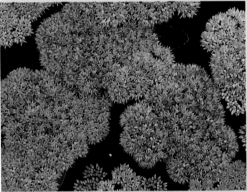

Sedum 'Autumn Joy' moves through each season with charm and character: spring (top), summer (middle), and winter (bottom).

PEAK SEASON
Midsummer to late fall

MY FAVORITES
Sedum 'Autumn Fire' is an improved 'Autumn Joy' with more robust heads of flowers. Height is 1 to 2 feet.

S. kamtschaticum 'Variegatum' grows to just 6 inches tall, bearing flashy white-edged leaves and striking yellow flowers in early summer.

S. spectabile 'Stardust' and 'Iceberg' have white flowers, and grow 18 inches high.

S. telephium 'Matrona' has shiny, wine red stems, deep gray leaves, and pale pink flowers. Height is 1 to 2 feet.

S. 'Vera Jameson' is upright but low-growing (to 9 inches). The color of its magnificent foliage defies description; imagine blue tinged with plum and a hint of green. The foliage sets off rose pink flowers that open in early August.

GARDEN COMPANIONS
Plant with
- black-eyed Susan (Rudbeckia)
- dwarf fountain grass (Pennisetum alopecuroides 'Little Bunny')
- feather reed grass (Calamagrostis × acutiflora)
- red-berried creeping cotoneaster (C. adpressa) for winter interest
- sages (Salvia)
- spurge (Euphorbia)

When Plant nursery-grown plants from containers in spring or summer. If you are planting in summer, wait for a cool, cloudy day and water well.

Where Choose a planting site in full sun with average to rich soil. Good soil drainage is important, especially in winter. Sedums will tolerate poor, dry soils better than wet soils, which can lead to root or crown rot. Use sedums in mass plantings, meadow gardens, rock gardens, or mixed borders.

How Amend the soil with organic matter before planting. Plant in groups of three, five, or more, space larger sedums 1½ to 2 feet apart, and smaller ones 6 to 9 inches apart. Water thoroughly and keep the soil moist until plants are established.

TLC Once the soil has warmed, apply a 1- to 2-inch layer of organic mulch to retain moisture, improve the soil, and reduce weeds. Sedums seldom require additional fertilizer; the stems tend to become lanky and flop if they have too much nitrogen. If it seems that the plants are stunted from lack of fertilizer, apply a light dressing of a balanced fertilizer such as 5-5-5, or an organic equivalent at spring cleanup time. Most come through our winters just fine without protection. Cut plants back to the ground in late winter or early spring, after you and the birds have enjoyed their attractive seed heads all winter. Divide plants in early spring if they become crowded.

Annuals are the lighthearted, no-commitment plants that make gardening fun and exciting. Every year they offer new opportunities to reinvent your gardens and window boxes with new plants. What's more, annuals such as cosmos, flowering tobacco, and verbena blend perfectly in a perennial border or vegetable garden and will provide flowers all summer until frost, something the more highly regarded perennials and shrubs can't do.

As their name implies, annuals are ephemeral. They germinate, flower, and die in a single growing season. Of course annuals often defy our categories, since many of our annuals are perennials in warmer regions.

PLANT SELECTION

There are hundreds of wonderful annuals that grow well in the Tri-State region. My aim is to get you started with a diverse selection. The annuals shown and described on the next few pages are for sun and shade and and express a diversity of color and form. Use this list to launch your own living experiment in texture, color, and fragrance.

The best annuals fill gaps and add lively color just when it's most needed, early summer through fall, when many perennial plants and shrubs remain static after spring flowering. Annuals with unusual leaf form and foliage color can greatly enhance the beauty of flowering plants by offering subtle or striking contrast.

It is exquisite torture to try and choose my favorite plants. In addition to their good looks, of the following 10 annuals have been selected primarily for their cultural ease and availability. Cultivars of a species vary greatly, as gardeners quickly learn by careful reading

of nursery catalogs and, most importantly, by trial and error.

PLANTING

Buy annuals as small plants or start them from seed. If buying plants, look for dense, fresh foliage and remove flowers and the top one-third of leggy plants to promote a fuller form. Also look for a healthy root system that is neither too small nor bursting out of the pot.

Many annuals are very easy to grow from seed, but avoid planting too early. Before sowing directly in the garden, check the seed packet and follow the instructions. Many common annuals are tropical, so they resent early planting. Incorporate organic material such as compost or leaf mulch as you plant, or prepare the soil beforehand by tilling in the amendments.

MAINTENANCE

Most annuals will tolerate dry soil for short periods, but supplemental water is usually needed, especially at planting time. Water plants thoroughly once or twice a week or as needed. Mulch beds with chopped leaves or similar material to retain moisture, control weeds, and

ABOVE: *Annuals include: tall, pink* Cleome, *yellow* Cosmos sulphureus *(right), blue* Verbena bonariensis *(left), and orange marigolds.* OPPOSITE PAGE: *Close-up of 'Carved Ivory' zinnia.*

improve the soil. Encourage branching by pinching tip growth to a lower set of leaves or buds on the stems. This method also works to rejuvenate a tired, end-of-the-season plant.

At planting time, use a controlled-release fertilizer that will last all season, or fertilize every 2 weeks with your favorite liquid fertilizer.

Annuals work hard to produce flowers and seeds. By removing faded flowers, or deadheading, you thwart the plant in its seed-making effort, and energy is directed into producing more flowers. Some annuals can be prolific self-sowers if they are left unchecked, which is either a delight or a nuisance, depending on how you feel about a particular plant popping up everywhere.

—NANCY SEATON

Coleus

Solenostemon scutellerioides

Coleus is an old-fashioned annual that is being rediscovered by a new generation of gardeners, and for a very simple reason. It is one of the most colorful and reliable plants to grow in a shade garden, where variations of green dominate. Many forms are easy to find now that the coleus revival is nearly a decade old.

Green and dark brown 'Inky Fingers' coleus is combined here with purple-leaved spiderwort (Tradescantia 'Purple Heart') and purple 'Million Bells' Calibrachoa.

Coleus is as popular today as it was in the Victorian era, when hothouse plants first became widely available to gardeners. It is a trouble-free, easy foliage plant that comes in enough sizes, shapes, and shades to please almost anybody. Distinct patterns of isolated colors have been developed, which are much different from the calico effect of magenta, white, green, and maroon on the coleus of my youth. Nurseries have even started creating small topiary "trees" with some of the fine-leafed cultivars.

Easy to grow, showy, and versatile: Today's coleus is a desirable annual indeed.

PEAK SEASON

Plants look good from planting
until frost.

MY FAVORITES

There are so many coleus cultivars
that naming favorites feels slightly
futile. Still, here are some that I've
grown, and will grow again.

'Alabama Sunset' is orange-red over
a chartreuse background.

'Inky Fingers' has petite, fingered
leaves of green and dark brown, each
one showing a distinct pattern.

'Pallisandra' has dark maroon leaves
that create either a shadow in the
garden, or a sobering anchor for the
wild colors of your other annuals.

'Sunset' is orange-red in the center
blending to dark red; leaf edges are
outlined in yellow.

'The Line' is chartreuse but with a
dark maroon rib down the middle of
each leaf.

GARDEN COMPANIONS

Coleus looks good with other tropical foliage plants such as caladium
(see page 212), and the shade-loving
flowering tobacco (see page 44).
The intense blue of amethyst flower
(*Browalia americana*) mixes nicely
with 'The Line' coleus, lighting up
a dark corner.

ABOVE: *Chartreuse 'The Line' coleus.*
RIGHT: *'Sunset', a crimson red hybrid coleus.*

When Coleus is a tender
tropical plant, so wait until
the beginning of June, once all
threat of cold weather is past,
to set plants into the ground.

Where Dappled shade is
best. Deep shade decreases
vigor and too much sun causes
sunburn. Similarly, plants need
moist soils, as their juicy stems
and generally broad leaves
suggest. This said, coleus is in
every other way a very adaptable plant.

How Buy plants or grow them from cuttings. The latter is
notoriously easy—coleus will root in a glass of water on the
windowsill. Or, stick 3- to 4-inch cuttings in builder's sand, and
keep moist. Plants will usually form roots within two weeks. If
nursery plants are tall and leggy, either pinch back to a lower
set of leaves, or bury the plant deeper in the ground.

TLC Water well and fertilize regularly. Deadhead flowers
when they appear. (I happen to like the flowers—a spike
of blue, sage-like blossoms—but removing them keeps the
leaves healthier.)

41

Cosmos
Cosmos bipinnatus

Cosmos deservedly hold a place as one of the more beloved annuals for their graceful habit and the animated movement of their pretty flowers in a slight breeze. They evoke cottage gardens, even when found on a rooftop garden in the city. Their simplicity is the epitome of easy summer days.

Each blossom is from 1 to 3 inches wide and has a central tuft of yellow stamens. Lavender, soft pink, and white are the prevailing colors, but strong, saturated rosy red and a range of hues from magenta through purple are also available to perk up an otherwise pastel palette. Newer strains even offer bicolor combinations. Plants are lacy and almost transparent, thanks to the finely divided, filigree leaves. Height varies between 1 and 4 feet, depending on the particular strain.

Cosmos deliver a nonstop floral show that can start in late spring and will extend into fall. If you let the late-summer flowers set seed, you'll have volunteer plants next year. And if you're lucky, you might see goldfinches feeding on the seeds in the meantime.

Pumpkin orange Cosmos sulphureus will add a blast of bright color to sunny corners of your garden.

PEAK SEASON

Flowering starts in early summer and continues until frost.

MY FAVORITES

The Sensation strain offers the full range of cosmos colors on plants that grow to 3 to 4 feet tall; selections include crimson red 'Dazzler' and red-centered pink 'Radiance'. The mixed-color Versailles strain grows to 3½ feet tall, bearing flowers on long, strong stems.

Plants of the mixed-color Sonata strain reach just 2 feet tall. Flowers of the novelty Seashell strain have quilled petals that look like slender cones; plants grow to 3 feet high.

Plants with multicolored blossoms include 4-foot 'Candystripe' (white and rose) and the 2-foot 'Picotee' (white petals edged in red).

The related species, *Cosmos sulphureus*, offers warm, luminous colors in yellow, orange, and red. The Bright Lights and Klondike strains can reach 4 feet tall; 'Polidor' and 'Dwarf Klondike' grow to 1½ feet.

GARDEN COMPANIONS

Good plants to combine with cosmos include:

- ornamental sage (*Salvia* 'Cardonna')
- peony (*Paeonia lactiflora*)
- catmint (*Nepeta* × *faassenii*)
- gaura (*Gaura lindheimeri*)

ABOVE: *'Seashells'*. TOP RIGHT: *'Early Sensation'*. MIDDLE RIGHT: *'Sonata White'*. BOTTOM RIGHT: Cosmos sulphureus.

When Sow seeds directly in the garden, or plant seedlings from cell-packs in spring as soon as danger of any frost is past. Plant them once and you'll have plants return year after year from their own seeds.

Where Cosmos thrive in full sun and in all climates. Average, well-drained soil is sufficient for good performance.

How Make a hole as deep as the plant's rootball. Remove the seedling from its container, and gently loosen roots that are tightly wound. Set the plant into the hole so that the top of the rootball is even with the soil's surface. Fill in with soil, then water.

TLC You'll need to water cosmos throughout the growing season—but just moderately. Tall plants may need staking in order to remain upright.

Flowering Tobacco
Nicotiana

Flowering tobacco has few peers as far as cultural ease and luminous beauty in shady situations. The sweet evening fragrance of *N. alata* and the ghostly appearance of its night-opening flowers make it the perfect annual for those of us who, like me, are away during the day and often enjoy our gardens at dusk. Their perfume is delightful and carries quite a distance. White-flowering varieties are more effective in the night garden than deeper colors, which tend to disappear.

Do not be mistaken, however, as many forms of flowering tobacco happily flower during the day and weave sinuously amongst other garden plants. Whereas many other plants look like interlopers in the woods, flowering tobacco is well suited to ferns and the like. Plants tolerate degrees of shade, but prefer dappled light.

And for some added value, hummingbirds and moths are attracted to the flowers.

The perfume of Nicotiana langsdorfii is light, but it is one of the best types of flowering tobacco for cutting and enjoying indoors. It grows anywhere from 3 to 6 feet high.

PEAK SEASON

Flowering starts in summer and continues until the first hard frost.

MY FAVORITES

Nicotiana alata 'Grandiflora' has the strongest, most penetrating scent. Flowers are white, star shaped, and tubular; plants grow to about 3 feet. 'Lime Green' flowers are chartreuse and less fragrant; plants are about 2 feet tall; similar 'Havana True Lime' flowers are pale green on plants about 15 inches high.

N. langsdorfii has small chartreuse bell-shaped flowers and blue anthers. It's perfect for blending strong colors, acting much like a foliage plant. It has no noticeable scent.

N. × *sanderae* is a shorter hybrid with denser flower spikes and a more narrow range of colors, mostly pink shades and whites. Plants grow to 10 inches.

N. sylvestris is the aristocrat of the group, growing easily to 4 feet, and in rich soil, to 6 feet. Pendulous, tubular white flowers cluster atop the tall stalk. Intensely fragrant and striking in the evening.

GARDEN COMPANIONS

Shade-garden plants, such as hosta (see page 26), as well as woodland ferns couple easily with flowering tobacco.

When Flowering tobacco is a tropical South American native and flourishes in the summer. Plant after all threat of frost has passed. It is also extremely easy to grow from seed and a promiscuous self-seeder—once planted, you will have many years of return.

LEFT: *Tall* Nicotiana sylvestris *has large, sticky leaves.* RIGHT: *Fragrant flowers of* N. sylvestris.

Where Plants need light shade and moist, fertile soil.

How Loosen the soil to a depth of 10 to 12 inches and work in 2 to 3 inches of compost or other organic matter. Seeds need light to germinate, so don't bury them. Lightly scratch them into surface of soil. Sow in place in late spring and thin seedlings so they are 8 to 12 inches apart; space the larger *N. sylvestris* further apart, to 18 inches. This spacing will look too far apart initially, but the more elbow room they have, the fuller the plants will grow.

TLC To renew plants at the end of July, prune the entire flower stalk to its base to promote fresh growth for the end of the season. I like tall plants for their movement, and I usually take my chances by not staking, and I have often suffered the consequences with blown-down plants. *N. sylvestris* in particular may require staking. The bright green basal rosettes of foliage on this species are a little sticky, like the foliage of its relative, petunia, which makes deadheading a messy affair.

Impatiens
Impatiens walleriana

Impatiens are just about the easiest plants to grow and are among the most reliable annuals for summer color in shade. These are not the graceful movement makers of the garden, which are my first loves, but I admire them nonetheless. They thrive in most conditions, including dense shade. They bloom constantly without deadheading, will double in size if fertilized, and never seem to get disease. Blooms are so prolific that the structure of the plant is obscured by the crown of bright flowers from early summer to a heavy frost. Impatiens grow equally well in pots and in the garden and fill spaces between other plants with its flowers.

Impatiens walleriana is a native of central Africa and loves heat. Before plant breeders came up with varieties that could stand a little chill, it was confined to the greenhouse or solarium. Imagine: impatiens a hothouse rarity! But it now thrives outdoors as an annual in our warm summer gardens and is consistently among the top-selling plants in North America. In the process, the plants seem to be getting tougher. I have seen impatiens blooming in Manhattan around Thanksgiving, and thriving in situations sunnier than I thought possible. Such is their vigor.

'Super Elfin Mix' fills a shady bed with color.

LEFT: *'Deco Rose' has good long-season performance.* RIGHT: *Impatiens edge a perennial bed.*

PEAK SEASON

Flowering starts in early summer and continues until frost.

MY FAVORITES

The Super Elfin strain is a garden-center staple with large flowers and a very tidy habit. Flower colors include white, pink, salmon, lavender, and red. There are many other popular strains: Firefly, 6 inches high, is the smallest, and Bruno and Pride, at 16 inches high, are the tallest.

Related species

The New Guinea hybrids are available in a slightly wider range of colors, including yellow, and generally are best displayed in containers.

Rare but extremely easy to grow and very sweet is *Impatiens zombiensis,* a delicate pink-flowered form that reseeds. It grows to 6 inches high; flowers are about ½ inch across.

I. balfourii and *I. glandulifera* are two other species that are easy to grow from seed if you can find them. Both are taller, make fewer flowers, and look something like the related native plant, jewelweed (*I. capensis*).

GARDEN COMPANIONS

Combine more than one color. The flowers—for some metaphysical reason—never clash, and combined they create a sizzling array of hues.

When Plant impatiens outside after all danger of frost has passed, on a cloudy day if possible to reduce transplant shock. Plants are readily available in nursery pots in spring, but they can be started from seeds sown indoors 10 to 12 weeks before the last frost date. Seeds need light to germinate, so press them just into the surface of the planting medium. Germination takes 2 to 3 weeks.

Where Plant in partial to full shade in fertile, well-drained soil. Impatiens are great for edging a pathway or planting in masses under large shade trees. This is the number-one choice for containers in the shade. New Guinea impatiens grow best in full sun to very light shade.

How Space plants 6 to 12 inches apart in the ground, closer in containers. Lightly fertilize with a controlled-release fertilizer after planting.

TLC Impatiens are truly low maintenance. The plants require no deadheading or pinching. They do need plenty of water, especially during the heat of summer. Plants will respond well to regular fertilizing.

Marigold
Tagetes

Many gardeners turn their noses up at the mention of marigolds, as I once did. So it may be appropriate to remind those who require a pedigree of good taste that the grande dame of horticulture herself, Gertrude Jekyll, incorporated marigolds into her planting schemes. She was a magnificent gardener who scientifically approached the optical effects flower colors have upon one another. She found that the sunshine spectrum of marigolds is a joyful relief from overly precious pinks and blues of flower borders. Marigolds have gusto.

African *(Tagetes erecta)* and French *(T. patula)* marigolds are neither from Africa nor France. Both are from Mexico. African marigolds are sturdy and large, with 2- to 3-inch flower heads in a range of yellows and oranges. French marigolds are short (below 1 foot) and offer darker colors, including a rich mahogany. Two of my new favorite cultivars are *T. erecta* 'Cempoalxochitl' and 'Moonlight', both of which carry single flowers on a shrublike armature of foliage. Perfect, miniature marigolds exist too, in *T. tenuifolia*, complete with fine, ferny foliage that is quite unmarigold-like.

Marigolds are also the flowers used in celebrations of the Day of the Dead in Mexico, and in wedding celebrations in India. So put your assumptions in a drawer and celebrate this glorious flower like the rest of the world. Think of Oaxaca as you gaze upon your carefree marigolds. But don't stay too close, because their fragrance can make you dizzy.

PEAK SEASON

Early summer and lasts until frost

MY FAVORITES

Among African marigolds, the Climax strain offers mixed colors on 3-foot plants; the Odorless strain is slightly shorter and the leaves lack the typical marigold scent. 'Moonlight' has a single, creamy flower head that seems to glow in the evening atop a 2- to 3-foot-tall plant. 'Cempoalxochitl' becomes a 4-foot-high shrub and is loaded with deep cadmium flowers; it requires support. In the 16- to 24-inch range are the mixed-color strains Galore, Jubilee, Lady, and Perfection.

Typical French marigold strains are Aurora, Hero, and Sophia; Bonanza and Janie are a bit shorter with smaller blossoms. Flowers are 2½ inches across on 1-foot-tall plants.

Mixed-color strains of Triploid hybrids are Nugget, Trinity, and Zenith; plants can reach 12 inches high.

Signet marigolds (T. tenuifolia) include 'Lemon Gem', a very sweet plant with fine foliage and the tiny single and bright yellow flowers.

GARDEN COMPANIONS

Combine marigolds with:

- mealycup sage (Salvia farinacea)
- chili pepper (Capsicum annuum)
- parsley (Petroselinum crispum)

OPPOSITE PAGE: *African marigolds have ball-like flowers.* ABOVE: *Coppery French marigolds.* RIGHT: *This low-growing marigold has red-orange flowers.*

When Plant marigolds as soon as all danger of frost is past. You'll find them available in cell-packs and 4-inch pots at the appropriate time in spring.

Where Sun, sun, sun! To stay so bright and sunny, they must have full sun.

How Start from seedling transplants or seeds. The latter cost less, are relatively large and easy to handle, and will readily germinate. Keep the soil moist until you see leaves emerge, and your seedlings become nice little plants. If you start with seedlings from the nursery you'll be limited to what it has on hand.

TLC Marigolds are drought tolerant once established, but benefit from water and applications of dilute fertilizer every other week. Stake tall varieties. Deadhead regularly. Shear the signet marigolds (T. tenuifolia); deadheading individual flowers would take forever. Many annuals tire as the season nears its close, and marigolds are no exception. To get the best look for the longest time, continue to fertilize until you must remove the entire plant.

Pansy
Viola × wittrockiana, V. cornuta

Pansies are one of the first plants I grew as a child, with the assistance of my mother, and they remain a favorite. Pansies are beloved by many for their cute flowers, or "faces"—the blotches of color suggesting human eyes, nose, and mouth. I especially love the smaller pansies that look like Johnny-jump-ups *(Viola tricolor)* for the sheer number of blossoms they produce and their small stature, though they unfortunately lack a face.

'Sorbet Sunny Royale' is like a supercharged Johnny-jump-up.

Pansies are hybrids of several *Viola* species, with slightly larger flowers and more complex, richer colors. Their flowers come in solid hues from white to almost black (including purples, reds, yellows, oranges, blues, and pinks), as well as bi- or tricolored patterns. They have a light, pleasing fragrance and are delightful plants for small bouquets.

Like violas, pansies are short-lived perennials that love cool weather. Excellent in containers, they're often set out in pots in early spring, and replaced in the heat of summer by petunias or other heat-loving plants.

'Pandora's Box' pansies come in warm colors and hold their flowers up high.

PEAK SEASON

Early spring until summer

MY FAVORITES

Pansies (Viola × wittrockiana) varieties include many named strains and cultivars. The Imperial Hybrids and Majestic Giants strains have the largest flowers, and the Joker strain, including 'Jolly Joker' and 'Joker Poker Face', has fun colors and patterns. The Universal strain is noted for cold and heat tolerance, and early bloom.

'Imperial Antique Shades' comes in warm pastels that look like a water-color painting. 'Flame Princess' has a color combination that's new to pansies: a bright red over a yellow background. 'Pandora's Box' flowers come in warm shades of pink, yellow, and red.

Violas (V. cornuta) include my absolute favorite: the Sorbet series. Its flowers feature charming color combinations and interesting whisker-like patterns.

GARDEN COMPANIONS

Pansies are great with spring bulbs of all kinds, especially daffodils and tulips. They also combine well with pot marigold (Calendula), love-in-a-mist (Nigella), and forget-me-nots (Myosotis).

When In New York City, I plant pansies in the autumn, at the same time I plant tulips. If I plant early enough in the fall, the pansies develop strong root systems and begin blooming very early, by late March. If you live where winters are colder, you can avoid any risk of winter damage by planting in early spring (March or April).

To start from seed, sow indoors eight to ten weeks before you want to move plants outdoors. Barely cover the tiny seeds with soil, place the seed flats in the refrigerator for a week to satisfy the seeds' requirement for chill, and then move them to a warm indoor spot. Seeds sprout in about 2 weeks. The seedlings tolerate cool temperatures, but if temperatures threaten to dip below freezing, they will need some protection.

Where Plant in full sun to partial shade in well-drained soil that is rich in humus. Summer plants will need shelter from afternoon sun. A pot of pansies is a must on the door-step in early spring. Include pansies in your edible landscape and harvest the colorful flowers for tasty additions to salads.

How Space plants 6 inches apart in the garden, closer in containers. (Incorporate a controlled-release fertilizer into containers before planting.) Lightly fertilize after planting.

TLC Water as needed to keep the soil evenly moist but not wet. If you didn't use a controlled-release fertilizer at planting time, fertilize every 2 weeks with a liquid fertilizer. Summer plants will need an organic mulch to help keep the soil cool. Deadhead regularly to prolong flowering, and cut back plants in late June to promote late-summer and autumn bloom (or buy new plants in the fall). Pansies are vigorous self-seeders and tend to show up in the least likely places, but they're always welcome.

Petunia

Petunia × hybrida

The petunia *used to* be a blowsy flower that tended to flop over in windy or wet weather, or get leggy and fall over if not frequently pinched back. New hybrids of this tender perennial offer smaller and sturdier flowers, a lusher growth habit, and a more stoic attitude in foul weather. They've retained their willingness to tough it out through heat spells, and to last longer than impatiens in the fall as cold weather comes on. Alas, the messy old-fashioned petunias had a spicy evening fragrance, which has been bred out of most new selections as toughness was bred in, while unfortunately retaining their sticky leaves.

Petunias are enormously popular, in the garden and in pots. Probably their single best feature is their incredible color range, which includes shades of white and yellow and the full spectrum of reds and blues. They may be striped, veined, edged in a different color, spotted, or splashed. The flowers may be single or double. Some have frilly edges; others are gently scalloped.

Wild Petunia integrifolia *trails vigorously.*

PEAK SEASON

Late spring or early summer and lasts until the first hard frost

MY FAVORITES

Grandifloras produce the fewest but largest flowers, 3 to 5 inches wide. Top series include: Aladdin, Dreams, Frost, Prism, Storm, Super Cascade, and Ultras. 'Prism Sunshine' is the first yellow in the category.

Multiflora plants are about the same size as grandifloras, but flowers are about 2 inches wide and are much more weather tolerant. Look for Celebrity, Madness, and Prime Time.

Trailing 'Purple Wave' is a vigorous plant with 2½- to 3-inch-wide flowers. The wild species, *Petunia integrifolia,* is a trailing petunia that is excellent when massed. It has small magenta or white blooms that don't need deadheading, and there is a new selection called 'Baby Pink'.

Milliflora petunias are smaller, more compact plants that produce tiny 1- to 1½-inch-wide flowers. The Fantasy series is available in nine colors.

GARDEN COMPANIONS

Plant petunias in a window box or in the ground with other flowering annuals like sage, zinnias, and *Verbena bonariensis,* and with trailing foliage plants like licorice plant *(Helichrysum petiolare).*

When Plant petunias outside after all danger of frost has passed, on a cloudy day if possible to reduce transplant shock. Sow seeds indoors 10 weeks before the last frost date. The seeds need light to germinate, so press them just into the surface of the planting medium. Germination takes one to three weeks.

Where Plant in full sun to light shade in average, well-drained soil. Petunias will tolerate poor soil, but too little light results in leggy plants. A spot out of the wind will help keep plants looking neat. Petunias are best suited to containers. A hanging basket makes a marvelous home for spreading, trailing types like 'Purple Wave'.

How Space plants 10 to 12 inches apart in the ground, closer in containers. Lightly fertilize after planting.

TLC Water as needed to keep the soil evenly moist but not wet. Pinch back young plants to encourage bushiness and more bloom. Deadhead the flowers regularly, and cut back plants in midsummer to encourage a second flush of bloom.

TOP: 'Prism Sunshine' is the first yellow grandiflora. BOTTOM: 'Lilac Wave' is a smaller-flowered multiflora petunia.

Sage
Salvia

Bright red scarlet sage 'Feugo' makes a fiery, compelling statement in the midsummer garden.

There was a time when only one type of sage was available, scarlet sage *(S. splendens)*. Its flowers are an assertive, in-your-face, fire-engine red, and are held in dense clusters atop short, stiff plants. Now there are easier and more elegant sages to grow.

For instance, tropical sage *(Salvia coccinea)* grows 2 to 3 feet high and produces bright red, orange-red, pink, or white flowers. It reliably provides a bright dash of color and may reseed from year to year. The 'Coral Nymph' variety is more compact and has more delicate colors than the common species.

Mealycup sage *(S. farinacea)* has cool-colored flowers that are velvety to the touch. Both tropical and mealycup sage look natural and mix well into established borders.

Silver sage *(S. argentea)* is primarily grown for its foliage of silky-haired, soft gray-green leaves. Technically a biennial, it produces tall spikes of white flowers in its second summer.

Even the well-known scarlet sage *(S. splendens)* has been improved by breeders to include an assortment of colors other than red, such as dusky purple, pink, orange, white, and bicolor variations.

The giant world of salvias can become an obsession, and once you have grown one you may want to try others as more species and cultivars become available.

PEAK SEASON

Summer is the main bloom period, but plants will continue blooming into fall until hit by a hard frost.

MY FAVORITES

Silver sage *(Salvia argentea)* is from southern Europe and northern Africa. It's very easy to grow, and has foliage like a giant lamb's ear *(Stachys)*. Prefers dry soil.

Tropical sage *(S. coccinea)* 'Lady in Red' is easy and reliable, and a favorite of monarch and swallowtail butterflies. 'Coral Nymph' has a shrimp and pink bicolor flower.

Mealycup sage *(S. farinacea)* 'Victoria', 'Sea Breeze', and 'Silvery White' are reliable and have cool colors.

Mexican bush sage *(S. leucantha)* is a long-lived perennial where it's native, but as an annual in our region, it provides an unexpected autumn crop of rich purple flowers.

Scarlet sage *(S. splendens)* 'Flare' or 'Fuego' are two new cherry red varieties of an old favorite.

GARDEN COMPANIONS

The most effective companion plants will offer shades of equal intensity: Mexican sunflower *(Tithonia rotundifolia)*, marigolds (page 48), zinnia (page 58), and amaranthus are just a few. Or accent annual sage by isolating a specimen amongst foliage plants.

When You'll find annual sages sold in cell-packs and 4-inch pots. Buy and plant when weather is warm and all danger of frost is past.

Where Sage wants full sun all day; it is adaptable to soil type and moisture levels.

How Space plants according to their size, providing enough room for them to reach maturity without crowding. Lightly fertilize with a controlled-release fertilizer after planting.

TLC Regular watering is the primary care for scarlet sage. Tropical and Mexican sages are largely drought tolerant once established. To boost growth of any type, begin fertilizing about a month after planting; either apply controlled-release fertilizer pellets or begin a program of diluted liquid fertilizer at regular intervals. Remove spent flower spikes to keep plants tidy and productive.

ABOVE: S. farinacea *'Silvery White'*. BELOW: S. splendens *'Sizzler Purple'*.

Spider Flower
Cleome hasslerana

The spider flower is aptly named, as both its flower and dangly seedpods resemble a spider's legs. Planted in a group, spider flower's tall, graceful forms sway toward one another in choreographed animation. The airy individual flowers are clustered atop a 3- to 5-foot stem, held above the string bean-like seedpods. The stamens and pistils protrude past the petals of each flower to form a large, 5-inch cluster of pink, purple, or white. Their hand-shaped leaves are also held away from the plant on long petioles. But despite its many charms, spider flower is stinky and thorny. Prickles run along the stem and leaves, and when rubbed, they emit a distinct skunk odor, so be careful when cutting the flowers. Otherwise, you needn't handle the plants much, as they are relatively trouble free.

Spider flower provides a colorful, unusual background for a large border; it is also attractive grown as an annual hedge or in a large container. Seeds are sold in mixed or individual colors.

OPPOSITE PAGE: *'Violet Queen' spider flower grows readily from seeds sown in early spring. It's not invasive, but plant it once and you'll likely have it year after year.* RIGHT: *Plant cleome generously, in large groups. They will grow tall enough to form a colorful back-drop to shorter flowers planted in front.*

PEAK SEASON

Plants are at their best from late spring through midsummer.

MY FAVORITES

You can choose from a number of varieties to grow from seed. Usually flower color is indicated by the name: 'Cherry Queen', 'Mauve Queen', 'Pink Queen', 'Purple Queen', 'Rose Queen', 'Ruby Queen', and 'Violet Queen' are all widely available. 'Helen Campbell' is snow white.

GARDEN COMPANIONS

Spider flower is best placed at the back of the border or against a hedge in order to show off the plant's habit. It looks attractive with many other annuals, including:

- Globe amaranth *(Gomphrena globosa)*
- *Malva sylvestris*
- Tropical sage *(Salvia coccinea)*
- Mealycup sage *(Salvia farinacea);* see pages 54 and 55 for more about sages.

When Sow seeds or nursery plants in place in spring, after Memorial Day. They'll sprout rapidly in the warming soil.

Where Plants are tolerant of all but a shady location. They can tolerate drought conditions once established, yet like most annuals, they are happy to receive a thorough watering. Spider flower is also forgiving of our hot and humid summers.

How Plant a foot apart, either as plants or seed once the ground has warmed up.

TLC Spider flower is quite liberal with its seed, which will return yearly if left to ripen. If you don't want self-sown plants next year, remove the ripening seedpods. Remove seeds as they ripen, but wait as long as you can because they become part of the ornamental nature of the plant. Deadheading isn't necessary, as new flowers develop at the top of the plant.

Zinnia
Zinnia

Zinnias rival cosmos for their popularity and iconic status as a flower of summer. Unlike cosmos, zinnias are not airy floaters swaying in the breeze. They are absurdly stiff, looking as if they were plucked from the Munchkin-land, not their actual home in the wilds of Mexico. Stems are popsicle-stick straight, and vivid, long-lasting blooms sit sunny-side up. Flowers come in red, pink, orange, white, and some bicolors. Flower form can be cactuslike (with spiky petals around a bright center), ruffled, or pom-pom shaped.

Taller zinnias perk up a fading flower border in late summer if planted in masses, but because they're prone to powdery mildew, plant them behind shorter plants that will hide their leaves. (Mildew doesn't affect the flowers.)

The extremely vigorous Profusion zinnias can be used in the front of a border. They also do well in pots.

The unusual pale green flowers of 'Envy' are beautiful in their own way, although I still prefer the rich color selections of zinnias in red, orange, and rose.

'Dreamland Mix' zinnia combines here with blue mealycup sage (Salvia farinacea).

TOP: 'Crystal White' is more disease and drought tolerant than common zinnias. BOTTOM: The unusual green 'Envy' grows 2 feet high.

PEAK SEASON

Midsummer to first frost

MY FAVORITES

Zinnia angustifolia Crystal series (also sold as the Star series) has a compact growth habit and orange, yellow, or white flowers that bloom constantly.

Z. elegans 'Envy' has pale chartreuse flowers. Blue Point zinnia series is tall, with giant, dahlia-type flowers that are perfect for cutting and indoor display. 'Dreamland Mix' grows about 1 foot high and has large flowers.

Profusion zinnias, award-winning hybrids between *Z. angustifolia* and *Z. elegans,* have prolific orange, cherry red, or white flowers that don't need deadheading and are an easy and satisfying group.

Zinnia haageana 'Old Mexico' and 'Persian Carpet' are old cultivars that come in a range of autumnal colors like gold and mahogany, with pointed petals. Many have double flowers.

GARDEN COMPANIONS

For a dazzling container, combine 'Profusion Orange' zinnia with lime green–leafed 'Margarita' sweet potato vine. This is my favorite combination, because 'Margarita' green makes all the zinnia colors vibrate with more intensity.

When Sow seeds of zinnias directly in the garden after the last frost, usually in late May or early June. The seeds sprout in a few days in warm soil, and flowers appear in 6 to 8 weeks. You can also start seeds indoors 4 to 6 weeks before the last frost date, but transplant carefully, as the young plants resent being moved. You can also buy seedlings at the nursery, but they don't transplant as easily as most other annuals, and the seed-started plants will catch up quickly.

Where Plant in full sun in well-drained, yet moist soil. Even partial shade will reduce flowering and weaken stems. Include taller varieties in your cut-flower garden.

How Keep the seedbed moist until seedlings appear. Once seedlings are up, thin to 4 to 18 inches apart depending on stem height; space shorter zinnias closer together than taller varieties. Water seedlings regularly with a weak solution of fertilizer.

TLC Water regularly. Powdery mildew can be a problem on zinnias. Reduce the risk of infection by providing ample spacing to increase air circulation. Deadhead faded flowers. Tall varieties may need staking.

TOP 10 Shrubs

Shrubs get no respect. We refer to them as bushes, prune them into the most unnatural shapes, or simply neglect them and then rip them out when they grow leggy and disheveled. Yet what would we do without forsythias, lilacs, spirea, and hydrangeas?

Unlike annuals and perennials, shrubs don't disappear in the fall. Evergreen broad-leaved shrubs and shrubby conifers remain much the same in winter and summer. Deciduous shrubs lose only their foliage in winter; the woody branches remain intact, along with the buds that will produce next season's leaves and flowers.

Whether planted as single specimens, in a mixed border, or as a hedge, shrubs give our gardens definition and structure. They create a sense of enclosure, screen out less desirable views, draw the eye to focal points, and offer shelter from winds. More than any other design element—including stone cherubs, tiered fountains, arbors, and gates—shrubs dictate a garden's mood and style: geometric shapes and tight pruning signal formality, while a more natural growth habit lends a garden an informal, relaxed air.

THINK AHEAD

Choosing the right shrubs for a particular site is critical. Select the plant whose mature size fits your space. Most of the shrubs listed here come in many sizes and shapes; if you fall in love with cotoneaster's leaf color and berries, you'll need to figure out if it would look best as an upright hedge or a low, spreading ground cover. Lilacs and hydrangeas are available in dwarf or tree forms. Also, if you want a flowering shrub to combine with perennials, make sure you know when it blooms, and don't make the mistake of pruning

at the wrong time and removing flower buds.

Careful pruning is the key to transforming a so-so shrub into a show-stopper. If you wish to create a tight formal hedge by shearing, be sure that you shear your plants so that the bottom is wider than the top, which allows sunlight to reach lower leaves. Shearing aside, most shrubs look best when pruned to their natural shape. The way to do this is by thinning: cutting off selected branches to the next living branch or by taking out specific stems all the way to the ground.

OFF TO A GOOD START

Shrubs are sold as bare-root, balled-and-burlapped, or container plants. Bare-root plants are sold in late winter and early spring. Their roots should be soaked in water for 2 hours or more before going into the ground. Plant container and balled-and-burlapped plants anytime, though early spring and early fall are best.

Make the planting hole no deeper than the rootball but twice as wide. This will allow

ABOVE: *Blue flowers of bigleaf hydrangea indicate acidic soil. Turn flowers red by liming soil.* OPPOSITE PAGE: *The crimson fall color of low-growing dwarf fothergilla is the equal of any sugar maple.*

the roots to spread out in an advantageous way. After setting the plant at the proper level, back-fill the hole with the soil that was removed from the planting hole. Some amendments, such as well-rotted leaf compost, may be added to the soil, but be careful not to make the planting soil so rich that the shrub is discouraged from anchoring itself in the undisturbed soil.

Shrubs need room to grow and good air circulation to ward off disease; space them according to label instructions. If you are making a hedge or screen, plants may be spaced a bit closer together. Give your shrubs adequate water and fertilize them now and then—but above all, appreciate them. They do work awfully hard.

— WAYNE CAHILLY

Azalea and Rhododendron

Rhododendron

Rhododendrons and azaleas used to be the sort of plants northern gardeners gazed at longingly in Southern gardens. The cold-hardy series, *Rhododendron* 'PJM' (named for Paul J. Mezett, a Massachusetts nurseryman), changed all that with an iridescent purple-flowering rhododendron that took the Northeast by storm. Likewise, when breeders at the Minnesota Landscape Arboretum introduced the hardy Northern Lights azaleas, scintillating shades of orange, yellow, red, and white were added to the color spectrum. There are now many varieties of cold-hardy rhododendrons and azaleas available in garden centers.

Azaleas are related to rhododendrons and are similar in many ways, but there are subtle differences. Rhododendrons are usually evergreens; their leaves are less pointy, darker green, and thicker—almost rubbery in texture. Many cold-tolerant azaleas are deciduous, losing their leaves in winter, and they have smaller leaves and flowers.

Be sure to choose only cold-tolerant varieties and give them an acid soil, partial shade, and consistent moisture. Alas, you still have to live in a warm climate to grow rhododendrons as big as a house, but with rosebay *(Rhododendron maximum)*, even northern gardeners can grow a rhododendron as big as half a house.

Partially deciduous Korean rhododendron bursts into bloom with the first warm weather of spring.

When Plant rhododendrons and azaleas in early spring.

Where Choose a site in partial shade, ideally on the north or east side of a building to prevent winter damage, but avoid deep shade. Deciduous azaleas can tolerate full sun if they receive ample water. All types need rich, well-drained soil high in organic matter. Rhododendrons are excellent as single specimens, but they also look great as massed plantings.

How All rhododendrons and azaleas require a pH of 4.5 to 5.5. Test the soil and amend as needed before planting. Plant at the same depth that shrubs were growing in the containers, spacing them according to the mature size of the plants. Plant balled-and-burlapped shrubs so that the top of the rootball is right at the soil surface. Remove as much of the burlap and wire holding the rootball as possible without injuring the roots. Fertilize after flowering with a complete fertilizer specifically formulated for acid-loving plants. Water the fertilizer in well after applying around the base of the plants.

TLC Keep the soil evenly moist from spring until fall, watering when the top 2 inches of the soil is dry. Once plants are established, keep 2 to 4 inches of an acidic mulch such as pine needles or shredded oak leaves around them throughout the growing season. Fertilize plants in the fall and again right after plants bloom. Stop watering in mid-September to encourage plants to begin hardening off for winter, but saturate the soil just before the first freeze to make sure plants go into winter with moisture around their roots. Remove dead or damaged branches anytime. Pruning should be restricted to cutting back overenthusiastic growth or selectively removing a few stems to open up the plant. This should be done immediately after flowering. Plants may be pinched after flowering to encourage bushiness as well.

PEAK SEASON
Late spring into summer

MY FAVORITES
Deciduous rhododendrons
Korean rhododendron (*R. mucronulatum*) produces delicate, pale magenta flowers that appear to float amid the dark gray stems.

Deciduous azaleas
Plumleaf azalea (*R. prunifolium*) is a native that produces orange-red flowers in July. It's also a parent of Northern Lights series ('Pink Lights', 'Rosy Lights', 'White Lights') that are very cold-hardy azaleas.

Evergreen rhododendrons
'PJM' is compact, has purple flowers in spring, and small, dark green leaves that turn bronzy purple in winter.

Rosebay rhododendron (*R. maximum*) grows 10 to 12 feet high and as wide. The small white flowers are produced after the new growth.

Evergreen azaleas
Hybrid azaleas include varieties such as 'Christmas Cheer', 'Appleblossom', 'Coral Bells', and 'Delaware Valley White'. Flowers range in color from deep reds to pure white.

GARDEN COMPANIONS
Mass azaleas and rhododendrons with woodland plants such as hostas, lungwort, and ginger (*Asarum*).

'Delaware Valley White' is one of the most popular evergreen azaleas in the Tri-State region.

Butterfly Bush

Buddleia davidii

While individual flowers of 'Burgundy' butterfly bush draw in butterflies with scent and nectar, the long blossom clusters make a convenient feeding platform for them.

Of all shrubs, butterfly bush is among the most aptly named. Its butterfly-drawing power is legendary, and it is a delight on a summer's day to watch all types of butterflies sip the nectar from the clustered flowers. Hummingbirds and moths also make occasional stops, especially in the evening. In our region, butterfly bush typically grows 3 to 8 feet tall.

Butterfly bush has tiny tubular florets that make up the blossom clusters. These clusters are quite long, up to 1½ feet in length, and they give off a uniquely sweet, lingering fragrance. Flowers of the original shrubs, which are native to China, were blue and mauve. Today, however, there are many different cultivars in pink, magenta, lilac, white, and a rich, deep indigo, often described as blue-black. Butterfly bush leaves are also handsome. They are long, slender, and fuzzy and have a faint silvery look. For anyone hoping to attract wildlife, butterfly bush is required.

When The best time to plant butterfly bush is early spring, but it can be planted all season long if it is watered well. Large plants can be easily transplanted in the spring if they are first cut back to within 1 foot of the ground, then dug and moved.

Where Butterfly bush needs full sun and thrives in enriched, well-drained soil. The shrub is awkward looking when not in flower and is best planted with other shrubs or perennials that will conceal the unsightly lower stems. I have seen fall-blooming clematis planted so it climbs through butterfly bush, blooming after the butterfly bush flowers have passed. Cut back both in the spring.

How Butterfly bush requires good soil with reasonable fertility. Plant in full sun or light shade. Water well the first two years and during drought periods.

TLC Mulch well for the winter. In the early spring, 3 or 4 weeks before growth can be expected to begin, cut back to within a foot or so of the ground. New shoots will develop from the woody stems and these should be thinned, leaving only 5 or 6 well-placed shoots. Fertilize in early spring, and water well throughout summer. Deadhead flower clusters throughout the summer by cutting back the blooming stems to a point where there are buds, and the shrub will bloom into fall. Cut back new flowering wood that develops after the first bloom to promote a healthy rebloom. Experiment; the plant is resilient and will respond if watered and fertilized. Its roots are hardy, but a winter mulch of straw, compost, or well-rotted leaf mulch gives extra protection.

'Petite Plum' butterfly bush with its languid flower clusters anchors this summer border, and provides nectar for butterflies, through summer's dog days.

PEAK SEASON
Summer to fall

MY FAVORITES
'Black Knight' is vigorous and hardy, but butterflies don't seem to like it as much as others.

'Burgundy' has burgundy red flowers, and is shorter than is typical.

'Empire Blue' has bright blue flowers with orange eyes and grows in a more or less upright form.

'Petite Plum' has fragrant, red-violet flowers, and grows about 5 feet high.

'Royal Red' has fragrant red-purple flowers and a tidy appearance.

'White Profusion' has large white flowers that can brighten a slightly shady location or focus attention on the back of a border.

The related fountain buddleia (*B. alternifolia* 'Argentea') is a graceful 8-foot-high and -wide shrub with dark green leaves and fragrant, lilac pink flowers.

GARDEN COMPANIONS
Buddleia combines well with many perennials. Plant with coneflower (*Echinacea*), yarrow (*Achillea*), or black-eyed Susan (*Rudbeckia*) in sunny locations. Or match it up with azaleas or juniper, or with taller shrubs such as blueberry or spirea.

Forsythia
Forsythia

Mother Nature knows just what we need after a long, hard winter: a few rays of golden sunshine. And forsythia's brilliant gold does a remarkably good imitation of sunlight. Its dazzling flowers bloom before the shrub leafs out and before most other shrubs flower. Though ubiquitous in regions where the plant is reliably hardy, forsythia still manages to lend a touch of the exotic to the late-winter landscape. Flowers range in color from a soft lemon yellow to bright gold, depending on the variety. Shrubs may be spreading or upright, dwarf or tall, and leaves are often variegated or turn purplish bronze in fall. Cut forsythia branches hold their flowers for weeks and are striking in a tall glass vase or in an arrangement with other spring bloomers. If you want to jump-start spring, you can force forsythia to bloom early by cutting branches when they're still in bud. The warmth indoors will trick the buds into thinking it's time to open.

OPPOSITE PAGE: *Loudly signaling spring's entrance and winter's demise is daffodil yellow 'Lynwood' forsythia.*

PEAK SEASON
Early spring

MY FAVORITES
'Golden Peep' is a dwarf shrub from France with profuse gold flowers; 'Golden Times' has green-and-gold variegated leaves; 'Meadowlark' has early yellow flowers and is very hardy; 'New Hampshire Gold' is extremely cold-hardy; 'Lynwood' (or 'Lynwood Gold') is an old-time favorite that grows upright to 7 feet high, and produces tawny yellow, storm-hardy flowers; and 'Spring Glory' reaches about 6 feet in height and is covered with sulfur yellow, 1½-inch-wide flowers.

GARDEN COMPANIONS
The yellow flowers of forsythia are wonderful with:

- early-spring bulbs that have blue flowers, such as Siberian squill, muscari, and hyacinths
- yellow and white daffodils
- tall, white tulips

Clusters of two to six yellow flowers burst into life by late March and last at least 2 weeks.

When The best time to plant forsythias is early spring, but they can be planted all season long if they are watered well.

Where To get the best show of flowers, plant forsythias in full sun. They prefer fertile, well-drained soil. Use them in mixed shrub borders where their foliage can fade into the background after they are finished blooming. They can also be used as hedge plants.

How Plant forsythias at the same depth that they were growing in the containers, spacing according to the mature size of the plants. Water immediately after planting.

TLC Consistent watering is especially important during the first two years. Once established, forsythias will tolerate dry spells, but are best in soil that is evenly moist from spring until the ground freezes. Once plants are established, apply 2 to 4 inches of shredded bark or wood-chip mulch around them as soon as the ground warms in spring and replenish as necessary throughout the growing season. Feed in spring with a 10-10-10 fertilizer or an organic equivalent sprinkled around the base of the plants and watered in well. The best bloom is on year-old wood. Cut one-third of the oldest stems back to the ground right after blooming to encourage new growth. Severely overgrown, untidy plants should be cut to the ground in spring before growth begins and allowed to grow back over the next few years. Plants may produce suckers, which can be dug up in early spring and replanted or discarded. Extreme winter temperatures or late-spring cold snaps can damage flower buds, reducing spring bloom.

Hydrangea

Hydrangea

Hydrangeas have a distinctly old-fashioned look. Their large blooms—some resembling lace caps, others like cotton candy viewed from a distance—are made up of thousands of delicate florets. These clusters may be white, blush pink, or sky blue.

The color of the flowers of bigleaf hydrangea *(H. macrophylla)* depends on the availability of aluminum in the soil, which is determined by soil pH. A soil pH greater than 6 will result in pink flowers, while a pH of less than 5.5 usually results in blue flowers. The flowers last for weeks and remain striking as they change color and begin to fade, holding up well in dried arrangements.

Hydrangea foliage is attractive and dense, and the shrubs come in various shapes and sizes. The peegee hydrangea makes a wonderful small specimen tree, especially when pruned to a horizontal canopy, and oakleaf hydrangea has beautiful bronze fall foliage and peeling bark (but may sustain some winter damage in coldest climates).

Hydrangeas complement other plants well and never look messy, though they will wilt in prolonged heat and drought. Place them where they'll get some afternoon shade and they'll be happy.

Enormous 12-inch-wide white flower clusters of 'Annabelle' hydrangea last for six weeks or more, then dry attractively.

PEAK SEASON

Mid- to late summer

MY FAVORITES

Bigleaf hydrangea (*H. macrophylla*) 'Blue Prince' produces dense flower heads and is among the hardiest of hydrangeas. 'Forever Pink' produces pink blooms earlier than other varieties. 'Sun Goddess' leaves emerge and remain bright yellow all season. 'Variegata' has creamy white-edged foliage on a 3-foot-tall shrub.

Oakleaf hydrangea (*H. quercifolia*) is a native shrub that produces white flowers above bold, dark green foliage that turn a brilliant burgundy in the fall. 'Snowflake' produces huge clusters of double flowers.

Smooth hydrangea (*H. arborescens*) 'Annabelle' produces snowball-like flowers up to 1 foot across that change from green to pure white. It tolerates light shade. 'White Dome' has white, lace cap–style blooms that give it a Victorian look.

GARDEN COMPANIONS

Plant hydrangeas in a mixed border with other shrubs, trees, and tall, slender hollyhocks or low, mounding perennials such as catmint and hardy geraniums. Plant 'Annabelle' behind a tightly pruned low box or cotoneaster hedge or, for a more informal look, 'Little Princess' spirea.

When The best time to plant hydrangeas is early spring. Planting later into summer is fine if plants are well watered.

Where Hydrangeas vary in their light requirements from full sun to partial shade. They all prefer well-drained soils high in organic matter. Their shade tolerance makes hydrangeas good candidates for the north side of buildings or under shade trees. Their late-summer color is a great addition to a mixed shrub border.

ABOVE: *'Forever Pink' maintains its color even in acid soil.* BELOW: *In fall the leaves of oakleaf hydrangea shift to a deep burgundy color.*

How Plant hydrangeas at the same depth that they were growing in the containers, spacing according to the mature size of the plants. Water immediately after planting.

TLC Consistent watering is especially important during the first two years, but even mature plants will wilt at the onset of drought. Keep the soil evenly moist from spring until the ground freezes, watering when the top 2 inches of the soil has dried out. Once plants are established, keep 2 to 4 inches of shredded bark, leaf compost, or wood-chip mulch around them throughout the growing season. In mid-June apply a 10-10-10 or or similar fertilizer around the base of the plants and water it in well. Prune anytime to remove dead or diseased wood and crossing branches. Some species may be cut to the ground in the early spring each year.

Kerria
Kerria japonica

Kerria is a tough and easy-care shrub that delights in spring by covering itself in daffodil yellow flowers that are similar to small roses. A plant that grows well in full sun or fairly deep shade, kerria produces a 6-foot-tall arching mound of slender, grass green stems covered with delicately toothed leaves. Usually, the leaves fall in winter but the stems remain green.

This shrub requires no special care or conditions, and is a good choice for a shady spot where other shrubs have failed. Kerria also works as a background shrub, with flowers that will brighten a dark corner of the garden, or in a location where the bare green stems will stand out during the winter months. After flowering, kerria fades into the background, presenting only a mass of tidy foliage.

The plant's only downside, if it is one, is its proclivity to spread beyond its original space via suckers. But this is rarely a serious problem.

LEFT: *After flowers fade, white-edged leaves of 'Picta' kerria add color interest that lasts until the end of the season.*
OPPOSITE PAGE: *This red brick wall provides contrast to bright yellow kerria flowers, and its striking green stems in winter.*

When Kerria is best planted in the spring but can be transplanted from containers at any time. Consistent watering during the first two years is key to establishment.

Where Give kerria room to display its arching form. It works well as a back-of-the-border shrub, where during the summer its foliage will form a background for other flowering plants. Some shade tolerance makes it useful in places where other flowering shrubs would become leggy or languish. The flowers hold their color and last longer in the shade than they do in full sun.

How Blooms develop on previous year's wood. Therefore, prune heavily after flowering, cutting out branches that have bloomed, all dead or weak wood, and suckers. Where winters are severe, some damage will occur; prune out the damaged wood before flowering to improve the shrub's appearance.

TLC Kerria requires a loamy soil that is well drained and only moderately fertile. Plant balled and burlapped or from containers and mulch with leaf compost or well-rotted wood chips. Lightly fertilize after flowering in the spring and then water well. Dead, white-brown stems are very noticeable, and often in the center of mature shrubs. Remove them annually in late winter or early spring.

PEAK SEASON

Bright yellow flowers bloom in spring, but the plant is handsome throughout the entire year.

MY FAVORITES

Kerria japonica produces bright yellow, five-petaled blooms that measure 1¼ to 1¾ inches across. 'Aureo-variegata' has 2-inch-long leaves edged in yellow; 'Picta' has variegated leaves; and 'Pleniflora' produces a profusion of double flowers that all but squeeze themselves off the stems in their robustness.

GARDEN COMPANIONS

Mahonia, with its bold evergreen foliage, red- or yellow-stemmed dogwoods, ferns, and ornamental grasses all work well as companions.

Lilac
Syringa vulgaris

Lilacs are said to be the most aromatic of all flowers, and I think that may be true. Their scent is the only flower fragrance I can conjure up, even in the dead of winter. And lilacs are long-lived. When you're walking in late spring in woods that cover former farmland, the scent of lilac is often your first clue that people once called the area home. I know of a place where there are no old fields, no houses, and many trees, yet near a depression that was once the site of a privy, a lilac blooms.

The old-fashioned common lilac *(Syringa vulgaris)* is a big, blowsy shrub that needs plenty of elbow room. The newer hybrids offer a range of sizes and bloom times, so you can extend the flowering period well into summer.

When The best time to plant lilacs is early spring, but they can be planted anytime during the growing season if they are watered well.

PEAK SEASON
Spring or early summer

MY FAVORITES
'Ludwig Spaeth' has single purple flowers; 'Madame Lemoine' is one of the hundreds of May-blooming French hybrids, and produces an outstanding display of double white flowers; 'President Lincoln' has flowers of a respectable blue; 'Sensation' produces lovely pinkish rose flowers edged in white.

Related species
Syringa meyeri 'Paliban' is a compact shrub seldom reaching 3 feet in height, with violet-purple flowers in early to mid-May. Zones 32, 34–43.

The summer-blooming Japanese tree lilac (*S. reticulata*) grows to 20 feet tall and is a dramatic small tree or alternative to the traditional lilac hedge.

GARDEN COMPANIONS
Plant lilacs with flowering crabapple trees or spring-flowering shrubs like sweet mock orange (*Philadelphus coronarius*), hydrangeas, and ferns.

OPPOSITE PAGE: *'Paliban' lilac is a shorter, neater version of common lilac. Its soft pink flowers are lightly scented.* RIGHT: *One of the many French hybrids, this white lilac is strongly fragrant.*

Where Lilacs grow best when they receive full sun at least 6 hours a day. Shrubs planted in partial shade will bloom less and are more susceptible to powdery mildew. Lilacs are lovely as specimen plants, in small groups, and in hedges. *Syringa meyeri* 'Paliban' combines well with perennials and other shrubs in a mixed border.

How Plant lilacs at the same depth that they were growing in the containers, spacing according to the mature size of the plants. Be sure to give all types ample space. Balled-and-burlapped shrubs should be planted so that the root flares are right at the soil surface. Remove as much of the burlap and wire holding the rootball as possible without injuring the roots. Water immediately after planting.

TLC Keep the soil evenly moist from spring until the ground freezes, watering when the top 2 inches has dried out. Once plants are established, keep 2 to 4 inches of shredded bark or wood-chip mulch around them throughout the growing season. Feed in spring with a 10-10-10 fertilizer, or organic equivalent. Remove spent blossoms right after blooming to encourage more blooms the next year. Prune dead or diseased branches anytime. To keep common lilacs from becoming overgrown, remove one-third of the older branches annually. Prune to reduce height and maintain form right after flowering. When pruning older lilacs that may be grafted, take care to remove

any shoots coming from below ground at the base of the plant. Grafted plants can be on the roots of another lilac, or they may be growing on the roots of an ash tree, which may begin to grow from the portion that is belowground.

73

Redtwig Dogwood
Cornus sericea

The most popular shrub dogwoods for Tri-State gardens are redtwig (or red-osier) dogwoods (*Cornus sericea,* formerly known as *C. stolonifera*). Redtwig dogwoods have an amazing ability to spread by stolons—stems that grow horizontally just below the soil surface. At joints or nodes on these stems, they send down roots and send up new shoots. Regular spade-work and pruning will keep these shrubs in check.

Redtwig dogwoods are famous for their brilliant crimson, purple, or yellow stems, which hold their color right through winter. Planting in a location where their stems contrast with the background is one of the ways to show these plants off well. Another is to plant them where you can easily see and appreciate them when there's snow on the ground.

ABOVE: *In summer the leaves of 'Silver and Gold' dogwood are the familiar green but accented with a colorful cream white border. In winter, its bare stems are yellow.* OPPOSITE PAGE: *The unmistakable color of redtwig dogwood dominates the scene in winter and early spring.*

When The best time to plant redtwig dogwoods is early spring, but they can be planted all season long if they are watered well.

Where Almost all dogwoods grow best in sun, but some will tolerate partial shade. Most prefer slightly acidic soil. Keep these thin-barked shrubs away from salted roadways. Place the colored-stem dogwoods where you can enjoy their color in winter.

How Plant dogwoods at the same depth that they were growing in the containers, spacing according to the mature size of the plants. Balled-and-burlapped shrubs should be planted so that the root flares are right at the soil surface. Remove as much of the burlap and wire holding the rootball as possible without injuring the roots. Water immediately after planting.

TLC Consistent watering is most important during the first 2 years. Keep the soil evenly moist from spring until the ground freezes, watering when the top 2 inches of the soil has dried out. Once plants are established, apply 2 to 4 inches of shredded bark, wood-chip mulch, or leaf compost around them as soon as the ground warms in spring and replenish as necessary throughout the growing season. Plants benefit from a spring application of 10-10-10 fertilizer or an organic equivalent applied around the base. Prune those that have colored stems by selectively removing the oldest stems to the ground before growth begins in the spring. Be careful not to remove more stems each year than are being produced, or your shrub will become rangy and unsightly. Remove dead, damaged, or diseased stems whenever they appear.

PEAK SEASON

Spring through late summer for foliage. Most also have spring flowers and late-summer fruits, but not all are showy. Some have colorful bark and interesting branching habits, which add winter interest.

MY FAVORITES

Yellow twig dogwood (*C. serica* 'Flaviramea') is a strong-growing shrub with yellow-green stems. 'Silver and Gold' has the same yellow stems but its green leaves have a creamy border.

Colorado redtwig (*C. s. coloradensis* 'Cheyenne') grows 3 to 4 feet high and has bloodred stems.

Related species

Tatarian dogwood (*C. alba* 'Argenteomarginata') stems are deep red, covered in slender green leaves edged in creamy white. 'Sibirica' has coral red stems and green leaves; 'Spaethii' has a strong yellow edge to the leaves.

C. racemosa and *C. amomum* are less showy, but both tolerate wet soils and partial shade, making them invaluable wherever those conditions prevail. Flowers are white in May and appear in flat-topped clusters.

GARDEN COMPANIONS

Use in borders with hydrangea, viburnum, and lilacs. Or use as hedges, and in mass plantings with ferns.

Smoke Tree
Cotinus coggygria

If you've got a spot in the yard for something really eye-catching and a little different, consider smoke tree. The colorful foliage of this unusual ornamental is attractive throughout the season but really heats up in fall, deepening to brilliant shades of purple, red, or orange-yellow, depending on the variety.

Don't let the common name, smoke tree, fool you. With some pruning you can create a single-trunked tree, but this is naturally a multi-stemmed plant—so, in my opinion, it's a shrub. If you want an interesting small tree, buy a smaller specimen and train it to one trunk. But treat it as a large shrub and you'll have a full, nicely rounded plant that's easily maintained.

The standard form of this shrub is an open, upright spreading mass of stems and foliage topped by the 8-inch clusters of blooms and their subsequent "smoky" heads. Leaves on the species are bluish green, rounded, and between 1 and 3 inches in length. As the large, loose clusters of tiny greenish flower blossoms fade, the flower stalks get longer and by midsummer are covered with fuzzy purple or pink hairs. These feathery trusses look like puffs of smoke, hence the common name. Even with these showy blossoms and vibrantly colored leaves, smoke tree is an easy plant to work into the landscape because it combines so readily with other shrubs and perennials.

When Plant balled-and-burlapped plants or from containers in the spring or summer. Water well after planting and through the first two growing seasons.

PEAK SEASON

Summer into fall

MY FAVORITES

'Velvet Cloak' is a spectacular addition to a shrub border or perennial garden. It grows to 10 feet high but can be kept to any size by pruning. Leaves are a handsome dark purple, turning reddish purple in the fall.

'Royal Purple' is unsurpassed for foliage color, with leaves opening maroon-red then changing to rich purple or nearly black. The foliage holds its color well through the summer and then offers a bright array of fall colors.

GARDEN COMPANIONS

Smoke tree fits well in shrub borders with hydrangea, or sand cherry, or with evergreens as a backdrop. It works very well as an accent plant in the perennial border accompanied by coneflower, ferns, or black-eyed Susans. Hostas tuck in nicely beneath the stems.

Where Plant where it will receive full sun and well-drained soil; dry, rocky locations are fine. Proper drainage is critical to avoid problems with verticillium wilt. If the plant does become infected with this soilborne fungus, it must be replaced. Otherwise, this is a disease- and insect-free plant. Unpruned, smoke tree is too large to be a foundation plant, unless planted on the corner where it can grow lavishly. But it is a good screening plant and works well on the edge of the property. Pruning to a framework of limbs allows smoke tree to be used nearly anywhere, making it one of the most desirable purple-foliaged accent plants.

How Plant at the same depth that plants grew in their container, and set balled-and-burlapped plants so that the root flares are right at the soil surface.

TLC In spring cut out the oldest, woodiest stems. If branches die to the ground, roots will survive and the plant will regrow. Cutting the plant to the ground in fall and mulching will produce a lush crop of leaves the following season, but no "smoke"—flowers come only on branches that are 2 years old.

OPPOSITE PAGE: *'Royal Purple' leaves begin red, mature to rich purple, and turn red, yellow, and orange in fall.* RIGHT: *'Velvet Cloak' leaves are red-purple all season, changing to dark red in fall.*

Spirea

Spiraea

There are two distinct kinds of spireas. The classic bridal wreath, *Spiraea × vanhouttei,* has clusters of white flowers that cascade down arching branches in spring or early summer. The way its late spring bloom is both casual but exuberant has earned it a place in gardens for generations.

The profuse pink flowers and blue-green leaves of 'Little Princess' grow on the same side of the arching branches, showing both to maximum effect.

The shrubby type, such as *S. japonica,* has pink, red, or white flowers clustered at branch ends in summer to fall. It combines the wispy charm of bridal wreath with more practical, trendier virtues like a tidy, low, mounding growth habit; light green (or bright gold) leaves against pinkish purple flowers; a long bloom time; and low maintenance. Give your 'Little Princess' lots of sun, along with a haircut every three years, and it will always look great.

Both kinds of spirea are tough, easy-to-grow, and unfussy plants that will reliably add color and charm to your garden.

PEAK SEASON
Midspring through summer

MY FAVORITES
Spiraea japonica 'Goldflame' has leaves that open a bronzy color, then spend most of summer chartreuse until shifting to red-orange in fall; flowers are pink. 'Goldmound' has similar yellow-chartreuse leaves and pink flowers. 'Little Princess' is a low, mounding shrub that grows to 2½ feet tall with small, pale lavender flowers at the stem ends. 'Magic Carpet' grows 1½ to 2 feet tall with brilliant yellow leaves and red leaf tips, and pinkish purple flowers.

S. × vanhouttei is the bridal wreath spirea, with white flowers on arching branches. It grows to 6 feet tall and 8 feet wide. 'Renaissance' is resistant to mildew and rust.

GARDEN COMPANIONS
Plant low, mounding types in front of a taller hedge of flowering hydrangeas or *Viburnum burkwoodii* 'Mohawk'. The dwarf 'Magic Carpet' looks great as a ground cover combined with hardy geraniums and rambling roses such as 'Sea Foam'.

TOP RIGHT: *'Goldmound' leaves are chartreuse-yellow.* BOTTOM RIGHT: *'Goldflame' leaves are bronze at first, chartreuse in summer, and red-orange in fall.*

When The best time to plant spireas is early spring, but they can be planted all season long if they are watered well.

Where Spireas grow best in full sun but will tolerate partial shade. They prefer fertile, well-drained soil. They will not do well in soils that are constantly wet or that are highly alkaline. Most low-growing spireas should be planted in groups for best effect, but bridal wreath types are often grown as specimen plants.

How Plant spireas at the same depth that they were growing in the containers, spacing according to the mature size of the plants.

TLC Keep the soil evenly moist from spring until the ground freezes, watering when the top 2 inches of the soil has dried out. Once plants are established, apply 2 to 4 inches of shredded bark or wood-chip mulch around them as soon as the ground warms in spring and replenish as necessary throughout the season. Feed in spring with a 10-10-10 fertilizer, or organic equivalent, sprinkled around the base of the plants and watered in. Prune summer-flowering spireas in late winter to avoid cutting off the current season's flower buds. Overgrown plants can be cut to the ground in early spring to control size or to rejuvenate. Prune to remove dead or diseased branches anytime. Remove faded flowers to keep plants tidy and encourage a second flush of flowers.

Viburnum

Viburnum

ABOVE: *The 3-inch-wide flower clusters of Korean spice viburnum are charming in spring, but the scent they spread over still evening air is intoxicating.* OPPOSITE PAGE: *'Shasta' doublefile viburnum covers itself in white flowers on horizontal branches in spring.*

If, like me, you share a special fondness for plants that attract birds and are easy to grow, be sure to give viburnums special consideration. This is such a large and varied group of plants it's likely that you can find at least one plant here that is exactly what your garden needs.

Most viburnums produce large white or pink, and sometimes fragrant, flowers in spring that are followed by clusters of red or black berries in late summer. Usually, the heaviest fruit set occurs when several different named varieties of seedlings that bloom at the same time are planted together. There are evergreen viburnums, but the ones that excel in our region are all deciduous.

All viburnums prefer slightly acid and well-drained soil, though most are also tolerant of heavy soil conditions and several grow well in soil with slow drainage. With few exceptions, these are unfussy, easy-to-grow shrubs.

When The best time to plant viburnums is early spring, but they can be planted all season long if they are watered well.

Where Most viburnums grow best in full sun, but many do well in partial to even full shade. They prefer well-drained, fertile, slightly acid soil, but are tolerant of less-than-ideal conditions, making them useful for hard-to-plant places. Use shrub-type viburnums in shrub borders, as hedges, or in mass plantings. Some can be pruned as small trees. Place the heavy-fruiting types where you can enjoy their fall and winter interest.

How Plant viburnums at the same depth that they were growing in the containers, and space plants according to their mature size. Water immediately after planting.

TLC Consistent watering is especially important during the first 2 years, but even mature plants will wilt in drought conditions. Keep the soil evenly moist from spring until the ground freezes, watering when the top 2 inches of the soil has dried out. Feed in spring with a 10-10-10 fertilizer or an organic equivalent sprinkled around the base of the plants and watered in well. Prune just after flowering to reduce height or improve form. Remove a few older stems every 2 or 3 years to keep plants vigorous. Viburnum leaf beetle is becoming a common pest in the Tri-State region. Doublefile, Korean, and tea viburnums are most resistant. Prune and destroy by burning or composting all infested twigs from October to April, after egg laying has ceased.

PEAK SEASON
Spring through fall

MY FAVORITES
Doublefile viburnum (*V. plicatum tomentosum* 'Shasta') carries flowers above the foliage in white, flat-topped clusters. Zones 32, 34–43.

European cranberry bush (*V. opulus*) has three-lobed leaves and flatish flower heads surrounded by showy sterile flower petals. Red fruits persist into winter. Zones 32, 34–45.

Korean spice viburnum (*V. carlesii*) forms a stiff, 6-foot-tall and -wide mound. Sweetly fragrant flowers come in spring. Zones 32, 34–43.

Linden viburnum (*V. dilatatum*) is an upright, 8- to 10-foot-high, slow-growing shrub. White, flat-topped flower clusters come in late May. Cherry red fruits persist into winter. Zones 32, 34–41.

Tea viburnum (*V. setigerum*) is an upright, sometimes leggy shrub with white flowers in flat-topped clusters followed by bright red fruit. Zones 32, 34–41.

GARDEN COMPANIONS
Plant with dogwood and lilac, or with low, bushy perennials like euphorbia. Viburnums do well under tall trees with azaleas and hydrangeas.

Evergreen Shrubs

Evergreen shrubs can be divided into two broad categories: broad-leaved plants that have leaves similar to deciduous shrubs (those that drop their leaves in the fall), and narrow-leaved plants with leaves that are like tiny overlapping scales or needles. Some broad-leaved evergreens, such as mountain laurel and some rhododendrons, provide us with the ability to screen views and divide garden spaces, and they have showy flowers as well. Growing conditions are important with broad-leaved evergreens; in particular, protect them from drying winds during the coldest portions of the winter.

Needle-leaved evergreen shrubs are usually conifers. Their flowers are inconspicuous and fruits are a cone. Most have finely textured needles or tiny leaves that overlap each other much as roofing shingles do. They are frequently tolerant of difficult planting conditions and may even do well in seaside locations.

These needle-leaved evergreens provide a range of foliage color, textural variation, and plant form, but the showy flowers in the garden will have to be provided by other plants, the broad-leaved evergreens.

COLOR AND FORM

Broad-leaved evergreen shrubs often grow into large, mounded plants, some reaching 10 or 15 feet in height. Others are small and compact, allowing them to be used as accent plants or sheared into tight formal hedges. This versatility is important because it allows you to change the mood of a garden without sacrificing enclosure.

Narrow-leaved evergreens range in form from prostrate shrubs that lie within inches of the ground and creep between rocks and over walls to wide-spreading or upright growers. Although they all have needlelike leaves, textures differ. Some have very small, sharp needles, while others have clusters of 2 inch-long needles.

Color is a key consideration when selecting evergreens. It is the element that will be there

OPPOSITE PAGE: *Flower buds of 'Dorothy Wyckoff' mountain pieris in snow.* RIGHT: *Juniper, dwarf pine, and dwarf spruce provide all-season structure to a garden.*

throughout the year, and the backdrop against which the other plants in a garden will be seen. Some evergreens are dark and foreboding, while others are light blue, cheerful, and upbeat in appearance. Some are yellow or have creamy-colored flecks in the foliage.

PLANTING

Early spring planting is ideal, although early fall is also a good time—and you'll find the best selection and lowest prices in fall. Be sure to select plants that appear to be well rooted and in good condition. As with deciduous trees and shrubs, don't go shopping until you know where sun and shade fall in your garden, how much space you have for each plant, and what size and shape your shrub will be when fully grown.

Shrubs are usually sold as container plants. Before planting, pull apart any tangled roots and spread them out, cutting those that are determined to grow in concentric circles, using a pruning knife or pruning shears. Plant as you would a deciduous tree or shrub, digging the hole no deeper than the rootball but at least twice as wide. Use the native soil excavated from the hole for backfill, amending only modestly, if at all.

Space evergreen shrubs as the plant labels advise unless you're planting a hedge, in which case you may want them closer together.

Continued on page 84

Evergreen Shrubs (continued)

EVERGREENS FAVORED MOSTLY FOR THEIR FLOWERS

Mountain laurel *(Kalmia latifolia)* is a large-growing, broad-leaved native reaching 10 feet in the wild, available in an increasingly large number of cultivars. Like its rhododendron relatives, mountain laurel requires moist, acid soil and some light shade. Showy flowers bloom on long stalks, with buds that look something like a turban, opening to chalice-shaped flowers with five starlike points. Zones 32, 34–41.

Mountain pieris *(Pieris floribunda)* is a compact, rounded, broad-leaved shrub that grows 3 to 6 feet high. It's related to, and needs the same conditions as, azaleas and rhododendrons, namely well-drained and acidic soil. Zones 34–43.

Glossy abelia *(Abelia × grandiflora)* is a spectacular broad-leaved shrub with shiny dark green leaves, pinkish white flowers, fine texture, and pinkish sepals that are as showy as the flowers. 'Sherwood' is a compact form seldom exceeding 3 feet by 4 feet. Zones 32, 34, 35.

EVERGREENS FAVORED MOSTLY FOR THEIR LEAVES

Barberry *(Berberis × gladwynensis)* 'William Penn' is a broad-leaved shrub that grows into a medium-textured mound of glossy green foliage on yellowish stems. Hidden beneath the foliage is an array of $\frac{3}{4}$-inch spines that will discourage the most determined trespasser. Use as a 4-foot-tall impenetrable hedge or as an accent plant. Zones 32, 34, 35, 39.

Boxwood *(Buxus microphylla)* 'Winter Green' and 'Winter Gem' are two slow-growing, broad-leaved, compact cultivars prized by northern gardeners for their winter hardiness. Able to handle our coldest Tri-State winters, 'Winter Green' is considered the best for tight shearing. *B. sempervirens* 'Green Velvet' is a similar plant that does not discolor to bronze in the winter cold. Zones 32, 34, 37.

Japanese euonymus *(Euonymus japonicus)* is a medium-textured, broad-leaved shrub that grows to 10 feet high and half as wide. This somewhat tender shrub forms a dense oval when grown in full sun. It is easily transplanted. Two popular

varieties are 'Albo-marginatus', which has leaves with a delicate edging of white, and 'Macrophyllus', with green leaves that are larger than those of the species. Zones 32, 34, 37.

Needle-leaved Chinese juniper *(Juniperus chinensis)* can grow to 50 feet high, but there are many shrubby cultivars. 'Hetzii' is a rapidly growing, wide-spreading, 15-foot shrub with blue-green foliage. 'Pfitzeriana', one of the most widely planted, grows 5 feet high by 10 feet wide. 'Compacta' is more prickly than the species, but stays a compact 1½ feet high by 5 feet wide. Zones 32, 34–43.

Oregon grape *(Mahonia aquifolium)* is a handsome, holly-like, broad-leaved evergreen that produces daffodil yellow flowers and fruits that look like blue-black olives. It is somewhat susceptible to winter damage, so provide some light shade and shelter. 'Compacta', a dwarf form that may reach 2 to 3 feet high, is more cold-hardy than the species. *M. bealei* is a large grower, capable of reaching 8 to 10 feet but seldom doing so. The flowers are showy and extremely fragrant. Zones 32, 34–41.

Mugo pine *(Pinus mugo mugo)* is a tidy, slow-growing pine that forms a medium-textured, 4-foot green mound; it is an excellent accent plant in gardens and at the ends of walkways. Zones 32, 34–45.

Yew *(Taxus baccata* 'Repandens') is the best evergreen for a dark corner of the garden. It is needle-leaved, slow growing, disease free, nearly prostrate, and reliable. *T. cuspidata* 'Capitata' can grow to 40 feet high, but with regular shearing is easily kept less than 10 feet tall. *T.* × *media* 'Densiformis' is a 4-foot-high by 6-foot-wide shrubby yew to use as a specimen plant or for large hedges; 'Hicksii' is a columnar form suitable for 10- to 12-foot-tall, narrow hedges or for use as an accent plant. Zones 32, 34.

Native Shrubs

Native shrubs may be evergreen or deciduous, but they all bear the distinction of originating from the Tri-State region. This comes with some distinct advantages. For example, a shrub that is from our region is most likely tolerant of the temperature and rainfall extremes that are typical here. Soil conditions, insects, and diseases are usually not problems for native plants the way they sometimes are with plants that originate a long way from home.

Native plants are sometimes maligned for not providing a sufficient "flower-fix" for gardeners who are enamored of showy cultivars. Some natives, however, have stunning flowers, and others provide fragrance, a trait that many showier plants do not.

Native shrubs vary as much as other plants; thus, a plant that fits your space can be found with sufficient searching. Some nurseries produce only native plants, and these are good places to begin your investigations. One warning: Don't go out to the local park or state forest and abscond with what you hope will be a prized native plant. Success is unlikely, and you may be assessed a hefty fine as well.

FAVORITE NATIVE SHRUBS

Bayberry *(Myrica pensylvanica)* is an underused, 5-foot semievergreen shrub. It has leathery leaves, and produces small fruits covered in wax from which bayberry

Long-lasting and sweetly fragrant flowers of summersweet are a powerful attraction to a wide variety of beneficial insects. The plant spreads slowly via underground roots to form a broad clump.

fragrance is derived. Prune it hard to produce dense growth. Zones 32, 34–44.

Blueberry *(Vaccinium corymbosum),* the blueberry grown commercially, is also an outstanding garden shrub. It has red twigs in winter, edible fruit, and spectacular orange-red fall color. Zones 32, 34–43. (For more about edible varieties, see page 236.)

Carolina allspice *(Calycanthus floridus)* grows 6 feet high, has an open form, and produces deep red, fragrant, unusual-looking flowers in June or July. 'Athens' has yellow-green flowers; 'Edith Wilder' has the most fragrant flowers. Zones 32, 34–41.

Fothergilla major is a rounded, dense shrub that grows 6 to 8 feet high. The white, fragrant flowers come in bottlebrush-like spikes in late spring. Fall colors of gold and red are outstanding. The dwarf, *F. gardenii,* grows about half as high. Zones 32, 34–39.

Witch hazel *(Hamamelis virginiana)* is a tall (to 25 feet) and sprawling woodland shrub with yellow flowers that bloom in November. Use it in a shrub border, or as an accent in a perennial border. Zones 32, 34–43.

Inkberry *(Ilex glabra)* earned its common name for its blue-black fruits. It grows 5 feet tall and is a valuable addition to the back-

ABOVE: *White, 2-inch-long, sweetly scented flowers of Fothergilla gardenii.*
ABOVE RIGHT: *Reddish brown flowers of Carolina allspice are strawberry scented.*
RIGHT: *Tiny, golden flowers of witch hazel in fall. The bark is the source of witch hazel liniment.*

ground planting of any garden. 'Compacta' is a 4-foot form. Zones 32, 34–43.

Winterberry *(Ilex verticillata)* is a 6- to 10-foot-tall deciduous holly. It produces long-lasting crimson fruit tightly held against nearly black stems. 'Red Sprite' has large berries and grows to 5 feet; 'Winter Red' has a heavier fruit set; 'Autumn Glow' produces excellent fall color and magnificent fruit; and 'Aurantiacum' has orange fruit that remain until January. All require a male variety for pollination. Zones 32, 34–43.

Summersweet *(Clethra alnifolia)* grows to 8 feet. It produces fragrant, white, spike-like flowers in June. It suckers freely and is great for streamside plantings. 'Pink Spires' is a compact pink-budded selection. Zones 32, 34–43.

Ground Covers

Ground covers are far more than just substitutes for lawn. In fact, their only feature in common with the familiar greensward is the ability to create a fairly uniform living blanket over bare earth. With these spreading ground cover plants, you can get infinite foliage variety, flowers, decorative fruits—and, yes, just plain green if you wish.

USING
GROUND COVERS

At the most mundane level, ground covers serve purely practical purposes. One of these is, of course, as a substitute for the water-guzzling, labor-intensive lawn. The less-thirsty ground covers are fine conservation alternatives wherever you want a low-growing foliage surface in an area that's unlikely to get any foot traffic. And in outlying areas of the garden, where keeping a lawn would be difficult, you can plant tough ground covers to beautify barren areas that otherwise would generate weeds and dust. In addition, many ground covers make neat, leafy carpets on sloping ground too steep for easy lawn maintenance;

some of these plants have dense root systems that will bind the soil and reduce erosion.

Ground covers also shine in a number of less utilitarian roles. Planted en masse, they can define spaces in the garden—separating areas or uniting them, depending on the garden design. They easily function as transition zones between other garden plantings and paving or lawn. A base of ground cover can immeasurably enhance the trees, shrubs, and even the garden ornaments, stone walls and rock outcrops rising above it. With a bit of ingenuity, you can create dynamic tapestry plantings by using two or more ground covers in combination within a given area.

OPPOSITE PAGE: *Red bishop's hat adds color to shady locations.* ABOVE: *Dwarf periwinkle.* BELOW: *'Blue Ridge' creeping phlox.*

While a shag-carpet lawn invites walking, most ground covers emphatically suggest "keep off." That traffic-control function can let you determine access patterns within a garden while maintaining a feeling of openness.

ESTABLISHING GROUND COVERS

Among my Top 10 ground covers, you'll find plants that need regular watering and those that need less—even to the extent of subsisting on rainfall alone. But regardless of a mature plant's water needs, young and small plants establish more quickly if soil is kept moist. Wide oscillations between wet and dry soil prolong the march to maturity, so you should pay close attention to watering during the first

year or two. In addition, it's a good idea to maintain a mulch on the soil in between plants until they fill in. This prevents rapid evaporation and fosters good root growth by keeping the soil more evenly moist and cool, and simultaneously suppresses unsightly moisture-usurping weeds. In time, the ground-cover growth will fill in to become its own living mulch.

— WAYNE CAHILLY

Bishop's Hat
Epimedium

A delicate tracery of handsome leaves and a pleasant display of spring flowers recommend bishop's hat for shaded or woodland gardens, where it spreads at a slow to moderate rate to form a carpet beneath plants that enjoy the same conditions, such as rhododendrons, mountain laurel, and mountain pieris.

A number of species and hybrids are available; they differ in details of foliage and flower, but all conform to the same general design. Growing from a dense network of underground stems, the leafstalks bear heart-shaped, 3-inch-long leaflets that overlap to form handsome clumps of foliage. New growth emerges bronzy pink, turns green by summer, then changes to reddish bronze in fall. In spring, wiry flower stems appear, holding airy blossom sprays either well above or just over the leaves, depending on the species. The waxy-textured flower may look like a cup and saucer or a saucer alone; in some species, flowers have spurs.

Bishop's hat grows well where many other ground covers can't: in the shade and dry soil under a tree.

When Plant in the spring in well-prepared soil.

Where All species need slightly acid soil liberally amended with organic matter. All species of bishop's hat prefer some shade, particularly in the afternoon.

How Prepare the area that will be planted by cultivating the soil 6 to 8 inches deep, unless planting under established shrubs and trees. In that instance, prepare planting holes spaced about a foot apart and amend the soil from each with compost. Position the plants at the same level that they were growing in the nursery containers, and then backfill with amended soil. Water thoroughly.

TLC Bishop's hat is remarkably adaptable. It does require good drainage, however, and failure to attend to this will lead to poor results. Maintenance is nonexistent once plants are established, but to keep deciduous and semievergreen plantings neat, some gardeners prefer to shear off the old growth at the end of the season or in spring before new growth begins.

PEAK SEASON

Flowers come in spring, but leaves are showy throughout the season.

MY FAVORITES

Epimedium alpinum spreads fast, making a carpet of leaves to about 9 inches high. Its small cup-and-saucer flowers are red and yellow.

E. grandiflorum bears the largest blooms. Flowers are red and violet with white spurs, and named selections in pink, lavender, or white are also available. Leaves reach 1 foot in height.

E. × canta-brigiense forms 8- to 12-inch clumps of olive-tinted foliage; two-tone flowers of red and yellow are held above the leaves.

E. × rubrum is red in both foliage and flower: its leaves have red veins and margins, while the showy blossoms are red with white to cream spurs.

E. × versicolor offers bronze-tinted leaves on a plant 12 to 15 inches tall; its vigorous yellow-flowered variety, 'Sulphureum', is widely grown.

Persian epimedium (*E. pinnatum*) grows 12 to 15 inches high, and produces brown-spurred yellow flowers.

GARDEN COMPANIONS

Plant bishop's hat to cover the ground under mountain laurel, rhododendrons, and even small trees such as flowering dogwood.

TOP: E. grandiflorum 'Rose Queen'.
BOTTOM: E. × versicolor 'Sulphureum'.

Creeping Lily Turf
Liriope spicata

You can't walk on this "turf," but you can enjoy the illusion of coarse, shaggy grass—plus a bonus of flowers that resemble those of grape hyacinth *(Muscari)*. Rather lax, strap-shaped, dark green leaves are just ½ inch wide and about a foot long, forming mounds to around 9 inches tall; they grow from underground stems that solidly colonize the soil in the manner of a spreading turfgrass, proceeding at a slow to moderate pace. In summer, dark stalks send up spikelike clusters of pale lilac to white flowers which peek through the foliage; they're attractive but not particularly showy. Berrylike black fruits may form after the flowers fade. During the cold months, the foliage takes on a bronzy cast.

Use creeping lily turf as a casual ground cover in small areas. It's also attractive as a border along paths, between a flower bed and lawn for instance. Creeping lily turf is attractive around garden pools or streams, and it looks good in rock gardens, spreading to fill gaps and crevices. Roots of creeping lily turf compete well with roots of other plants, so planting around the base of trees and shrubs is likely to be more successful than with other ground covers.

Creeping lily turf spreads by means of underground runners, creating a dense mat.

RIGHT: *Big blue lily turf in flower.*

PEAK SEASON

The foliage looks best in summer after the new growth has covered any winter damage or the "crew cut" of a sheared bed in spring. In late summer the blue flowers show off against the dark green leaves.

MY FAVORITES

'Franklin Mint' leaves are a little wider and the color green a bit darker.

'Silver Dragon' has white stripes the length of its dark green leaves; remove all-green shoots that appear.

RELATED SPECIES

Big blue lily turf (*L. muscari*) is so similar to creeping lily turf that it is often confused with it. Most significantly, it doesn't spread to create an even mat of foliage, growing instead in slowly expanding clumps. It is also a few inches taller and slightly less cold hardy, to zone 39.

GARDEN COMPANIONS

Creeping lily turf makes an excellent ground cover under peonies and other long-lived perennials that seldom require dividing. Use it as an edging along the front of the perennial border, but take care to keep it in check. Plant grape hyacinth or daffodils into it or use it under shrubs such as viburnums.

When Plant from pots or from six-packs in the spring or anytime.

Where Provide filtered sun to full shade, though plants will tolerate more sun in cool-summer areas. Use as an underplanting for woody plants or large perennials. Or, plant beneath trees in light shade or along the bottom of a wall to soften the edge.

How Plant at the same level that the plants were growing in pots. For the first season a mulch may be necessary between the plants until they become established and fill the space between them. Water well after planting and weekly when there is little or no rain.

TLC Once established, creeping lily turf requires little care during the growing season. In the spring before growth begins, shear the winter-damaged foliage with hedge shears or a lawn mower to remove the tattered ends. New growth will cover the cut foliage in a few weeks. Fertilize the initial planting with a slow-release fertilizer or organic equivalent.

93

Dwarf Periwinkle
Vinca minor

Dwarf periwinkle's charming looks mask a thoroughly tough constitution. Spreading or arching green stems, clothed in paired shiny, oval leaves, may root at the joints or even at the tips when they touch moist soil; each newly rooted part is then another plant, ready to send out additional stems. Bloom time comes in early spring, when the foliage cover is adorned with single, phloxlike flowers of a medium-light lilac blue—the color known as periwinkle blue.

I know of several locations where substantial houses once stood and now all that is left are foundations draped in dwarf periwinkle. The ability of this plant to outlive its planter is legendary.

Dwarf periwinkle is widely adapted and available in many varieties. Dark green, narrowly oval leaves are ¾ to 1 inch long and are spaced fairly close together on the trailing stems. Plants make a carpet of stems and leaves 4 to 6 inches high, against which the blossoms stage their show.

The plant has no distinct soil preference, and even competes well with tree roots. Plants will take full sun as well as any amount of shade.

PEAK SEASON

Flowers appear in spring, but dark green leaves are attractive all season.

MY FAVORITES

There are several good cultivars of dwarf periwinkle for you to consider.

'Alba' is notable for its white flowers.

'Atropurpurea' flowers are a rich burgundy.

'Bowlesii' has deeper blue flowers and larger leaves, compared with the common form. It is also slower growing and more apt to remain in a clump, which is why it's also useful as a low-growing perennial. (If you see a plant named 'La Grave', it's either the same as 'Bowlesii' or indistinguishable from it.)

'Miss Jekyll' (also called 'Gertrude Jekyll') has white blooms on a very low-growing plant.

'Ralph Shugert' features white-margined leaves, and it reblooms in fall.

GARDEN COMPANIONS

Interplant with naturalizing bulbs such as daffodils, Siberian squill, or white crocus.

OPPOSITE PAGE: *'Atropurpurea'.*
TOP: *Dwarf periwinkle.*
BOTTOM: *'Miss Jekyll'.*

When Early spring is preferred, but well-rooted plants can be set out until midsummer if adequate water is provided.

Where Any soil, sun or shade. Plants establish most quickly with at least 6 hours of sun per day.

How Set out plants from pots, spacing them about 1½ feet apart, or closer for faster coverage. I have planted periwinkle on 8-inch centers in the spring and had nearly complete coverage of the ground by that same fall.

TLC Water newly planted periwinkle for the first two summers and fertilize lightly with a controlled-release fertilizer or organic equivalent. Whenever plantings mound too high or become layered with old stems, shear or mow them in late

summer to stimulate new growth from ground level. Light fertilization after a severe renovation of the planting will encourage strong new growth.

Dwarf Plumbago
Ceratostigma plumbaginoides

Dwarf plumbago provides a patch of vivid blue in the garden from midsummer to midautumn, when cool colors are especially welcome. Its leaves are 3-inch-long, bronzy green ovals that ascend wiry, 6- to 12-inch stems; they turn to bronzy red when frosty weather begins. At bloom time, loose clusters of phlox-like flowers in an intense bluebird blue appear at the stem ends. Bloom is heaviest and longest lasting where the growing season is long. The plant reaches about 10 inches tall and is semievergreen in our region. It will lose all of its leaves in a severe winter. It is a free spreader that provides several seasons of interest for the price of one plant.

Dwarf plumbago is as durable as English ivy, but is certainly not planted as frequently. It grows very well in our region and is definitely much underappreciated.

When Plant in the spring or early summer about the time spring growth begins.

Where Dwarf plumbago grows well in a range of soils (from clayey to sandy types) but spreads fastest in light soils. It will overwhelm smaller annuals and perennials, so it is best used by itself or beneath shrubs or trees.

How Set out plants from pots about 1 foot apart, those from 1-gallon containers 1½ feet apart. Plant at the same depth that the plants were growing in their pots. Fertilize with a complete fertilizer or organic equivalent at the time of planting, and every other spring thereafter. A light mulch between plants may be necessary to keep soil moist until the plants have filled out.

TLC At some point in fall, plants begin to look shabby as stems die to the ground; shear or mow the planting to remove dead stems and foliage before new growth resumes the following spring. Plantings will eventually become over-crowded and begin to show sparse or dead patches. When that happens, dig and replant rooted divisions at the start of the growing season.

PEAK SEASON

Foliage provides some interest throughout the growing season, but the midsummer blast of gentian blue flowers is hard to beat.

GARDEN COMPANIONS

Plant under small trees and gray-stemmed shrubs such as hornbeam, witch hazel, and viburnum. Interplant with bulbs; dwarf plumbago leafs out late in the spring, allowing the bulbs to push through without damage.

OPPOSITE PAGE: *Plumbago grows well in the partial shade of a tree.* BELOW: *Rich blue plumbago flowers start in summer and continue into fall.*

English Ivy
Hedera helix

Some gardeners swear by ivy; others swear at it! Depending on whom you ask, it's either the perfect vine and ground cover or one of the most troublesome. Once established, ivy is relentless and seemingly immortal. Ground-cover plantings will head upward if given the chance, clinging tightly by aerial rootlets to climb any vertical surface—fences, walls, tree trunks, shrub stems, flowerpots, even garden furniture. And vertically growing vining plants, if not curbed periodically, will embark on ground-level conquests, spreading out over the soil and rooting as they go. In short, ivy requires vigilance and management.

The plant's very aggressiveness and tenacity, however, can offer a distinct advantage in certain situations. As a ground cover, English ivy roots densely and deeply, providing an ideal erosion-control blanket. Vining ivy transforms any chain-link fence into a living green wall of handsome foliage. Solid walls, too, can be beautified by a dense cloak of ivy leaves, though wood surfaces and masonry joints will eventually suffer from the plant's aerial rootlets and the moist atmosphere created by its thick foliage. It's best to keep English ivy out of shade trees. Although trees are only seldom damaged, its dense foliage may mask structural problems in the tree and so lead to problems.

PEAK SEASON

Summer, when the dark blanket of leaves covers the soil.

MY FAVORITES

'238th Street' is a particular favorite, mostly because it was first collected from a Bronx churchyard on that street.

'Baltica' is somewhat more cold hardy than other cultivars, and has whitish-veined leaves just half the usual size.

'Glacier' leaves are small and silver gray. The plant makes a good ground cover for small areas. It will climb up masonry walls but is easy to keep in check.

'Thorndale' features vivid creamy white veins on extra-large, rich green leaves. It also offers improved cold hardiness.

Persian ivy *(Hedera colchica)* is less cold hardy than English ivy, so in our area it is limited to zones 32 and 34. It is the giant of the genus, with heart-shaped to oval, glossy, dark green leaves that can reach up to 7 inches across and 10 inches in length.

GARDEN COMPANIONS

Crocuses, daffodils, and snowdrops will push through a bed of ivy in the spring, bringing the bed to life. Use English ivy as an effective ground cover under showy shrubs such as witch hazel or pussy willow.

When Plant in the spring, if possible, so plants have an entire season to root. A late-summer or early-fall planting can work if some additional winter protection is provided.

Where Full sun to light shade, in well-drained soil. Use on banks and in places where soil anchorage must be ensured. Be careful not to plant English ivy where it can cover ground-level utilities that may need to be accessed, such as water valves and irrigation controllers.

How Plant from pots, plugs, or six-packs into prepared soil. Amend soil with compost and a controlled-released fertilizer prior to planting. Space plants 8 to 12 inches apart, closer for faster coverage and on slopes and banks.

ABOVE: *'Glacier' English ivy.* OPPOSITE PAGE: *English ivy serves as a ground cover under a Norway spruce and wooden bench.*

TLC English ivy is not particular about soil. For ground-cover plantings, though, a bit of preparation ensures a good start. Begin by digging or tilling the soil deeply (to 8 to 12 inches, if possible) and incorporating a generous quantity of organic matter. To decrease the mortality rate, thoroughly moisten roots and stems—and the soil—before planting. English ivy can manage with moderate watering in cool-summer locations but needs regular moisture where summers are hot. Give any ivy, whether ground cover or individual vine, regular watering during its first year to get roots established. Thereafter, Persian ivy prefers regular watering. After several years, ground-cover plantings will build up a deep thatch of stems with foliage riding on the surface—a haven for snails, slugs, and even rodents. At that point, shear the planting back to ground level or mow it with a heavy-duty mower. Do this job in early spring, and fertilize immediately afterward so new growth will quickly cover the scalped stems.

Japanese Spurge
Pachysandra terminalis

Count on Japanese spurge to bring a touch of elegance to shaded gardens. Lustrous, oval, deep green leaves, carried in whorls toward the ends of upright stems, form an even carpet about 10 inches high in full shade, about 6 inches tall with more light. The plant spreads by underground runners at a moderate rate, even competing well with tree roots. The fluffy spikes of tiny white flowers that come in late spring or early summer (sometimes followed by small white fruits) are a bonus, but Japanese spurge's main virtue is its neat, trim, good looks throughout the season.

'Silver Edge' Japanese spurge brightens shady locations by reflecting more light than varieties that are all green.

PEAK SEASON

All year, although spring has the added benefit of flowers.

MY FAVORITES

'Cut Leaf' has deeply dissected leaf margins.

'Green Carpet' features darker, glossier, denser foliage on stems that grow to about 4 inches tall. It is more compact and slower growing than the species.

'Green Sheen' is slow spreading and has notably shiny foliage, looking almost as if it is made of plastic.

'Silver Edge' ('Variegata'), a selection with creamy white leaf margins, lends an attractive sparkle to fully shaded locations. It's a bit more fussy to establish, however.

GARDEN COMPANIONS

Interplant small bulbs to provide additional interest to a pachysandra bed. Siberian squill, grape hyacinth, and glory-of-the-snow all will bloom in and among the leaves, adding springtime interest to the bed. Japanese spurge does well under large trees such as oaks and maples.

ABOVE RIGHT: *Sawtooth leaf edges and flower buds of Japanese spurge.* RIGHT: *Japanese spurge teams with other shade lovers such as hosta and mountain laurel.*

When Plant in spring or summer, at least 6 weeks before the onset of cold weather in fall.

Where Plant Japanese spurge in slightly acid, organically amended soil. It prefers partial shade.

How Plant out in individual holes, or preferably in a prepared bed. Cultivate soil about 6 inches deep and amend with compost and a controlled-release fertilizer. Plant 6 to 8 inches apart (from cuttings or flats) or 10 inches apart (from well-rooted plants). Water well and consistently during the first season.

TLC Japanese spurge needs little attention once established. During the establishment period, an annual fertilizing with a controlled-release complete fertilizer or organic equivalent in the early spring will keep the color rich and encourage spreading. Water thoroughly whenever drought threatens. Tame errant plants that creep over walls or onto walks by cutting back to another shoot inside the bed.

Juniper
Juniperus

Junipers are the universal ground covers, and they flourish throughout the Tri-State region. At least three virtues account for their popularity: ease of growing, neat appearance, and an enormous number of varieties.

Another of juniper's strong points is adaptability. As its geographic range makes clear, there's a kind for almost any climatic combination of cool and hot or moist and dry; beyond that, juniper takes soils ranging from light to heavy, acid to alkaline, even seashore conditions. Where summers are hot (especially if they're dry as well), junipers prefer partial shade; in cooler regions, they'll accept some shade but will grow better in full sun. In warm-summer areas, moderate watering will see most junipers through the dry months; in cool-summer areas, plants growing in loamy to claylike soil will likely get by with no supplemental moisture. All junipers are intolerant of water-logged soil, which will rot their roots.

Compared with other shore junipers, 'Blue Pacific' has especially dense blue-green leaves. It is more heat tolerant than other shore junipers.

PEAK SEASON

Juniper foliage is attractive year-round.

MY FAVORITES

Japanese garden juniper (*J. procumbens*) has feathery blue-green foliage and reaches to 3 feet high and up to 20 feet across. All zones.

Juniperus horizontalis offers the greatest number of cultivars for ground-cover use, a few of which are true ground-huggers that never exceed 6 inches in height. All zones.

Prostrate juniper (*Juniperus chinensis* 'Parsonii') is a slow grower that reaches 8 feet across and 1½ feet high, with stiffly horizontal main limbs densely clothed in dark foliage. All zones.

Shore juniper (*J. conferta*) has soft, bright green needles covering a trailing plant that reaches 8 feet across and 1 foot high. Zones 32, 34, 39.

Sargent juniper (*J. sargentii*) has feathery gray-green foliage on plants to 1 foot high and 10 feet across. All zones.

GARDEN COMPANIONS

Ground-cover junipers combine well with upright shrubs such as hydrangea, viburnum, and even blueberries. Avoid combining junipers and apple trees because the fungus that spreads cedar-apple rust disease uses some junipers as an alternate host.

When Spring planting is preferable, though container-grown plants may be planted anytime up until early fall.

Where Plant in full sun to part shade, depending upon the variety. Plant ground-hugging junipers so that they can spill over walls or clamber among rocks for an interesting effect.

TOP: *Bright green 'Emerald Sea' shore juniper is attractive under snow.* ABOVE: Juniperus procumbens 'Nana' *spills over a low wall.*

How Though junipers usually spread at a slow to moderate rate, it's best to set out plants from 1-gallon containers 5 to 6 feet apart to avoid overcrowding in the future. Or set plants 3 to 4 feet apart for a faster cover, then remove every other one when they start to crowd each other. Mulch between them until they fill in.

TLC Junipers are reliably carefree plants once established. Prune out broken or dead branches as they appear, typically in spring.

Lawn Grasses

The classic lawn—lush, green, and crisply mowed—has long been a basic landscaping element. Today, however, water conservation is an important issue everywhere, and attention has naturally focused on the huge amount of water needed to keep lawns alive and green. Research has shown that the traditionally favored lawngrasses (Kentucky bluegrass, bent grasses, fine fescues, and perennial ryegrass) require more water per square foot than almost any other kind of garden plant.

If you plan to include a lawn in your landscape, you can do more to save on time and water than just keeping it small. Opt for a simple geometric shape; it will allow you to irrigate without overspray, and it's easier to mow. Keeping the lawn fairly level makes good sense too; it minimizes runoff and makes mowing safer. Finally, be sure you prepare and plant the site carefully, and maintain the lawn properly.

Grass mixes used in the Northeast should contain a variety of grasses. Single-species lawns are susceptible to disease and may not do uniformly well across your entire planting area.

A lawn connects flower beds to each other as well as merging house and yard.

MY FAVORITES

Kentucky bluegrass *(Poa pratensis)* is a part of most every grass-seed mix for our region. A mix that is identified for sunny areas should have mostly bluegrass, because it grows well in sun. 'Arcadia', 'Blue Velvet', 'Midnight', and 'Princeton 105' are some of the best varieties.

Fine fescues *(Festuca rubra* and others) are notable for doing reasonably well in shaded areas, so they are always a large portion of any seed mix for shaded lawns. They're distinguished from other lawn grasses by their fine, almost needlelike blades. Red fescue, chewings, and hard fescue are favorites. 'Ambassador', 'Jamestown II', and 'Longfellow' are often recommended.

Perennial ryegrass *(Lolium perenne)* looks very much like Kentucky bluegrass, but it germinates and grows much faster. It is a part of many seed mixes because of that quick germination. It also doesn't spread the way Kentucky bluegrass and fescue do, and is somewhat less cold hardy. 'Applaud', 'Charismatic', 'Exacta', 'Manhattan', 'Palmer', 'Pennant', and 'Pizzazz' are top rated.

When Plant lawns from seed about 6 weeks before the typical date of first frost in fall, or about mid-September. Spring-seeded lawns can be successful but will require more effort to control weeds.

Where Lawn grasses need full sun to grow well. If your area is shaded by trees or tall buildings, consider a shade-tolerant ground cover instead. Lawns also need well-drained soil that has a slightly acidic pH.

How Proper site preparation is essential. Remove any existing sod with a sod cutter, and have the soil's pH tested. Spread a 3- to 4-inch layer of an organic amendment, such

An expanse of lawn is calming.

as commercial compost, and then till the site to a depth of about 8 inches. Apply a fertilizer and any other materials recommended by the soil test lab to adjust the pH, such as limestone. Till again; rake the area smooth, water, and then let the soil settle for a few days before planting.

TLC To encourage deep rooting, irrigate lawns deeply and infrequently. To determine how thirsty the lawn really is, note how it springs back from your footprint: If it doesn't, water. Most lawns require regular applications of high-nitrogen fertilizer. Ideally, fertilize twice in spring and twice in fall. Numerous kinds of bagged lawn fertilizers, both synthetic and natural, are available; check the packages for application rates. Mow regularly; grass is weakened if allowed to grow too long between mowings. Unless the clippings are quite long, leave them on the lawn to decompose and add nutrients to the soil (long clippings might smother the grass). Lawn care is a science unto itself. For the latest and most accurate information about lawn care for our region, check with your local cooperative extension office.

Siberian Carpet Cypress

Microbiota decussata

If I had to have only one plant in my garden that would demand no labor or care from me, and would bring my gardening friends to a screeching halt when they saw it, it would be a Siberian carpet cypress. This soft-textured evergreen, with both scalelike and needlelike leaves, forms a low mound of overlapping ferny foliage that may reach 6 feet across.

Siberian carpet cypress spills attractively over the edge of a flagstone pathway.

The effect is an outward-flowing fountain of branches arching gracefully to the ground. In the winter, the leaves turn a deep wine color, in striking contrast to their dull green summer color.

Siberian carpet cypress is hardy to a fault, able to tolerate temperatures to −30°F/ −34°C without effort. It grows naturally on the snow-covered and windswept barren plains of southern Siberia, and will thrive if given similar conditions in a suburban yard here.

When Set out container plants in spring.

Where Plant in partial shade, providing some shelter from the heat of the afternoon. Use to soften the top of a wall or at the corner of a planting bed along a walkway where the soft foliage and winter color can be fully appreciated. This plant will do well in most soils that drain, however a slightly acidic soil with a pH of 6.5 or below is preferable.

How Plant at the same depth that the plant was growing in the container. Provide a reasonably fertile, well-drained soil amended with peat or leaf compost.

TLC Siberian carpet cypress makes its best show when left unpruned and given adequate space to grow. It is insect and

Bright green Siberian carpet cypress provides an all-season contrast to trunks of white birch, and is a seasonal backdrop to hydrangea.

disease free, able to withstand just about any abuse except foot traffic. Although a little slow to establish, it requires little of the gardener other than a moderately fertile, well-drained site. During the first two years, provide water during periods of drought or when the top 2 inches of the soil begins to dry. Pruning is restricted to removing broken or damaged branches, and if size must be controlled, give the plant a light shearing in the spring just before growth begins.

PEAK SEASON

Siberian carpet cypress is an outstandingly tidy, handsome plant in summer. But I think that its best season is winter, when the foliage has turned reddish and a bit of snow dusts the ground and surrounding plants and rocks.

GARDEN COMPANIONS

Siberian carpet cypress combines well with upright and wide-spreading junipers and flowering shrubs such as *Rhododendron carolinianum* and oak-leaf hydrangea (*Hydrangea quercifolia*).

Sweet Woodruff

Galium odoratum

A patch of sweet woodruff always suggests the coolness of a shady woodland. Closely set whorls of narrow bright green leaves clothe slender, 6- to 12-inch stems, forming a dense carpet. From late spring into summer, this lush mat is dotted with tiny, four-petaled white flowers. Dried sweet woodruff leaves are the traditional flavoring for May wine.

Like many other woodland natives, sweet woodruff needs reasonably good, organically enriched soil and a steady supply of moisture. Given these conditions, it will spread rapidly by rooting stems, even becoming somewhat invasive. Its shallow, noncompetitive root system makes it easy to contain, though—and also makes it a fine underplanting for shade-loving trees, shrubs, and larger perennials.

PEAK SEASON

Spring when the flowers bloom, adding another dimension to sweet woodruff's uniform foliage. Summer for its neat and tidy appearance.

RELATED SPECIES

Galium mollugo and *G. aristatum* are European natives that grow well here. The first is so well adapted that it has naturalized throughout much of North America. Both have white flowers. They grow to 1 foot or more in height, so work better in a rock garden or perennial border than as a ground cover.

Yellow or ladies' bedstraw (*G. vernum*) is another European, North African, and Asian native. It produces sprawling mats of foliage decorated with yellow flowers.

GARDEN COMPANIONS

Plant sweet woodruff under shallowly rooted trees such as red maple and beech, or on slopes, provided adequate moisture can be maintained. Native perennials such as jack-in-the-pulpit and toothwort (*Dentaria heterophylla*) grow through sweet woodruff to nice effect.

OPPOSITE PAGE: *White spring flowers of sweet woodruff have a pleasant vanilla scent.* RIGHT: *Sweet woodruff's delicate look belies its wiry stems and tough nature.*

When Plant sweet woodruff in the spring or early summer.

Where Plant in a moist soil that includes plenty of organic matter. Woodland soils are ideal, but any soil will suffice if sufficient well-rotted compost is incorporated. Sweet woodruff prefers light shade but will do adequately in full sun if given a moist location with some protection from wind. Use to soften a woodland edge or as an underplanting for taller woody plants.

How Plant from pots, flats, or plugs at the same level that the plants were growing in the nursery containers. Space plants 6 to 9 inches apart, water well, and lightly fertilize with a controlled-release complete fertilizer or organic equivalent about a month after planting.

TLC Little additional care is required. Some cleanup of old foliage and stems in the fall may be necessary to tidy up the garden, and a light fertilization early each spring will enhance growth.

Spillers and Fillers

Some plants lend themselves to tight and tidy places along the edge of the walk or next to the door. They stay where you put them, do what you ask of them, and provide flowers or fruit with clockwork predictability. Other plants that cascade over an edge or spread between pavers are valued for their ability to tough it out where more delicate plants may fail. Use these "spillers and fillers" to soften edges, to hide the unsightly parts of a masonry wall, or to cover a slope that would be unsuitable for more formal treatments.

Bugleweed *(Ajuga reptans)* is capable of filling in between practically anything. Usually only 1 to 3 inches tall, its purple leaves are decorative throughout the seasons, but do be careful: it can creep away if unattended. All zones.

Lady's mantle *(Alchemilla mollis)* forms a dome-shaped mound of gray-green foliage that will hold the last drops of rain or dew to sparkle in the sunshine. It has chartreuse

flowers and makes a very nice edging in hard-to-maintain locations. Zones 32, 34–43.

Coreopsis verticillata 'Moonbeam' is a tall ground cover (14 or 15 inches in height). It will willingly fill the space in front of a wall or between rocks and boulders where other plants would not. All zones.

Cotoneaster dammeri 'Coral Beauty' and *C. apiculatus* are low-growing, spreading shrubs that hang down over the edge of a wall and scramble between rocks. Foliage is tidy and provides good fall color; fruits range from clear red to an attractive coral. Zones 32, 34–41.

Forsythia suspensa and *F.* 'Arnold Dwarf' are low and draping versions of forsythia that are hard to beat for covering an unmanageable bank or rock outcrop. Planted above, *F. suspensa* will drape 6 to 10 feet, and blooms yellow in early spring. *F.* 'Arnold Dwarf' is daintier, but

a reliable performer in smaller spaces. Zones 32, 34–41.

Coralbells (*Heuchera sanguinea* 'Apple Blossom', 'Bressingham Blaze' and 'Mt. St. Helens') provide wonderful foliage in green or deep purple, with tiny swaying flowers in pink, coral, or red. For hard-to-fill crevices where you need an 8-inch-tall plant with 12-inch-tall flowers, coralbells answer the call. All zones.

Aaron's beard (*Hypericum calycinum*) grows 1 foot tall (or more), but it is prized for its ability to fill in among rocks and tree trunks and along steps. Tender in the northern range, it may die to the ground in winter. It bears brilliant yellow flowers most of the summer. Zones 32, 34.

Winter jasmine (*Jasminum nudiflorum*) is a near perfect bank-cloaking plant. Its pendulous green stems are interesting to look at in winter and summer, and the yellow flowers on warm days in the dead of winter are a joy to behold. Zones 32, 34, 39.

Drooping leucothoe (*Leucothoe fontanesiana* 'Nana' and 'Scarletta') drapes readily over walls and banks and provides white flowers against green or variegated foliage. Winter color on this evergreen is a deep wine or purple. Zones 32, 34–43.

Wire vine (*Mazus reptans*) has purple flowers and such cheerful green foliage that you'd never suspect its potential to spread quickly and become weedy if not managed wisely. It is outstanding in shady places where other plants would not thrive. Zones 32, 34, 39.

Creeping phlox (*Phlox stolonifera*) and moss pink (*P. subulata*) are valued members of the "rock and wall planting" list. Both are hardy to below zero, and both prefer rich organic soil. All zones.

Creeping thyme (*Thymus serpyllum* 'Albus' and 'Roseus') is the perfect plant to fill between flagstones and pavers, and to cover any place where walking on it or brushing against it will release the wonderful fragrance. My mother-in-law's entire front yard is creeping thyme. All zones.

Native Ground Covers

Native ground covers bear the distinction of being adapted to the region in which we Tri-Staters are gardening. This can ease the burden of garden maintenance and care when establishing a new garden or provide a sense of integration in a woodland garden. Native plants are adapted to the soil, moisture, and sunlight conditions that you have in your garden. In contrast, plants from the other side of the globe may be attractive and interesting enough to find their way to your local nursery, but ultimately may be difficult to grow or prone to pest problems.

Bearberry *(Arctostaphylos uva-ursi)* is a ground-cover vine that forms a mat 6 to 8 feet wide. Leaves are small and green with a purple tinge; fruit is red and edible but mild tasting. Zones 34, 37–44.

Wild ginger *(Asarum canadense)* is the aristocrat of the woodlands. It is slow growing with glossy leaves, and once established it requires no maintenance. It thrives in a woodland garden, or nestled into a special shady niche where its interesting bell-shaped flowers can delight. Zones 32, 34–44.

Golden star *(Chrysogonum virginianum)* is a flowering woodland spreader that makes an excellent filler in a native or naturalistic garden setting. It combines nicely with evergreen shrubs. Golden yellow, star-shaped flowers come in spring and fall. Zones 32, 34–39.

Blooming fringed bleeding heart is backed by ostrich fern.

Golden star blooms in both spring and fall.

Bunchberry *(Cornus canadensis)* is a true ground-cover dogwood and a prize to have in a woodland or shady garden. White flowers cover the plant in late spring. The diminutive, 6- to 9-inch-high spreader requires rich organic soil and consistent moisture to flourish. All zones.

Dwarf redtwig dogwood (*Cornus sericea* 'Kelseyi') is a wide spreading, 18-inch-tall version of the common redtwig dogwood (see pages 74 and 75). In addition to its low stature, 'Kelseyi' is prized for its dense mound of arching foliage. Plant it at the top of a wall in full sun. White flowers in spring are secondary to the fine foliage. All zones.

Fringed bleeding heart *(Dicentra eximia)* is a graceful flowering woodland plant that produces a raft of heart-shaped pink flowers from midspring to early fall. The delicate foliage mixes well with ferns in locations where other plants would appear cramped or stiff, such as between rocks and along steps. All zones.

Fragrant sumac *(Rhus aromatica)* is a tidy, mound-forming, 3- to 5-foot-high shrub that will drift over walls and rocks. Tiny yellowish flowers come in spring, and in fall, the fragrant leaves turn a stunning orange-red. Zones 32, 34–43.

113

Deciduous Trees

Try to imagine your neighborhood stripped of its trees: You would feel exposed and, the natural landscape would seem out of kilter. ˙ees settle our homes and gardens into the larger landscape, giving ˙ sense of our world as a three-dimensional space. They put ceilings ˙ gardens. They turn our streets into green cathedrals.

Trees have many practical virtues too. They help clean the air by cycling pollutants through their leaves, and their roots help prevent erosion by holding soil in place. Trees also serve as windbreaks, and their nuts and berries are dietary staples for countless species of birds and other small creatures.

Deciduous trees retain their branches and stems year-round but lose all their foliage in autumn with the onset of cold weather. In spring, new leaves unfurl from leaf buds that formed the previous summer. Trees of this type form flower buds as well, which bloom in spring, summer, or fall, depending on the species.

TYPES OF TREES

What distinguishes trees from shrubs is their growth habit. Shrubs are bushy, with numerous stems growing up from the base of the plants, and seldom exceed 15 feet in height. Trees with a single trunk typically grow much taller, and branches higher up on the trunk create a dense canopy. The branches may curve gently upward from the trunk to form the shape of a vase; they may grow out from the trunk horizontally; or they may even have a "weeping" habit, meaning that the branches actually grow downward. Some trees' branches grow out and then up, like the candle holders on a menorah.

Most trees look best and stay healthiest when they are allowed to assume their natural shape and are pruned only to remove diseased or damaged limbs or to thin the canopy just a little so more sunlight can reach the interior branches. That means choosing the right tree in the first place. All too often, I see what could have been a spectacular crabapple, magnolia, or cherry tree that has been aggressively pruned, resulting in a tightly packed web of shoots and suckers that destroys its beauty. Select a tree with a mature size that fits the space you have. Prune in moderation, unless of course you are creating an espalier or other rigidly formal art form with the plant.

PLANTING A TREE

Trees are sold as bare-root, balled-and-burlapped, or container plants. Bare-root plants must be planted immediately. Burlap should be removed or folded back before planting, or it will wick water away from the roots. Avoid root-bound container plants if you can. If that's not possible, you'll need to force roots that are

ABOVE: *Especially bright green leaves unfurl from this pin oak in spring.* OPPOSITE PAGE: *Mature dogwood trees at the peak of their spring bloom shelter azaleas.*

growing in circles to change course, even if this means cutting them with pruning shears.

Make planting holes two or three times wider than the rootball, and backfill with the excavated soil, moderately amended at most. Bare-root trees may need to be staked. If you suspect rodents are nibbling at a trunk, you can deter them by applying a tree wrap or plastic tree guard. A circle of mulch will keep down weeds at the base of the tree and, more important, protect the trunk from your lawn mower. Though young trees benefit from some fertilizing and a cover of mulch to hold in moisture, the trees I'm recommending here shouldn't need much of your time to maintain excellent health if thoughtfully placed and properly planted.

—WAYNE CAHILLY

Dogwood
Cornus

ABOVE: *Yellow flowers of Cornelian cherry contrast with bulb flowers.* OPPOSITE PAGE: *Pink flower bracts of 'Rubra' dogwood.*

Native to the eastern United States from New England to central florida, flowering dogwood *(Cornus florida)* has been called the most beautiful native tree of North America. In some situations, it grows 40 feet tall and as wide, but closer to half that size is more typical. The tree branches low to the ground and sends branches out horizontally, turning up at the tips. The effect is a distinctive appearance through the growing season, and an equally unique and good-looking winter silhouette.

But the flowers that come in spring are the main attraction. The 2- to 4-inch-wide flowers (or more accurately, bracts) cover the tree in midspring before leaves have fully emerged. The typical color is white, but there are numerous named selections that have colors ranging between white and red. Dogwoods provide more than just a springtime show. In fall, leaves turn a glowing red before falling, and then clusters of small, oval, scarlet fruits remain for weeks.

The only shadow over this otherwise outstanding tree is a fungus disease called anthracnose. The Kousa dogwood, and hybrids of it and *C. florida,* are largely resistant to the disease. Other dogwoods offer greater hardiness and a variety of other ornamental features.

When Plant in spring before growth begins if planting balled-and-burlapped trees. Plant anytime until midsummer from containers if adequate water can be provided during the heat of summer.

Where Select a location with some afternoon shade. Although dogwoods will do adequately in full sun, some, such as *C. florida*, are understory trees preferring to have the shelter of larger trees. Plant in good garden soil modestly amended with leaf compost. Use as a focal point at the end of a garden, or to flank a long path backed by larger trees such as oaks and maples.

How Plant dogwoods at the same depth that they were growing at the nursery. Dig the planting hole at least twice as wide as the rootball or container but only as deep as the rootball. Position the plant and straighten it by moving the ball, not by holding the stem. Backfill the hole halfway, then firm the soil with your hands. Finish filling the hole and firm the remaining soil, then water thoroughly.

TLC Water dogwoods well through the first two growing seasons, never allowing them to suffer from drought. Fertilize in the fall after leaves fall with a controlled-release fertilizer or organic equivalent and water it in. Prune dead, damaged, or diseased wood, and remove crossing branches that rub each other, causing wounds. When pruning, take care to not remove too many branches at one time or water sprouts—upright growing shoots that are out of character with the plant's form—will result.

PEAK SEASON
Spring and fall

MY FAVORITES
'Rubra' is my favorite flowering dogwood. I especially like its pink flowers, and the winter flower buds. Zones 32, 34–41.

Cornelian cherry (*Cornus mas*) has yellow flowers early in spring that are followed by red fruits. Zones 32, 34–41.

Kousa dogwood (*C. kousa*) can reach 30 feet high and 20 feet wide, and blooms a month after *C. florida*. It is resistant to anthracnose disease. Zones 32 and 34.

Pagoda dogwood (*C. alternifolia*) grows 15 to 20 feet high by 12 to 15 feet wide. Tiny white flowers come in attractive flat heads that are about 4 inches across. Zones 32, 34–43.

Stellar dogwood (*C. × rutgersensis*) has good resistance to anthracnose disease and blooms midseason, thus filling a gap usually reserved for crabapples and cherries. Zones 32, 34–41.

GARDEN COMPANIONS
Dogwoods are excellent small to mid-size garden trees that look appealing with a ground cover of ivy or pachysandra. Plant them with low perennials such as astilbe or meadow phlox, or foliage plants such as hosta.

Eastern Redbud

Cercis canadensis

T hough the tree is called redbud, the buds of this native tree are pink-purple, not red. They open in early spring on bare branches, just as most other trees and shrubs are beginning to leaf out. The exquisite flowers are followed by large, heart-shaped leaves and interesting flat, beanlike pods that may cling to the tree well into winter.

Redbuds and daffodils color a perfect spring day.

Eastern redbud has a rounded head and grows quickly to 30 feet in height. It is rapidly gaining popularity, as much for its stately, upright posture and spreading branches as for its flowers. It is happiest in a woodland setting. Redbud is a beloved harbinger of spring. In the coldest parts of our region, the flowers are always at risk of being nipped by a late frost, which is why gardeners in zone 43 should purchase only the Northland strain eastern redbud and plant it in a protected site. That small risk aside, flowers in March or early April are worth the risk of losing them to an early frost.

PEAK SEASON

Flowers come in spring, but the tree looks good in all seasons.

MY FAVORITES

'Flame' has double pink flowers and grows vigorously. The branching is more upright than the species and flowering is a bit later, thus this cultivar is rarely damaged by frost.

'Forest Pansy' has pink-purple flowers and deep purple foliage that remains purple through the heat of summer. Fall color is a purple-red. A very nice accent plant for use in perennial gardens or borders.

'Royal White' is a rare white-flowered cultivar that flowers heavily. 'Alba' is more readily available than 'Royal White' and its white flowers contrast sharply with its nearly black stems.

'Silver Cloud' has striking variegated foliage that is marbled with silvery white. The plant is less vigorous than the species and flowers are a bit on the sparse side, but when the tree is grown in part shade, the foliage will light up a garden corner nicely.

GARDEN COMPANIONS

Plant redbud in front of tall evergreens to accent flowers. Under-plant with bunchberry (C. canadensis) or sweet woodruff (Galium odoratum). In a more formal setting, blue junipers contrast well.

When Plant balled-and-burlapped trees as soon as you can work the ground in spring, or from containers into midsummer. Avoid fall planting.

Where Partial shade is preferred, but full sun or shade will do. Rebud grows best in moist but well-drained soil that is high in organic matter. Plant a single redbud as a focal point where it will have plenty of room to grow into its lovely mature form, or plant it in groups at a forest edge.

White-flowered 'Alba' redbud.

How Remove the tree from its container carefully, keeping the rootball intact. Plant at the same depth that it was growing in the container, in a hole as deep as the rootball and wide enough to accommodate the roots without crowding. Plant a balled-and-burlapped tree so that the root flare is right at the soil surface, cutting and removing as much of the burlap and wire as possible without injuring roots. Gently firm soil around the roots and water thoroughly, making sure there are no air pockets.

TLC Keep the soil evenly moist from spring until the ground freezes in fall, especially during the first 2 years. Water deeply to encourage deep root growth. Apply 2 to 4 inches of organic mulch such as shredded bark or wood chips and replenish as needed throughout the growing season. Trees will benefit if fertilized every other spring just before growth begins. You may prune off dead, damaged, or diseased branches anytime.

The Northland strain of eastern redbud is hardy to zone 43.

European Beech
Fagus sylvatica

A mature European beech has a mammoth, stout trunk covered with very smooth gray bark and wide-spreading branches that sweep to the ground. Leaves are dark glossy green and toothed, though cut-leaved forms with dark purple summer foliage are popular too.

European beeches are ornamental through the year. When leafless in the winter, their majestic silhouettes are shown off in full glory. A European beech is late to leaf out in spring, and the new foliage is often copper-colored, especially in the purple-leaved forms. Leaves may cling to the branches well into winter. The tiny triangular nuts are edible.

Leaves of fernleaf beech, F. sylvatica 'Asplenifolia', are deeply lobed, nearly to the midrib.

120

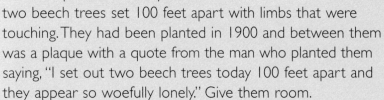

When Plant in the early spring. Beeches resent transplanting, but if planted early before they begin to leaf out they move well.

Where Use as a specimen where the tree will have full sun, well-drained soil, and space to develop. I have seen two beech trees set 100 feet apart with limbs that were touching. They had been planted in 1900 and between them was a plaque with a quote from the man who planted them saying, "I set out two beech trees today 100 feet apart and they appear so woefully lonely." Give them room.

How Place the plant so that the top of the rootball is even with or slightly above the surrounding soil, in a location where adequate moisture is available. Amend the soil slightly if at all, and water well to eliminate air pockets. If the plant was grown in a container, be sure to cut roots that have begun to circle in the pot. Once they begin to grow in a circular pattern, they will not branch out into the surrounding soil unless cut.

TLC Cover the ground beneath a beech with a mulch; don't try to grow anything there. Prune away sprouts that arise from the base or roots. Watering during dry spells is critical. Beech trees normally grow in a forest bottomland where moisture is abundant. Although they tolerate garden conditions well, additional care in watering will ensure establishment and success. Prune only to remove dead, damaged, or diseased branches, or those that are rubbing against others, causing damage.

PEAK SEASON

Foliage is excellent spring through fall; winter silhouette is stately.

MY FAVORITES

'Dawyck' is a living exclamation point, usually only 15 to 20 feet wide while reaching 50 feet in height.

'Laciniata' is a catchall name for the many cut-leaved beeches sold under names such as 'Asplenifolia' (the fernleaf beech). Leaves have 7 to 9 sharply pointed lobes. The tree grows 80 feet high and 40 feet wide.

'Pendula' looks droopy at first, but grows 50 feet high and 60 feet wide, appearing to pile up on itself in successive waves of gray branches and green foliage.

'Purpurea' produces foliage ranging from coppery bronze to deep purple. There are several related cultivars, such as darker 'Purpurea Spaethiana'. They all grow to the full proportions of the green-leaved species, reaching 80 feet by 50 feet.

'Tricolor' grows to 25 feet at most. It produces leaves edged in pink in the spring, but turning white or cream by midsummer.

GARDEN COMPANIONS

Beeches can provide a dramatic backdrop for flowering trees such as crabapples or dogwoods, and a foil for midsized evergreens.

With leaves edged in pink, white, or cream, the tricolor beech (F. sylvatica 'Tricolor') is a showy accent.

121

Flowering Cherry

Prunus

Think pink. Each spring at daffodil and tulip time, flowering cherry trees erupt into giant puffs of horticultural cotton candy. These trees are graceful and varied, coming in many shapes and many shades from white to pink, with either single or double blossoms that, in some selections, are carried in pendant clusters. Fruits are negligible to nonexistent.

Japanese flowering cherry *(Prunus serrulata)* offers the most variations, though the prevailing dimensions are to about 25 feet high and 20 feet wide. Narrowly oval leaves emerge bronzy green or green and remain lustrous green through the growing season, until fall changes them to bronzy red. Yoshino flowering cherry *(P. × yedoensis)* is a rounded, 40- by 30-foot, horizontally branched tree bearing pale pink to white blossoms. In gardens, it is best known by its selection 'Akebono', a cloud of pale pink blossoms on a tree that reaches 25 feet in both directions.

When Flowering cherries are sold as bare-root trees during the winter dormant period. Buy and plant as early as possible during that time so trees have the longest possible stretch of cool weather in which to put out new roots.

Where Plant cherries in full sun where the ground can be kept moist but not wet. Good soil aeration is key to success with flowering cherries, so avoid locations where soil is compacted or waterlogged.

How The day before planting, soak the roots of a bare-root tree in water to make sure tissues are fully plumped up. Then dig a planting hole two or three times as wide as the tree's root system but a bit shallower. Dig deeper around the hole's inside edge to leave a firm center, then form a firm soil cone and spread the tree's roots over it, adjusting so the juncture of roots and trunk will be just slightly above the soil grade. Fill in with soil, firming it as you go. Water the newly planted tree thoroughly, then stake it for the first year or two so it won't be badly buffeted in strong winds. Plant container or balled-and-burlapped trees at the depth that they were growing in the container or nursery. Dig a hole that is just as deep but at least twice as wide as the rootball. Backfill with soil that is well broken up, and firm lightly but sufficiently for the plant to stand straight. Water well to eliminate air pockets.

PEAK SEASON

Early spring is the big show. Leaves turn yellow, orange, or red in fall.

MY FAVORITES

'Accolade', a hybrid, is broadly pendulous with dark pink buds opening to pink blossoms.

Autumn cherry (*Prunus subhirtella* 'Autumnalis') is a small tree that flowers both in fall and in spring. 'Autumnalis Rosea' is the pink form.

Japanese flowering cherry (*P. serrulata*) is known for its large trusses of white or pink flowers. Cultivars include 'Beni Hoshi', 'Kwanzan', 'Shogetsu, and 'Snow Fountains'.

Weeping Higan cherry (*P. subhirtella* 'Pendula') is one of many weeping trees with pale pink flowers and 20-foot-high and -wide growth habit.

Yoshino flowering cherry (*P. × yedoensis* 'Akebono', sometimes sold as 'Daybreak') is the flowering cherry planted in the tidal basin display in Washington, D.C.

GARDEN COMPANIONS

Flowering cherries are striking when underplanted with early spring bulbs such as yellow daffodils, blue grape hyacinth, or Siberian squill. Choice shrub companions include azalea, rhododendron, mountain laurel, or bayberry.

OPPOSITE PAGE: *Close-up of flowers of weeping Higan cherry.* BELOW: *'Kwanzan' cherry at peak bloom.*

TLC Flowering cherries need only moderate watering after the first two growing seasons. Prune only to guide framework development, remove badly placed branches, and eliminate deadwood as it occurs. Overpruning results in the reduction of flowers and the proliferation of water sprouts and other unsightly growth.

Flowering Crabapple
Malus

This genus includes many different kinds of apple trees. Some bear the familiar large apples, others produce smaller crabapples for eating and cooking, and some—the flowering crabapples—are grown for their spectacular show of flowers.

Some flowering crabapples have a horizontal branching habit that is well suited to the tranquil mood and flowing lines of a Japanese garden; others stand tall and erect and look wonderful in rows along a street, driveway, or fence. The flowers come in white, pink, or various shades of red, and are usually followed by attractive fruits that vary in size and color depending on the species and variety. Branch color ranges from tan to gray to purplish red.

Wonderful as crabapples are, in the Tri-States apple scab disease is common and sometimes serious enough to completely disfigure the trees. The disease causes dark brown or black discolored spots on leaves. And cedar apple rust, which causes coppery bull's-eye spots on leaves, is also common. But there is a remedy for both: disease-resistant cultivars. If you are planning to plant a flowering crabapple, choose one, such as those recommended here, that is resistant to one or both of these diseases.

ABOVE: *Light pink flowers of 'Sugar Tyme'.*
OPPOSITE PAGE: *Sargent crabapple at peak bloom.*

PEAK SEASON

Flowers in spring, fruits in winter

MY FAVORITES

'Dolgo' blooms early and produces large edible fruits; 25 feet high by 35 feet wide.

'Red Jade' is a spectacular white-flowered weeping tree; 15 feet high and wide.

'Donald Wyman' has a broad canopy, carmine buds opening to white flowers, long-lasting fruit, and glossy leaves; 20 feet high by 25 feet wide.

'Prairifire' has a rounded canopy, pink flowers, and exceptional disease tolerance; 20 feet high and wide.

Sargent crabapple (*Malus sargentii*) is a small, 15-foot-high and -wide tree with a dense branching habit and profuse white flowers.

'Snowdrift' has copious pink buds opening to white flowers that are followed by long-lasting orange fruit; 20 foot high and wide.

'Sugar Tyme' has an upright, oval shape; pink flowers age to white; red fruits are long lasting; 18 feet high by 15 feet wide.

GARDEN COMPANIONS

Beneath your crabapple trees, plant spring bloomers such as these:

• primroses
• early-spring bulbs
• shade-loving annuals like impatiens

When Plant bare-root flowering crab-apples as soon as you can work the ground in spring, soaking roots in water for 2 hours first. Plant container trees anytime until early fall. Water as needed for the first 2 years.

Where Best flowering is in full sun. A site with good air circulation decreases the chance of leaf spot disease. Give trees well-drained soil with a slightly acidic pH.

How Plant at the same depth as it was in the field or container, in a hole deep and wide enough to accommodate the roots without crowding. Gently firm soil around the roots and water thoroughly, making sure there are no air pockets.

TLC Keep the soil evenly moist from spring until the ground freezes in fall, especially during the first 2 years. Water deeply to encourage deep root growth. Apply 2 to 4 inches of organic mulch, such as shredded bark or wood chips, and replenish as needed throughout the growing season. Fertilize annually, in spring before growth begins; or use an organic or controlled-release fertilizer in the fall just after leaves drop. Protect the thin bark of young trees from chewing critters by wrapping the lower trunk with a commercially available plastic cylinder or hardware cloth. Prune only to remove dead, damaged, and diseased branches or to eliminate crossing branches that are damaging others. Overly aggressive pruning results in the single biggest disappointment in growing crabapples—the proliferation of water sprouts.

Some varieties, including 'Donald Wyman' and 'Snowdrift', are hardy to zone 44.

Heritage River Birch

Betula nigra 'Heritage'

It's unusual to recommend just one specific cultivar of a Top 10 tree, but this tree is indeed one of a kind.

The heritage river birch does have many relatives that are good ornamental trees, but none compare favorably to this most famous member of the clan. Whereas most trees have a single trunk, heritage river birch likes to fork at ground level, forming several spreading trunks, an advantage because their golden, peeling bark is one of this tree's chief attractions.

Heritage river birch loves our hot, humid summers and is able to tolerate poor drainage. It also looks great in winter, when its bark becomes very prominent.

River birch is native to the eastern United States and grows quickly in its youth. Over time, it will reach 50 feet high or more. Dark green leaves are diamond-shaped and 1 to 3 inches long. Young bark is smooth and shiny, and apricot- to pink-colored. On older trees, random sections of the bark curl off in sheets revealing a cinnamon brown to blackish inner bark.

If you're looking for a well-behaved and easy-to-grow tree for your yard, give this one serious consideration.

PEAK SEASON

Its ragged bark is attractive all year and is complemented in summer by clean, green foliage.

RELATED SPECIES

'Crispa' European white birch (*Betula pendula* 'Crispa') is a cut-leaved birch with a white trunk and pendulous growth habit. 'Youngii' is a strong weeper frequently grafted onto a 5- or 6-foot stem.

B. jacquemontii is a variable species, some with chalk white bark and others more gray-white. Twiggy almost to a fault, this tree produces a moderately heavy crown for a birch and should be used as a midsized shade tree if grown in the open.

Monarch birch (*B. maximowicziana*) is a long-lived tree with a gray-white trunk that reaches 50 or more feet in height with graceful, slender branches and roundish leaves.

GARDEN COMPANIONS

River birch looks good in an informal setting with flowering dogwoods, as well as with a backdrop of evergreens such as Norway spruce or underplanted with large-leaved hostas or ferns.

When Plant river birch as soon as you can work the ground in spring.

Where River birch prefers sun but will grow in partial shade. It likes well-drained, slightly acidic to average soil. It tolerates moist or even wet sites but not drought. Plant it where you can enjoy the interesting bark.

How Remove the tree from its container carefully, keeping the rootball intact. Plant at the same depth that it was growing in the container, in a hole as deep and two to three times as wide as the rootball. Plant a balled-and-burlapped tree so that the root flare is right at the soil surface, cutting and removing as much of the burlap and wire as possible without injuring roots. Gently firm soil around the roots and water thoroughly, making sure there are no air pockets. A controlled-release fertilizer or organic equivalent may be applied in the fall after leaves have dropped.

TLC Keep the soil evenly moist from spring until the ground freezes in fall, especially during the first 2 years. Water

deeply to encourage adequate root growth. Maintain 2 to 4 inches of organic mulch such as shredded bark, leaf compost, or wood chips throughout the growing season. Do annual shaping in summer to avoid heavy sap flow.

LEFT: *Peeling bark is showy in winter.* OPPOSITE PAGE: *River birch in early spring.*

Hornbeam

Carpinus

Hornbeam is compact and tidy, with a dense, leafy canopy and pretty, nutlike fruits that hang in drooping clusters. The leaves last well into fall, and the trunk's smooth, gray-blue bark lends an air of sophistication to the garden. Hornbeam is excellent both as a boulevard plant and for making allées, along a driveway, for example. You can use these trees to make "hedges on stilts" by planting them close together in straight rows and training the canopies to grow together through frequent shearing.

The European species *(Carpinus betulus)* has a tighter, more pyramidal shape than the native American hornbeam *(C. caroliniana)*. American hornbeam tolerates both sun and heavy shade, doesn't mind being waterlogged, and is often found along rivers as an understory plant. Its leaves fall off earlier than the European hornbeam's do; otherwise the two species are quite similar. Both have very hard wood and grow fairly slowly.

LEFT: *Leaves of American hornbeam turn attractive shades of yellow, orange, and red in fall.* OPPOSITE PAGE: *'Fastigiata' European hornbeam in early spring.*

PEAK SEASON

Undulations in hornbeam's smooth, slate gray bark look good year-round, and the dark green leaves turn yellow, orange, and red in fall.

MY FAVORITES

European hornbeam (*Carpinus betulus* 'Fastigiata') is most common and has a striking flamelike shape. This cultivar begins as a narrow, tightly growing, upright plant, but as it reaches middle age, it begins to spread until it is 30 feet tall and 18 or 20 feet wide. It stays so neat and uniform you might think it had been sheared. Zones 32, 34–41.

American hornbeam (*C. caroliniana*) is native and very hardy. It grows 20 to 30 feet high and wide, has a round shape, and makes a good tall hedge. It's slightly hardier than European hornbeam, to zone 43. I know of one such hedge that is 15 feet high and 6 feet wide, and has been maintained since the early 1940s. Zones 32, 34–43.

GARDEN COMPANIONS

European hornbeams are right at home in a formal setting with clipped conifers, boxwood hedges, and perfect lawns. Plant American hornbeams in a more natural setting with moisture-loving shrubs such as shrubby dogwood, bayberry, or spice bush and trees such as willows or river birch.

When Set out young plants in early spring for best results.

Where Hornbeams prefer sun to partial shade, but American hornbeam will grow in heavy shade below taller trees. All need well-drained, slightly acidic soil. American hornbeam is a great small tree in naturalized landscapes and mixes well with native shrubs and ground covers. Use the more upright European hornbeam as a landscape specimen.

How Remove the tree from its container carefully, keeping the rootball intact. Plant at the same depth that it was growing in the container, in a hole big enough to accommodate the roots without crowding. Plant a balled-and-burlapped tree so that the root flare is right at the soil surface; cut and remove as much of the burlap and wire as possible without injuring roots. Gently firm soil around the roots and water thoroughly, making sure there are no air pockets.

TLC Keep the soil evenly moist from spring until the ground freezes in fall, especially during the first 2 years. Water deeply to encourage deep root growth. Apply 2 to 4 inches of organic mulch such as shredded bark, leaf compost, or wood chips around the base of European hornbeam. Remove any root suckers that appear, and don't mulch—that tends to encourage them. Fertilization is rarely required, except perhaps the first year and then only when poor growth indicates need. Annual shaping can be done in late winter. Prune off dead, damaged, or diseased branches anytime. European hornbeam tolerates clipping, and young branches can be interwoven to form an effective barrier.

Katsura Tree

Cercidiphyllum japonicum

Katsura tree is a formal-looking tree with a tall, pyramidal shape that becomes broader with age. In fall, when the foliage of many trees is colorful, there are still very few that can rival a katsura tree. Colors are a brilliant orange to red, or a clear yellow.

This species has the potential to become a landscape giant if given the room and an appropriate location. I know of one that is over 60 feet in width and nearly as tall, with huge, multiple trunks.

Cinnamon-scented leaves are heart-shaped and dense. They emerge reddish purple and gradually change to dark green.

Katsura tree is well mannered and has strikingly attractive leaves.

PEAK SEASON

Fall is the peak season, but summer foliage is neat and trim.

MY FAVORITES

'Magnificum Pendulum' is a weeping form with slightly larger leaves.

'Pendulum' is a weeping form, though it still becomes quite large. A very beautiful specimen tree, it can spread to 40 feet wide.

GARDEN COMPANIONS

Katsura tree looks excellent with sugar maples and fothergilla, both of which also turn wonderful shades of red and orange in the fall.

BELOW LEFT: *In fall, the leaves of katsura tree turn brilliant colors.* BELOW RIGHT: *In spring, emerging leaves show a purple tint before becoming green.*

When Katsura trees are best planted when small, as they resent transplanting. Plant in spring before leaves emerge if the plant is balled-and-burlapped, or any-time until midsummer if container-grown. Avoid fall planting if pos-sible, as this species needs to root sufficiently to make it successfully through the winter in severe climates.

Where Katsura trees need moist, well-drained soil. Drought, even if only occasional, will set them back. Give this tree room. It requires full sun and good air circulation. Use as a specimen, or to block an unattractive view.

How Plant at the same depth that the tree was growing in the nursery or in the container. Dig the hole at least two to three times as wide as the rootball and amend the soil with well-rotted compost. Backfill the hole and water well.

TLC To enhance fall color, withhold water somewhat in late summer if possible (but don't cause the plant to wilt). Soil that is acidic will also enhance fall color. Fertilize once every two or three years with an organic or controlled-release fertil-izer applied in the fall after leaves have dropped. Mulch with 2 inches of well-rotted leaf compost or wood chips. Keep the lawn mower away from the base of the tree; Katsura trees will frequently produce roots near the surface, and lawn mower damage to these roots should be avoided.

Magnolia
Magnolia

While the classic southern magnolia *(Magnolia grandiflora)* is rightly appreciated and well known, there are many other magnolias that thrive in our region. Most notable of these is the star magnolia *(M. stellata)*, whose flowers are shaped like stars and come in white, pink, yellow, or lavender. The flowers bloom early, before the leaves unfurl. This makes for some anxious moments when late frosts are forecast, for once the flowers are nipped by frost they're done for. Fortunately, flowers aren't star magnolias' only virtue.

Flowers of native sweet bay *(M. virginiana)* are fragrant and hardy throughout much of the Tri-State region. This tree is typically semievergreen, although it may drop all of its leaves in the colder locations.

The spring display of 'Rosea' star magnolia equals any rhododendron.

The saucer magnolias *(M. × soulangeana)* present 6-inch goblet-shaped blooms on bare limbs in early spring. Flower colors range from pure white through yellow, pink, and red.

PEAK SEASON

Showy flowers appear in early spring, usually before the leaves.

MY FAVORITES

Magnolia loebneri blooms with fragrant flowers on a tree that can reach 25 feet in height and spread. 'Merrill' grows fast and covers itself in blooms in April. Zones 32, 34–41.

Star magnolia (*M. stellata*) grows 20 feet high. Its flowers appear in April and are sometimes nipped by a late frost. 'Rosea' is a pink-budded cultivar. Zones 32, 34–41.

Saucer magnolia (*M. soulangiana*) is a wide-spreading tree (illustrated above right) with pinkish purple flower buds that open to reveal a snow white interior. Many cultivars are available. Zones 32, 34–41.

The Kosar-DeVos hybrids include 'Ann' (purplish red) and 'Jane' (pink). Their flowers open later in spring and are less likely to be nipped by frost. Zones 32, 34–43.

Sweet bay (*M. virginiana*) has creamy white flowers that bloom sporadically all summer and have a sweet fragrance. Zones 32, 34, 37.

GARDEN COMPANIONS

Plant in mixed borders where the magnolia's flowers can enjoy the company of early-spring bulbs like scilla, daffodils, and early tulips.

TOP: *The seed pod of sweet magnolia.*
BOTTOM: *The pearly white flower of 'Merrill'.*

When Plant or transplant all magnolias in early spring. This is counter to much garden literature but is backed by experience showing that the rate of planting and transplanting success increases considerably in early spring, peaking when this species blooms, then diminishes quickly as leaves emerge.

Where Plant in full sun at a location protected from winter winds, to help protect flower buds. Avoid planting in low-lying areas that can trap cold air in late spring. Magnolias grow best in soil that is rich with organic matter and has a slightly acidic to nearly neutral pH.

How Plant the tree at the same depth that it was growing in the container, in a hole deep and wide enough to accommodate the roots without crowding. Plant a balled-and-burlapped tree so that the root flare is right at the soil surface, cutting and removing as much of the burlap and wire as possible. Gently firm soil around the roots and water thoroughly, making sure there are no air pockets.

TLC Keep the soil evenly moist from spring until the ground freezes in fall, especially during the first 2 years. Water deeply to encourage deep root growth. Maintain 2 to 4 inches of organic mulch such as shredded bark or wood chips throughout the growing season. Fertilize in early spring with a controlled-release fertilizer or an organic equivalent. Prune right after flowering.

Maple

Acer

ABOVE: *'Dissectum' Japanese maple combines elegant, sculptural shape with brilliant color to make a dramatic garden statement.* OPPOSITE PAGE: *Red stems of 'Sango Kaku' Japanese maple contrast leaves.*

While not as grand as an oak or as elegant as a river birch, maples do just about everything a tree is supposed to do. Their full, round canopies sit atop a straight trunk. Their large, almost-pointy leaves, recognizable at once to anyone who loves maple syrup, supply dense shade in summer. Then fall comes and turns the canopy into a ball of flame.

Although I love the autumn brilliance of sugar and red maples, their shallow roots and heavy shade can make it tough to grow anything beneath them. In smaller gardens, Japanese maples are a better choice than the large forest trees. With delicate leaves, seeds, and stems, they make a wonderful addition to a perennial garden or as specimen trees.

PEAK SEASON

Fall when leaves change colors.

MY FAVORITES

Freeman maple (*Acer* × *freemanii* 'Autumn Blaze') forms a tall conical-shaped tree that turns red and orange in the fall. Zones 32, 34–44.

Fullmoon maple (*A. japonicum*) grows 20 to 30 feet tall with feathery leaves and a graceful habit. Zones 32, 34–41.

Japanese maple (*A. palmatum*) cultivars are more common than the species; 'Bloodgood' has bold purple-red leaves; 'Dissectum' has lacy leaves that layer one over the other; and 'Sango Kaku' has coral red stems. Zones 32, 34–41.

Red maple (*A. rubrum*) is one of the most prominent and beautiful native trees in fall. 'Red Sunset' is an exceptional cultivar. Zones 32, 34–44.

Sugar maple (*A. saccharum*) is one of the most important trees of North America. 'Bonfire' has spectacular fall color. Zones 32, 34–44.

GARDEN COMPANIONS

Combine smaller maples in the dappled light of a woodland garden with hostas, bishop's hat (*Epimedium*), and ferns. Plant Japanese maples with witch hazel or with velvety, deep green Hinoki false cypress.

When Plant maples as soon as you can work the ground in spring. Set out container plants into midsummer. Maples are relatively easy to move and they re-establish well.

Where Most maples prefer full sun but will grow in partial shade. Young trees like well-drained, slightly acidic soil. Their brilliant fall color makes them good as specimen plants in mixed borders. Japanese maples grow well under a high forest canopy, providing a second level of foliage under which woodland wildflowers thrive.

How Remove the tree from its container carefully, keeping the rootball intact. Plant at the same depth that it was growing in the container, in a hole deep and wide enough to accommodate the roots without crowding. Plant a balled-and-burlapped tree so that the root flare is right at the soil surface, cutting and removing as much of the burlap and wire as possible without injuring roots. Gently firm soil around the roots and water thoroughly, making sure there are no air pockets.

TLC Keep the soil evenly moist from spring until the ground freezes in fall, especially during the first 2 years. Water deeply to encourage deep root growth. Apply 2 to 4 inches of organic mulch such as shredded bark, leaf compost, or wood chips and replenish as needed throughout the growing season. Maples rarely require fertilizer, but if slow growth indicates some is needed, apply a 10-10-10 (or organic equivalent) in spring. Scatter the fertilizer around the base of the tree and water it in. Avoid major pruning in late winter and early spring, but cut off dead, damaged, or diseased branches anytime. The thin bark of young maples is susceptible to damage from winter sun and string trimmers. Protect trunks of young trees with plastic cylinders, or plant trees in locations where the trunks are not vulnerable to marauding animals or power equipment.

Native Deciduous Trees

The native trees that are adapted to live in our region are the same ones that will perform best with the least amount of care. In the Northeast, native trees range from understory types, such as flowering dogwood, to the massive and stately red oak. The dogwoods' attributes go beyond adaptability; it's also one of the finest garden trees available, which is why it's included as a Top 10 (on pages 116 and 117). Not all of the trees on the following list are strictly native in the sense that you might stumble upon one in the forest. Some are cultivars of natives that have been selected by nursery professionals for some outstanding attribute.

When growing a native tree, consider for a moment where it would likely grow were it on its own and not in your garden. This bit of contemplation and research can go far in the direction of placing trees where the resources that they require are available. Shadbush *(Amelanchier canadensis)*, for example, is the native tree that blooms in New England at the same time the shad are swimming upstream to spawn. In its natural habitat will often be located along a stream where sunlight is strong and water readily available; a similar location in your yard may be on the downhill side of the property near where the downspout discharges from the roof gutters. Other plants may resent the periodic inundation, but shadbush will appreciate it.

Shadbush has white, five-petaled flowers and round blue-green leaves that turn rusty red in the fall. 'Spring Glory' is a tall, narrow form, and 'Tradition' has a strong single trunk, good branching structure, and blueberry-sized fruit. The related apple serviceberry (*A. × grandiflora* 'Princess Diana') has excellent fall color that is longer lasting than most. 'Cumulus' is less disease resistant but is very flowerful and has good fall color. Zones 32, 34–44.

Fringe tree (*Chionanthus virginicus*) has attractive, stout, purple twigs and dark green foliage, but it is the dangling clusters of white flufflike flowers in late spring that have the greatest appeal. Fruits are blue-black berries. Zones 32, 34–41.

Green ash (*Fraxinus pennsylvanica*) can reach 50 feet in height with pale green compound leaves. Reportedly less affected than white ash by ash decline or ash yellows, this tree casts light shade and grows well in average soil. 'Marshall's Seedless' is a seedless selection that has become the most frequently planted selection of green ash. Zones 32, 34–44.

Native oaks (*Quercus*) are too many to list here, but here are my favorites. At the top of my list is the red oak (*Q. rubra*), the patriarch of northeastern forests. It grows quickly to 60 feet and will soar to more than 100 feet in time. Scarlet oak (*Q. coccinea*), a close runner-up, is not quite as tall and is noted especially for its scarlet fall color. Pin oak (*Q. palustris*) is most common in the nursery trade and, compared with the others, branches close to the ground and prefers deep lowland soils where there is plenty of moisture. Leaves of all three color well in fall, and all oaks have deep roots that make them suitable for use in gardens and in lawns. Zones 32, 34–44.

Evergreen Trees

The defining feature of evergreen trees is that they look pretty much the same in every season. As such, they provide the essential landscape function of a backdrop. In front of evergreens, flowering trees, shrubs, and perennials show off to maximum effect. The consistency of evergreens also gives a garden a feel of permanence.

On a more utilitarian front, evergreens screen unwanted views, which is no small matter in our densely populated region. Whether you love them or even notice them in summer is one thing. But in winter, when deciduous plants lose their leaves and annuals and herbaceous perennials have disappeared, it is the evergreens that remain, sentrylike, waiting until spring returns.

Don't confuse the evergreen-conifer connection. Conifers are a type of evergreen. Most conifers are evergreens, but many evergreens are not conifers. Conifers are cone-bearing plants, with leaves

that are shaped like needles. Most conifers carry their seeds in woody cones, and others bear them in structures that are more like berries or fruit. Junipers, for example, bear clusters of dense, pale blue berries; yews produce fleshy red berries.

While conifer leaves are usually needlelike, many evergreen leaves are broad and flat.

Aside from European and American hollies, which have long been a backbone of gardening in our region and will undoubtedly remain so, there are few other broad-leaved evergreens for our area. But several new selections of southern magnolia (see

OPPOSITE PAGE: *An eastern white pine covered with fresh snow becomes a delicate winter sculpture.* RIGHT: *Golden false cypress and Leyland cypress combine to make an all-year screen.*

pages 154 and 155), which promise the ability to cope with northern winters, are a promising exception.

Evergreen trees are not necessarily less messy than deciduous trees. All trees drop leaves and other debris. It's just that deciduous trees do it all at once, in fall, and evergreens drop leaves more or less continuously.

This characteristic eases the annual chore of raking and bagging leaves, and the decomposing needles enrich the soil as well as maintain the low pH most conifers prefer. Some needles make an attractive mulch that keeps down weeds and holds moisture in the soil.

COLOR AND FORM

If you don't look at individual evergreens, you might assume that they are all green. Not so. Colors range from silvery blue through blue-green and yellow-green. Texture is important to consider as well; it ranges from the coarse character of southern magnolia to the delicate texture of some pines.

Consider how much space you have, and what size and shape each plant will be when fully grown. Taller evergreens tend to grow upright, like spires or pyramids, taking on interesting silhouettes as they mature; a few, notably spruce, never lose their Christmas-tree shape. Others have a ball shape when young but will eventually strike out for the sky.

PLANTING

Early spring planting is best. Fall is frequently recommended, but evergreen plants require a longer establishment period than deciduous types, so I think it's best to avoid planting them in fall. Don't go shopping, however, until you know where sun and shade fall in your garden, and how much light each tree needs.

—WAYNE CAHILLY

American Arborvitae
Thuja occidentalis

American arborvitae has flat sprays of feathery foliage and tiny cones. Like yews (see pages 158 and 159), it is staid and structural. But unlike yews, it can't take much shade, and its leaves are softer, smoother, more pliable, and a lighter green. American arborvitae comes in a variety of interesting shapes. These include spheres, cones, slender columns, and plump pyramids, all in various sizes (which means no clipping is necessary to shape your shrub into a ball, if that's what you want).

In fact, little pruning is required, but an annual haircut is a good idea if you need to keep your plant in bounds. Plants take pruning well, but don't cut away too much foliage or brown spots will show. Prune so that the plant is always wider at the bottom than at the top. This allows the lower leaves to receive sufficient sunlight and thus remain green and healthy.

PEAK SEASON

Year-round

MY FAVORITES

'Columbia' is a tall, narrow-growing tree with a columnar habit. New growth emerges white in the spring and early summer, then darkens, and lightens again to near white or gray in winter. 'Wintergreen' is a fast-growing dark green tree that develops a conical shape with age.

'Aurea Nana' is one of the best-known smaller forms.

Related species

Western red cedar (*Thuja plicata*) is a huge tree in its native range, sometimes reaching 150 to 200 feet. In gardens it usually stays under 80 feet, but that is still a lot to handle. It is a medium-textured tree with flat sprays of foliage that are frequently pendulous and drape from horizontal branches. Zones 32, 34–37, 39.

GARDEN COMPANIONS

Arborvitae anchors beds of mounding and creeping plants like hardy geraniums, shrub roses, catmint, and low-growing false cypress. Grown as a tall hedge, it makes an excellent backdrop for tall perennials like delphiniums, phlox, and lilies. The cone-shaped types look good framing masses of lavender.

When Plant as soon as you can work the ground in spring. Arbor-vitae also can be successfully planted in early fall if given ample water.

Where Choose a location that receives full sun and has fertile, well-drained soil. These are popular plants for hedges, foundation plantings, screens, and windbreaks.

ABOVE: *Golden foliage of a mature 'Aurea Nana' American arborvitae combines well with other evergreens.* OPPOSITE PAGE: *A columnar dwarf cultivar of American arborvitae partially hides arbor supports.*

How Carefully remove each plant from its container, keeping the rootball intact. Plant at the same depth that it was growing in the container, in a hole deep and wide enough to accommodate the roots without crowding. Plant balled-and-burlapped trees so that the root flares are right at the soil surface, cutting and removing as much of the burlap and wire as possible without injuring roots. Gently firm the soil around the roots and water thoroughly, making sure there are no air pockets.

TLC Keep the soil evenly moist from spring until the ground freezes in fall, especially during the first 2 years. Water deeply to encourage root growth. Apply 2 to 4 inches of organic mulch such as shredded bark or wood chips and replenish as needed throughout the growing season. Cut off winter burn in early spring. Prune just after new growth has emerged. Prune formal hedges again later in the season, but not after mid-August.

Atlas Cedar

Cedrus atlantica

Hailing from the Atlas Mountains of Tunisia, Algeria, and Morocco, Atlas cedar is one of the few conifers native to Africa. This is not a small tree. I have seen individuals with a branch spread exceeding 100 feet and a height of 75 feet. Unfortunately though, I frequently see Atlas cedar planted in small places, straining at its bounds and otherwise not looking its best.

Branches are horizontal, then curving up. The foliage is clustered on branches, giving the tree a rather bristly appearance, sort of like a bottle brush with some missing bristles.

Although the species plant can be found in nurseries if you search, you more frequently see the blue-foliaged cultivar 'Glauca'. This has a steel blue or nearly blue-white color and is singularly striking when grown to full proportion and placed where it can be seen from a distance.

When Plant in early spring from nursery-grown container stock, being careful to select well-rooted plants. Or plant balled-and-burlapped trees; handle them carefully to avoid damaging the rootball.

PEAK SEASON

Foliage and form are this plant's best qualities, and it is consistently attractive year-round.

MY FAVORITES

'Glauca' is the blue form, and "blue" is used advisedly. It's silvery blue, and individual trees vary as well. Notwithstanding, the color is best if the plant grows in full sun. Otherwise, this cultivar is the same as the species.

'Glauca Fastigiata' has the same silvery blue color, but is much narrower. The branches are so strongly upswept that a 60-foot-tall tree may be only 10 to 12 feet wide. Just the opposite is 'Glauca Pendula': its branches droop and trail such that it requires staking to remain upright.

GARDEN COMPANIONS

Best planted as a specimen with space around it, but this tree also sits comfortably in a carpet of ground-hugging junipers or other low ground cover.

RIGHT: *Clusters of Atlas cedar needles grow from woody pegs.* OPPOSITE PAGE: *'Glauca' Atlas cedar makes a striking specimen tree.*

Where Provide a site that has sufficient room for this tree to develop to its full potential, and that offers full sun and good air circulation. This tree does not appreciate sitting in a cold air pocket and does much better in our region if placed on a rise from which cold air will quickly drain. A range of soil types is fine, including clay or sandy soil, but avoid wet or poorly drained sites. Use as a backdrop for other plants or to block an undesirable view.

How Plant balled-and-burlapped or container plants at the same level that they were growing at the nursery or in the container. Dig the hole just as deep as the rootball but two to three times as wide. Although Atlas cedar is not particular about soil, it does appreciate organic material incorporated into the soil used to backfill the hole. Use a well-rotted leaf compost if available, and mix it in thoroughly before backfilling. Water well immediately after planting and apply a controlled-release fertilizer or organic equivalent in the fall, when deciduous plants are beginning to go dormant.

TLC Water through dry spells and particularly during the first 2 years after planting. Atlas cedars require little fertilization when planted in average garden soil. If annual growth seems to be slow, a fall fertilization with a controlled-release fertilizer every other year will likely help. Prune only those branches that die or are broken. The natural form of this plant is one of its greatest assets, so let it be.

English Holly
Ilex aquifolium

nglish holly is the traditional Christmas holly used in wreaths and holiday decorations. Its dark blue-green foliage is not quite as prickly at maturity as that of our native American holly, and the shiny leaves appear to have been buffed to achieve such a noteworthy luster. The fruit is green during the summer and seldom noticed until it turns crimson red in the fall, contrasting effectively with the dark green leaves. The fruit of English holly is produced on the twigs that formed the previous year, thus some of the berries may be masked by foliage; take care when pruning or you may cut off the flower buds for next year's berry crop. Trees are either male or female, and both are required to produce fruit.

The English holly is the classic evergreen for winter good looks.

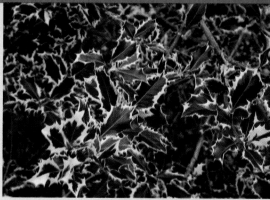

'Argentea Marginata' leaves have wide, creamy white edges.

PEAK SEASON

Berries provide welcome color in winter, but the glossy leaves are good-looking year-round.

MY FAVORITES

'Argentea Marginata' is a female plant with red berries that contrast the variegated leaves.

'Sparkler' is a spectacular cultivar that grows quickly, fills out solidly, and produces heavy crops of berries annually. Fruit usually turns from green to red earlier than other hollies.

Related species

Chinese holly *(Ilex cornuta)* is an interesting and somewhat peculiar-looking plant with leaves best described as square. This species is marginally hardy here in the Tri-State region but is worth a try if you have a sheltered location. Coldest winters will damage leaves. Zone 32.

GARDEN COMPANIONS

English holly makes an excellent background plant for flowering and fruiting shrubs such as chokeberry *(Prunus virginiana)* or winterberry *(Ilex verticillata)*. Shrubs with colored foliage or stems, such as red- or yellowtwig dogwood *(Cornus sericea)*, also make good companions.

When Plant English holly in spring from balled-and-burlapped or container plants. Fall planting is not recommended because of the need for plants to be well established prior to winter.

Where Plant in full sun whenever possible, but partial shade is okay. Trees planted in shade will have less foliage and fruit and will not appear as robust. Plant in deep, rich soil that is well drained and slightly acidic.

How Plant at the same depth that they grew in the container or at the nursery. Dig a hole that is only as deep as the rootball but at least two times as wide. Backfill with native soil amended with leaf or other organic compost to improve both water holding and drainage. Keep the soil uniformly moist from spring until the soil freezes in the fall, especially for the first two growing seasons.

TLC English holly is adaptable but a bit difficult to establish. Take care to place holly where drying winds are minimal, especially in the winter when plants may dry out and suffer damage during the first year. Uniform watering is essential for the first 2 years, after which plants will tolerate some period of drought during summer. Prune selectively to remove dead, damaged, or diseased branches or any overly exuberant growth. Holly can be sheared but the larger-leaved forms look terrible after the leaves have been cut by hedge shears, so it's better to maintain the size of these varieties by selective pruning. Cut back severely only to rejuvenate old plants. Fertilize in the fall of the first and second year after planting, and every other year thereafter if growth is slow. Apply a controlled-release fertilizer after deciduous trees drop their leaves, and water it in well.

False Cypress
Chamaecyparis

False cypress come from North America and Asia, primarily lands bordering the Pacific Ocean, with the notable exception of the eastern white cedar (*Chamaecyparis thyoidies*), which is native to our region (see page 160). These are tall trees with a graceful outline that tapers to a point; when growing in stands or groves, trees produce long, slender trunks that reach over 100 feet in height. But in gardens, false cypress are shorter, rarely exceeding 50 feet high. This is an advantage to gardeners who can't accommodate a 100-foot tree.

False cypress have delicate feathery foliage that is held in flattened sprays on pendulous branches; some also have pendulous branches

ABOVE: *'Lane' false cypress has a predictable trim shape that complements many kinds of gardens.* OPPOSITE PAGE: *Leaves and cones of false cypress.*

that give the plant the appearance of being draped in foliage. They all have thin peeling bark that is soft to the touch and reddish in appearance, and all are fine-textured trees that can tolerate some shade and won't be damaged by snow or ice.

When Plant in early spring as soon as the ground can be worked; avoid planting in late fall.

Where False cypress appreciate full sun but will tolerate some shade. They prefer acid soil that is rich and deep but not wet. Use as accent plants or as specimens. They work well as background plants to screen unwanted views; being single stemmed, cypress are not bent over by heavy snow, an advantage over several other evergreens.

How Plant from containers or balled-and-burlapped nursery stock in a hole that is just as deep as the rootball but two to three times as wide. If plants have been in containers, cut any roots that circle inside the pot. Backfill the hole with excavated soil amended with some well-rotted leaf compost. Water thoroughly throughout the first 2 years.

TLC False cypress seldom make many demands on the gardener once established. Water well during the first 2 years and during drought in successive years. Pruning should be minimal, being restricted to dead, damaged, or diseased branches. Think ahead before planting the larger-growing forms, as they do take up a lot of room and are damaged by undue pruning.

PEAK SEASON

False cypress are very attractive in winter, with a dusting of snow resting on their dark green foliage.

MY FAVORITES

Port Orford cedar (*Chamaecyparis lawsoniana*) has short ascending branches that droop at the ends. It grows about 50 feet high. Of the many cultivars, my favorites include broadly upright 'Pyramidalis' and 'Lane' with its golden new foliage. Zones 32, 34–41.

Nootka cypress (*C. nootkatensis*) is a giant of the Pacific Rim. In the wild, it is tall and a somewhat dull blue-green. The tree is adaptable to gardens. Zones 32, 34–41.

Hinoki false cypress (*C. obtusa*) is a small and slow-growing tree that grows only 20 feet or so after 20 years. Foliage is green and frondlike, and the short branchlets are pendulous. Zones 32, 34–45.

Sawara false cypress (*C. pisifera*) grows 20 feet wide and 60 feet tall. Loose and open in habit, it does not form a totally solid screen. Zones 32, 34–45.

GARDEN COMPANIONS

Plant as a backdrop for flowering perennials, or as an accent plant in shrub borders. Plant taller selections alone as specimens.

Japanese Cedar
Cryptomeria japonica

Japanese cedar is a plant of contrasts; the foliage is fine-textured, but the overall texture of the plant is often rather coarse. That aside, this is an outstanding evergreen tree of abundant character. It has long been the backbone of Japanese gardens and landscapes where a plant that was just a little different could happily reside.

There are only two species of *Cryptomeria* and both come from Japan and southwestern China. The Chinese cedar *(C. fortunei)* is not reliably hardy in our area, thus it is seldom seen outside of botanical collections. The Japanese cedar *(C. japonica)* is hardy much farther north and can be counted on to survive our winters in style.

This tree grows with a strong central trunk and develops into a tall, conical tree. The foliage varies in color from yellow to gray to dark coppery brown, and from graceful and tidy to something reminiscent of a bad hair day. Needles are only about ⅜ inch long and densely clothe the twigs.

LEFT: *Japanese cedar in a shrub border.*
OPPOSITE PAGE: *The small cones are borne at the tips of densely needled branches.*

PEAK SEASON

Japanese cedar looks good all year; however, the peak for some cultivars is during the spring flush of growth.

MY FAVORITES

'Elegans' is a tall-growing tree capable of reaching 75 feet with sufficient age but usually grows much smaller under garden conditions. It produces long, soft needles that are bluish green during the growing season, changing to an attractive red-brown during winter.

'Lycopodioides' becomes a tree with long, unbranched twigs that resemble some species of club moss (*Lycopodium*). It is small, growing only 15 to 20 feet tall, and appears a bit tousled most of the time.

'Sakkan-sugi' is a rare and slow-growing conifer that has yellowish new growth in the spring. The foliage is very effective at brightening a dark corner of the garden; however, the plant is shown to best effect if grown in full sun, where it seems to glow.

GARDEN COMPANIONS

Look for plants that contrast with the texture or color of Japanese cedar. Blue spruce, both in tree form as a backdrop or as dwarf or semidwarf shrub in the foreground, works well. Among perennials, boldly foliaged hostas and tall plants such as delphiniums are good companions.

When Plant in early spring as soon as the ground can be worked. Planting can continue into mid- to late spring. Avoid fall planting if possible, as the plant may have insufficient time to establish before cold weather.

Where Plant in full sun to light shade, and in well-drained soil. Provide some shelter from winter wind to avoid winter burn. Japanese cedar grows well in average garden soil but needs good drainage.

How Dig a planting hole that is the same depth as the rootball and two to three times as wide. Remove the plant from the container carefully so that the soil around the roots is not disturbed. If roots have begun to encircle the inside of the container, cut them off. Place the plant so that the root crown is even with the surrounding soil and backfill the hole with the excavated soil. Water deeply and thoroughly during the first two growing seasons, never allowing the soil to become totally dry.

TLC During the early spring, remove any foliage that may have been killed or damaged during the winter, and inspect the tree for branches that may have broken in heavy snow. Pruning should be limited to the removal of this dead, damaged, or diseased foliage and to minor shaping as needed. Some cultivars may become congested with dead foliage and thus benefit from a cleaning out once every 2 or 3 years. Apply fertilizer in the early spring or late fall; use a balanced, controlled-release fertilizer (or organic equivalent) that is intended for shrubs or trees, and water it in immediately after applying.

149

Leyland Cypress
Cupressocyparis leylandii

If you need an evergreen that will grow fast, fill lots of space, and tolerate salt spray, shade, and poor soil (and look good on top of it), search no further. Leyland cypress is a hybrid between the Alaska cedar and the Monterey cypress *(Chamaecyparis nootkatensis × Cupressus macrocarpa)* and has the best qualities of both parents.

Leyland cypress grows fast, really fast—48 feet in 16 years has been recorded, and I've seen these trees put on 2 feet of growth the year after planting. Leaves are fine textured and feathery, and the bark is reddish. This is not a tree for a tight space. In most landscapes, you can expect an ultimate height of 60 to 70 feet, and perhaps more. The tree's only downside is its potential for winter damage during our worst cold spells.

This cypress transplants easily and is adaptable to a variety of soil conditions. Leyland cypress is very effective as either a specimen or planted in groups of three or five.

When Plant trees in early spring. In our region, a long establishment period during the first growing season very much aids their survival through the first winter.

PEAK SEASON

Summer, when trees provide a background or screen with grace and style. They allow the fussier foreground plants to show off against a backdrop of uniform green.

MY FAVORITES

Most often I prefer the regular species of the plant because its color combines easily with neighboring plants. Two cultivars deserve mention:

'Leighton Green' has a columnar form and excellent green foliage that is held in flat sprays.

'Naylor's Blue' is a blue-green cultivar that is also very narrow, providing a bluish accent particularly in winter.

GARDEN COMPANIONS

Leyland cypress works well with other needled evergreens in mass plantings, as well as in a row to make a hedge or screen. Plant dwarf blue spruce (*Picea pungens* 'Fat Albert') or false cypress in front of it for contrast. Underplant with English ivy or dwarf periwinkle, and accent with blue-flowering spring bulbs such as bluebell or grape hyacinth (*Muscari*).

OPPOSITE PAGE: *Fast-growing Leyland cypress grows 25 feet tall in as few as five years, and will continue much higher if left unpruned.* RIGHT: *Close-up of snow-covered Leyland cypress leaves.*

Where Plant in soil that can be kept evenly moist during the first two years. Full sun is generally best, but a location that is somewhat sheltered from afternoon sun will limit the possibility of winter sunburn. Avoid windy locations as well as areas that are poorly drained, soggy, or prone to flooding. Plant in the back of a border, individually or grouped to make a screen, or alone as a specimen.

How Dig a hole that is the same depth as the rootball but at least two to three times as wide. Backfill with excavated soil and water well to eliminate air pockets. Fertilize with a water-soluble complete fertilizer at planting time and follow up with an application of a controlled-release fertilizer (or organic equivalent) in the fall.

TLC Leyland cypress is not particular about soil once established, but mulching with 2 to 3 inches of shredded bark, composted leaves, or wood chips will help to keep soil evenly moist. Prune selectively to cut out damaged branches as necessary. Fertilize every other year in the fall at half the recommended rate if growth is slow.

Norway Spruce
Picea abies

Ask a child to draw a picture of an evergreen and you will get a Christmas tree every time, one that looks exactly like a spruce. Other evergreens may make better Christmas trees, but spruce is still the prototype, thanks to its perfectly symmetrical pyramid shape and the way its cones hang like, well, Christmas ornaments.

But Norway spruce is far more useful in the landscape than in the living room. It is hard to beat when you want a tall, graceful, dark green conifer that requires minimal care. Its pendulous branches that turn up at the tips are very graceful, and the dark green foliage is attractively marked with white on the underside.

By the way, it's easy to distinguish spruce from fir, their look-alike cousins. Simply pull off one needle and look at where it attaches to the twig. If it looks like a peg with a little bit of bark still attached, it's a spruce. If it looks like a suction cup, it's a fir.

PEAK SEASON

Looks good year-round but particularly in winter with a dusting of snow.

RELATED SPECIES

White spruce *(Picea glauca)* makes an especially good windbreak because frigid, sweeping winds have little effect on it. 'Conica' is a dwarf form reaching 10 to 15 feet in the garden but is more frequently seen growing in pots on a doorstep.

Colorado spruce *(P. pungens)* is the common spruce. 'Hoopsii' has dense growth that is nearly sky blue. 'Koster' is frequently sold in nurseries but what is provided under that name varies; the only consistent characteristic is blue foliage.

Oriental spruce *(P. orientalis)* is a dense, cone-shaped tree that grows to 60 feet tall with short needles and branch tips that turn up at the ends. 'Aurea' has new growth that emerges golden yellow and then fades to green as the growing season progresses. 'Skylands' has golden foliage year-round and grows to 20 feet tall.

GARDEN COMPANIONS

All spruce are excellent lawn specimens. Plant 'Conica' white spruce with low-growing perennials such as lamb's ears *(Stachys)* or coral bells *(Heuchera)*. Plant smaller bulbs such as grape hyacinth or glory-of-the-snow *(Chinodoxa)* around them.

ABOVE: *Leaves and new growth of Oriental spruce.* OPPOSITE PAGE: *Norway spruce needs space to grow.*

When Plant in spring as soon as you can work the ground.

Where Choose a location in full sun; even partial shade will result in thinner foliage. Norway spruce prefers slightly acidic soil with some organic matter mixed in. Good drainage is essential, and avoid sites with drying winds. Landscape uses include hedges, windbreaks, and background plantings. Smaller related species are good accent plants. Avoid planting spruce trees too close to buildings.

How Carefully remove the plant from its container, keeping the rootball intact. Plant at the same depth that it was growing in the container, in a hole deep and wide enough to accommodate the roots without crowding. Plant a balled-and-burlapped tree so that the root flare is right at the soil surface, cutting and removing as much of the burlap and wire as possible without injuring roots. Gently firm soil around the roots and water thoroughly, making sure there are no air pockets. Water in a starter fertilizer solution (diluted according to the product's instructions) around the base.

TLC Keep the soil evenly moist from spring until the ground freezes in fall, especially during the first 2 years. Water deeply to encourage root growth. Apply 2 to 4 inches of organic mulch such as shredded bark or wood chips and replenish as needed throughout the growing season. Spruces benefit from a spring application of an acidic fertilizer. Most require very little pruning and are best left to grow into their natural shape. Any pruning to shape trees should be done in late spring; snip off no more than one-third of the new growth.

Southern Magnolia
Magnolia grandiflora

ABOVE: *A diminutive cultivar of southern magnolia, 'Little Gem' produces flowers in spring and again in fall.* OPPOSITE PAGE: *Close-up of southern magnolia's elegant flower.*

Southern magnolia's sumptuous, silken blossoms have been called the most elegant floral offerings found on any tree. "Breathtaking" definitely sums up their beauty. Their bold broad-leaved foliage is coarse in texture and couldn't contrast more with the needled evergreens that are usually used for screening and as specimens.

Southern magnolia is a stately, dense tree, featuring broadly oval, leathery, glossy dark green leaves that are green on top and rusty brown underneath. The leaves can grow to 8 inches long—a classy backdrop to the nearly foot-wide glistening white flowers, which exude a heady perfume. Flowering can begin in spring and continue through summer into early fall. In favored locations, this tree may eventually reach 80 feet high with a spread of 60 feet. But in our region, which is near magnolia's northern limit, I'm not aware of any trees reaching that size, and the ones that are best adapted are much smaller.

PEAK SEASON

White flowers bloom in spring, summer, and fall. Leathery leaves are good-looking year-round.

MY FAVORITES

'Bracken's Brown Beauty' has proved to be one of the most cold-hardy cultivars of southern magnolia currently in the nursery trade. A distinctly upright grower with a tight, dense habit, this tree grows to about 30 feet in height, fitting nicely in the midsized garden. I have planted one that is now 20 feet tall, is mostly unprotected, and has withstood temperatures down to $-2°F/-18°C$ with no winter damage.

'Bronze Beauty' is similar but less cold hardy, in my experience.

'Little Gem' is a grafted dwarf version that has slightly smaller leaves and a more compact, narrower form. In our region, it will reach 20 feet tall and half as wide.

GARDEN COMPANIONS

Magnolias have sensitive surface roots, so choose companions that can be planted at the same time as the tree. Permanent ground covers that do well beneath southern magnolias include:

- ivy (Hedera)
- Japanese spurge (Pachysandra)

When Southern magnolias are sold as container-grown plants. Plant them in early spring, when temperatures are coolest and soil is moist.

Where Southern magnolias grow in full sun or partial shade. For best results, they need well-drained soil. Plant in locations where they are protected from drying winds in winter. Summer heat is not an issue, provided soil can be kept moist.

How Dig a planting hole at least twice the width of the plant's container and slightly shallower than the original rootball; dig slightly deeper around the perimeter of the hole and create a firm central core. Carefully remove the magnolia from its container, making sure not to damage the fleshy, brittle roots; set the rootball on the central core, then fill in the hole with soil amended with organic matter. Make sure the juncture of trunk and roots is slightly above the surrounding soil grade to allow for settling. Water well and mulch with 2 inches of organic mulch.

TLC Southern magnolias grow best in soil that's moist but not saturated; water regularly, adjusting the frequency to your soil type. While plants are young, mulch the soil around them to conserve moisture and to maintain cooler soil temperature during the warm months. Avoid digging or cultivating beneath a magnolia, as this could damage the fleshy surface roots. If growth is sparse or weak, apply a controlled-release fertilizer (or organic equivalent). Prune only to shape trees or to remove lower branches on the trunk as the tree gains height.

White Pine
Pinus strobus

White pines are pretty ordinary conifers at first. They begin life as rather scruffy, pyramid-shaped plants, and grow a bit more interesting as their upper branches open up or develop a more rounded habit. But with time, white pines become one of the most majestic of all trees. Given enough time, some individuals grow over 220 feet high. In our region, white pine is the tallest evergreen tree.

Given its potential size, white pine is best either in woodlands or in very large gardens or parks. However, dwarf, weeping, and trailing types are available and quite lovely in smaller gardens. Dwarf varieties of other species such as mugo pine (see page 85) are also excellent, especially in rock gardens; their deep green, tuftlike needle clusters and twisting branches add a touch of the exotic.

When Plant as soon as you can work the ground in spring. Early fall planting can be successful if you're careful to provide plenty of water.

Where All pines grow best in full sun in acidic soil. They are very sensitive to salt damage from roadways. Use in the landscape as hedges, windbreaks, and background plantings; smaller cultivars make good accent plants. Avoid the temptation to use pines to fill in under taller trees to form a screen. They require full sun and are usually disappointing as understory plants.

How Carefully remove the pine from its container, keeping the rootball intact. Plant at the same depth that it was growing in the container, in a hole deep and wide enough to accommodate the roots without crowding. Plant a balled-and-burlapped tree so that the root flare is right at the soil surface, cutting and removing as much of the burlap and wire as possible without injuring roots. Firm soil around the roots and water thoroughly, making sure there are no air pockets. Water in a starter fertilizer solution, diluted according to the product's instructions, around the base of the plant.

ABOVE: *Curled and twisted needles of 'Contorta' white pine.* OPPOSITE PAGE: *'Pendula' white pine as part of a border.*

PEAK SEASON

Year-round, but particularly in winter covered with a dusting of snow.

MY FAVORITES

'Pendula' is more architectural statement than garden ornament. It will look awkward at first, but its weeping trunk and branches gradually become a real showstopper. Soft green cones are borne in clusters of five.

'Contorta' (or 'Torulosa') is a medium-sized tree with twisted needles. I grow this tree just to collect the fallen needles for mulching the perennial garden; it's by far the most interesting-looking mulch there is. But the tree is beautiful enough to be grown as a large specimen too.

Related species

Japanese white pine (*Pinus parviflora*) has a natural windswept appearance that is enhanced by pruning and training.

Swiss stone pine (*P. cembra*) is hardy and slow growing, to 70 feet or more, although most of the ones I have seen in our region are less than 30 feet in 90 years. This species is great in small gardens.

GARDEN COMPANIONS

Plant ground covers of ivy (*Hedera*) or dwarf periwinkle (*Vinca*) once the pine tree is established.

TLC Keep the soil evenly moist from spring until the ground freezes in fall, especially during the first 2 years. Water deeply to encourage deep root growth. Apply 2 to 4 inches of organic mulch such as shredded bark or wood chips and replenish as needed throughout the growing season. Remove winter-burned branches in early spring. Pines benefit from a spring application of an acidic fertilizer. Prune annually in early summer by cutting back the upward-growing new growth ("candles") by half. This will limit the size of smaller trees but of course is impractical for large trees.

Yew

Taxus

Yews as we know them are often sheared into a knee-high hedge of less than stunning character. This is an unfortunate case of plants being used for what they can be made to do, while being neglected for those things they can readily do on their own. Left to its own devices, a yew becomes a single- or multistemmed tree that may reach 25 or 30 feet in height. Depending on the cultivar, the tree may also have horizontal branches reaching outward for 20 feet, draped in slender, pendulous twigs covered in dark green foliage. Choose a different cultivar, and the results may be upward-sweeping branches forming a green, teardrop-shaped globe.

Yew is perhaps the one plant most associated with England (with the possible exception of oak). Yew was the wood of the English longbow, the 12th century's weapon of mass destruction, and has long been the stately tree of well-appointed gardens. In England, yew is now used to divide garden spaces, to create impossibly tall hedges, and to quietly erase views that do not enhance the garden atmosphere. They do wonders in our gardens too, albeit on a smaller scale.

When Plant yews as soon as you can work the ground in spring, so they have sufficient time to become established before winter.

Where Yews will grow in sun or shade, but they don't tolerate drying winds. Preferred soils have excellent drainage and are high in organic matter.

How Carefully remove the plant from its container, keeping the rootball intact. Plant at the same depth that it was growing in the container, in a hole deep and wide enough to accommodate the roots without crowding. Plant a balled-and-burlapped tree so that the root flare is right at the soil surface, cutting and removing as much of the burlap and wire as possible without injuring roots. Gently firm soil around the roots and water thoroughly, making sure there are no air pockets. Give each tree plenty of space to grow to its full height and width.

TLC The only two reliable ways to fail with yews are to plant them too late in the fall, or to plant them where they are subject to flooding. A yew in good health can adapt to nearly any other combination of conditions. Keep the soil evenly moist from spring until the ground freezes in fall, especially during the first 2 years. Water deeply to encourage deep root growth. Apply 2 to 4 inches of an organic mulch such as shredded bark or wood chips, and replenish as needed throughout the growing season. Yews benefit from a spring application of fertilizer. Spreading types should be allowed to grow naturally with very little pruning. Shear upright forms in spring and again in midsummer if necessary. Yews are a favorite food of deer; they may require protection.

OPPOSITE PAGE: *'Capitata' can serve as a large shrub, a screen, or as a small tree beneath larger deciduous trees.* BELOW RIGHT: *Red fruits are characteristic of yews.*

PEAK SEASON

Year-round. The scented, spreading branches have attractive leaves that are dark green on top and lighter green on their undersides.

MY FAVORITES

Japanese yew (*Taxus cuspidata*) is a small, spreading tree with dark green needles and arching branches. 'Capitata' will grow to 25 feet tall unless new growth is pinched back; it has a pyramidal form and profuse red berries. Zones 32, 34–41.

English yew (*T. baccata* 'Stricta', also called 'Fastigiata') grows to 20 feet or more. It's reliably hardy in zone 32 and the warmest parts of 34.

T. × media is used for hedging in our area, but the cultivar 'Hicksii' will form a tall shrub or small multi-stemmed tree that is narrow toward the bottom and arches outward at the top, somewhat like a vase. Zones 32, 34–41.

GARDEN COMPANIONS

Use the upright types as screens or hedges or as a backdrop for perennials. Grow the spreading types among ferns, hostas, and lily-of-the-valley.

Native Evergreen Trees

Native evergreen trees often have distinct advantages over their exotic cousins. For one, a native tree is thoroughly adapted to the growing conditions in our region. Also, some occupy a niche in our environment that is hard to fill with a nonnative. For example, the native habitat of eastern white cedar is bogs along the East Coast. Few trees grow as well in our wettest soils, though this cedar grows well in dryer soil too.

Eastern white cedar *(Chamaecyparis thyoides)* is a tall-growing, moderately dense evergreen with dark bluish green leaves that resemble flattened scales more than they do needles. The trunk bark is reddish brown and forms thin, outward-peeling strips that give the plant a slightly roughened appearance. It requires regular moisture and will grow well in locations that remain wet for long periods. Eastern white cedar requires full sun to grow and look its best. Zones 32, 34, 37–42.

American holly *(Ilex opaca)* is a wonderful broad-leaved evergreen tree reaching 40 or more feet in height, given sufficient time to do so. Leaves are leathery, shiny, and armed with conspicuous spines. Relatively large, ½-inch-diameter fruits turn bright red or yellow in the fall; they're carried on the current year's growth, making the overall effect showier than the English holly (see page 144). Plants prefer moist growing conditions and full sun, but can take partial shade. Zones 32, 34, 35, 39.

Eastern red cedar *(Juniperus virginiana)* forms a dense, dark green canopy of prickly leaves. It can tolerate very poor, neglected sites; the one requirement is full sun. 'Glauca' is a bluish-colored selection with a narrow, upright form and

Pitch pine cones are oval and about 4 inches long. The tree becomes gnarled with age, often assuming a sculptural and windswept appearance.

scalelike leaves. 'Pendula' is a green form with horizontal branches and pendulous branchlets. Zones 32, 34–43.

Pitch pine *(Pinus rigida),* a coastal species of pine, is the dominant tree of the famous Pine Barrens of southern New Jersey, eastern Long Island, and Cape Cod. It is an irregularly shaped tree with a yellow-green coloration, long needles in bundles of three, and handsome, light brown cones. It tolerates sandy soil and salt spray better than most pines. The Jersey or Virginia pine *(P. virginiana)* is a similar coastal species, but it is not found in extensive and uniform stands the way pitch pine is. It also has an irregular shape and short, green needles in bundles of two. The narrow, prickly pinecones hang on the tree for several years. Zones 32, 34–43.

TOP LEFT: *Many cultivars of American holly are available, with red or yellow berries and various combinations of leaf markings.* TOP RIGHT: *Scaly leaves of eastern red cedar turn reddish in cold weather.* ABOVE: *All holly berries are borne on female plants that require a male pollinating plant.*

American arborvitae, one of our outstanding evergreen trees, also just happens to be a native. It's described in more detail on page 140.

161

Vines

Climbing vines have a special charm that goes beyond adding vertical interest to a garden. I think it has to do with the way they reach out to others to form endearing partnerships: if you let me cling to you, I'll make you look beautiful. You see it in the way they embrace arbors, trellises, fences, houses, even the trunks of trees.

Vines may seem hopelessly dependent, but I see them as resourceful and tough. After a little help getting started, such as a bit of twine to hold them in place, you'll be reaching for the pruners more often than the scissors and twine ball. Vines are programmed to grow toward the sun.

TYPES OF VINES

Vines such as English or Boston ivy, whose leaves form a thick, carpet-like mass of green, cling to even the slickest surfaces, engaging every crevice they encounter. Holdfasts, tendrils with adhesive discs at the end, "glue" the plant to any surface it touches. Climbing hydrangeas and trumpet creepers are clingers too, with twining stems and "sticky feet." When grown along a fence or wall, or

trained to gracefully drape over an arbor, the clinging stems help these plants to remain attached to these supports. Clematis and grapevines send out slender tendrils that will curl around a strand of wire, a bamboo pole, a slat in a trellis, or a twig. Honeysuckle and wisteria depend solely on twining stems to hold them in place.

SEEDS OR PLANTS?

Perennial vines are typically slow to get established. If you've decided to grow one of the perennial vines on my Top 10 list, start with a potted plant, not seeds—unless you don't mind waiting 3 or more years for the vine to flower. If the vine is already growing up a trellis or stake in the container, the support should be

OPPOSITE PAGE: *Anemone clematis climbs behind dwarf Korean lilac and barberry.* RIGHT: *Few spring flower displays exceed that of fragrant Japanese wisteria. This vine is supported by a cedar post.*

transplanted into the garden with the plant, but you'll need to help the vine make the transition to its permanent support. If planting against a house, consider that the eaves sometimes protect the soil against the foundation from rainfall and the area may be as dry as a desert. You may have more success planting a little bit away from the foundation and then guiding your new vine to the support you have provided on the wall.

Annual vines (for more, see pages 184–185) are easy to grow from seed. They flower in mid- to late summer and often self-sow. Some have seedpods as handsome as their flowers. Many annual vines also happen to have exceptional foliage and are quite attractive even when they're not in bloom.

PRUNING

All the vines featured here were chosen for their beauty and their reputations as reliable performers. Given the right location and just a little bit of guidance, they'll do well in your garden. A few of them are pretty aggressive, and you will need to rein them in now and then.

Wisteria, for example, made the list in spite of its sometimes rather brutish nature, because this spectacular vine is well worth the effort it takes to keep its growth in check. Clematis needs occasional pruning too, but to remove crowded and aging stems, not to curb an invasive streak. Well-timed pruning improves its flowering and vigor. In the TLC sections I'll tell you how to prune each vine that needs it. Gardening, after all, isn't entirely labor free—nor is wisteria as scary as people may tell you it is.

— WAYNE CAHILLY

Akebia
Akebia quinata

Distinctive, attractive flowers and fruit make this vine a certain conversation piece, but in the landscape it is valued chiefly for its lovely, fine-textured foliage. Even a large vine has a delicate look. Each leaf resembles a clover leaf, with five oval leaflets up to 2 inches long radiating out from the end of a long leafstalk. The leaves are a cool mint green that seems to reduce the temperature of an overheated garden space. Pendant clusters of vanilla-scented blossoms appear in spring. Female flowers (toward the cluster base) consist of three shell-like segments in an odd chocolate purple color; smaller male flowers in rosy purple appear farther down. Purplish, sausage-shaped, 4-inch fruits—edible but insipid—may appear in summer. Both flowers and fruit are somewhat obscured by the foliage. White- and pink-flowered forms exist but are not widely available.

Akebia is semievergreen, but in our region usually drops most of its leaves in fall.

ABOVE: *Flowers of akebia are either male (smaller and rosy purple), or female (larger and chocolate purple). But both kinds offer the same vanilla scent.* OPPOSITE PAGE, TOP: *A curving akebia stem wraps around a pair of leaves.* OPPOSITE PAGE, BOTTOM: *Snow-covered and semievergreen akebia drapes over a deck railing.*

PEAK SEASON

Spring, although attractive foliage makes this a three-season vine.

RELATED SPECIES

Three-leaf akebia (*Akebia trifoliata*) is similar to *A. quinata* but has three instead of five leaves, and *A. × pentaphylla,* a hybrid between the former two, has larger fruits.

GARDEN COMPANIONS

Akebia grows well when allowed to climb into crabapples such as white-flowering *Malus* 'Snowdrift', or the large tree-form hydrangeas. The best nonplant companion for akebia is a wrought-iron fence, along which it can drape and show off its leaves and interesting flowers.

When Plant nursery-grown plants anytime in spring.

Where Plant in average, well-drained soil. The vigorous stems easily twine to 30 feet if given some support; arbors, walls, and trees are all suitable. The plant also makes a fine 1-foot-high ground cover for large and especially sloping areas. If you use it this way, try to locate it on its own, since it is likely to overwhelm most other plants in its path.

How Set out plants from 1-gallon containers about 6 feet apart along a wall, or where desired if being used as a ground cover. Akebia can be an aggressive ground cover, so be careful to consider how you will keep it in the space provided before you plant. For upright plants, provide newly planted vines with a means of reaching a wall or tree to climb—a bamboo stake between the plant and wall for example, or by installing a length of twine between a tree branch and the vine. Plant akebia in pairs of the same species if fruit is desired.

TLC Do major thinning and pruning during winter. Thin out superfluous and tangling stems while plants are growing actively. Fertilizing the vines occasionally will improve their vigor; however, unless the soil in which you planted them is very poor, fertilization is rarely required. During the first year after planting, attend to watering during any period of drought; even a stretch of 4 or 5 days without rain can slow the growth and stunt the plants during the first year. Once established, watering during severe drought will ensure that the foliage remains attractive and the vines vigorous.

Boston Ivy
Parthenocissus tricuspidata

Some vines are treasured for their floral displays. Boston ivy, however, is valued for its foliage: demure green throughout spring and summer, turning to dazzling orange and red in fall. This is the "ivy" of the Ivy League.

In fall, crimson leaves of Boston ivy contrast sharply with evergreen English ivy on a stucco wall. Once leaves fall, the remaining intricate network of branches becomes visible.

Boston ivy has broad, three-lobed leaves that grow up to 8 inches wide. Unlike its relative Virginia creeper, it produces a solid foliage cover. Holdfast discs and stem rootlets give Boston ivy a tenacious grip on just about any vertical surface, so think twice before letting it attach to shingle or clapboard—the firm attachment accelerates the deterioration of wood and mortar. By comparison, Virginia creeper needs a rough surface to adhere to because its tendrils are less clingy than those of Boston ivy.

Both Boston ivy and Virginia creeper are famed for their vigor and potential size; they can cover multistory walls and clothe tree trunks, and Virginia creeper can also blanket open ground. Silvervein creeper is something of a wimp by comparison (though it too climbs by means of tendrils tipped with holdfast discs), but its leaves are more decorative.

PEAK SEASON

Fall, once leaves show red colors

MY FAVORITES

'Beverly Brooks' and 'Green Showers' are large-leafed selections of Boston ivy, the former offering especially bright fall color. For smaller leaves on less rampant vines, look for 'Lowii' and 'Veitchii'.

RELATED SPECIES

Virginia creeper *(Parthenocissus quinquefolia)* leaves are bronze tinted when new, dark green by summer, and crimson and burgundy in fall. Plant with care as it may be invasive.

Silvervein creeper *(P. henryana)* grows in the warmer parts of zone 32. It is the species of choice where space is limited because its maximum height and width is only about 20 feet. Leaves look like Virginia creeper, but leaflets are smaller (to just 2 inches long). Leaves are purplish when new, mature to dark bronzy green with a network of pronounced silver veining, and turn rich red in fall.

GARDEN COMPANIONS

Let Boston ivy climb an old tree stump or tree that's beyond renovating. Combine with akebia (pages 164–165) or trumpet creeper (pages 180–181) for contrasts in foliage color and texture.

When Plant in the spring from well-rooted container plants. Fall planting works in warmer locations, but for best results, a full growing season for establishment in the garden is required.

Where Plant in full sun for the best growth, but partial shade will result in better leaf color. Particularly with 'Silvervein Creeper', partial shade is required or the leaves will bleach and look sunburned. Provide the vines with an average garden soil and regular watering through the first two years until established.

How Plant vines at the same level that they were growing in the containers. Dig holes that are twice as wide but just as deep as the rootball and backfill with the native soil amended with some well-rotted leaf compost. Water well immediately after planting. Fertilize at the end of the first growing season with a balanced fertilizer. Provide a means for vines to reach the surface they are to climb upon, and they are off and running.

TLC Boston ivy requires little care after initial establishment. Ground cover plantings may require some trimming at the ends to encourage branching and filling in. Pruning is usually restricted to removing dead or broken stems or stems that have come loose from the structure to which they have attached. Some thinning and directing of stems will be beneficial in the first few years.

Boston ivy's summer look is a cool dark green, here covering a stone garden wall.

Clematis
Clematis

When I'm out plant shopping, I can always spot beginning gardeners in the first flush of an infatuation with clematis. They gaze longingly at the elegant petals and the charming way the perennial vine scales its miniature plastic trellis. Then, after a few deep sighs, they move on. I know just what they're thinking: Someday I'll be skilled enough to take one of these beauties home. Someday I'll have clematis cascading over the mailbox, or threading through a tall shrub rose, or scrambling up the trunk of a flowering crabapple tree—just as it does in the garden books. But clematis is for experts, not for know-nothing gardeners like me. Take heart: nobody has told the clematis you are a beginner, and with a little forethought you can keep it fooled.

But the fact is, clematis gets a bad rap. If you choose the right variety for your climate, soil, and site, and if you prune it properly and make sure its roots are protected, you'll find that clematis is among the easiest and most rewarding of all flowering plants to grow.

Yes, even if you're a novice. In fact, *especially* if you're a novice, as experienced gardeners won't feel a tenth as proud as you will when friends come over to admire your clematis at its floriferous peak.

Sweet autumn clematis produces creamy white, fragrant, 1-inch-wide flowers in late summer or fall. The vine is rampant and will cover a substantial trellis.

TOP TO BOTTOM: 'Nelly Moser', a long-blooming favorite; 'General Sikorski' flowers are 6 to 8 inches wide; and 'Marie Boisselot' may be 9 inches wide.

PEAK SEASON

Flowers bloom in early spring, summer, or fall, depending on variety, followed by wispy seedpods that can be as showy as the flowers.

MY FAVORITES

Anemone clematis (C. montana) is easy to grow and produces huge numbers of flowers in spring. Many varieties are available.

Hybrid 'General Sikorski' blooms intermittently beginning in June and into September producing many lavender blue flowers.

Hybrid 'Nelly Moser' has large mauve to pink flowers with a dark pink stripe on each petal. It blooms in summer, on new spring growth.

'Marie Boisselot' (C. jackmanii) has pure white flowers with cream-colored stamens. Prune right after flowers fade for best flowering the following year.

Sweet autumn clematis (C. terniflora) blooms prolifically in fall. Given a fence or garden shed to devour, this clematis is truly outstanding at summer's end.

GARDEN COMPANIONS

Clematis does wonders for a mailbox or lamppost, especially when combined with a climbing rose or morning glory. Or combine with lilies, peonies, and 'Annabelle' hydrangeas.

When The best time to plant nursery-grown clematis is early spring.

Where Plant in rich, loose, fast-draining soil in full sun or light shade. Roots like to be cool, but leaves require 6 to 8 hours of sun. An eastern exposure is best. Mulch south- and west-facing plantings to keep roots cool. Plant vines next to a trellis or tree trunk to provide support.

How Loosen soil to a depth of 10 to 12 inches and work in generous amounts of compost or other organic material. Incorporate a controlled-release fertilizer into the soil before planting. Plant vines at the same depth that they were growing in the container. Water deeply and consistently through summer: allow soil to partially dry and then follow with a soaking.

TLC Keep the soil evenly moist from spring until the ground freezes, watering when the top 2 inches of soil has dried out. Apply 2 to 4 inches of shredded leaves, bark, or wood-chip mulch around plants as soon as the ground warms in spring, and replenish as necessary throughout the growing season. Give plants a complete liquid fertilizer monthly during the growing season. Stems are easily broken, so use care when attaching to supports. The twisting leafstalks may need help climbing. Pruning varies with the type of clematis. Spring bloomers flower on old wood; prune them a month after flowering to restrict sprawl. Summer and fall bloomers flower on new stems; prune them in spring before leaf and flower buds swell.

Climbing Hydrangea
Hydrangea anomala petiolaris

Most gardeners first learn about climbing hydrangea when they're looking to add a vertical dimension to a shady garden. Few flowering vines do well in shade, but climbing hydrangea actually thrives in it. Another virtue is its versatility as a climber. Its aerial rootlets cling tenaciously to wood, brick, or stone. A climbing hydrangea can also be trained to a trellis or other support.

Among the most spectacular examples of this vine that I have seen is one that clothes the lower portion of a nearby stone house. The stems of the vine are 3 inches in diameter and its length is undoubtedly 75 or 80 feet. When it blooms in summer, the entire house appears to be floating on a pillow of blossoms. The flowers appear in flat-topped clusters, called corymbs, held outward from the plant and parallel to the ground. The buds are round and greenish white, opening to a dull white. The outer flowers are sterile and showy, similar in appearance to the lace-cap varieties of shrubby hydrangea.

Climbing hydrangea is slow to get established and may not flower for the first several years, but once adapted to its site, the vine is a showstopper.

PEAK SEASON

Dark green foliage is attractive all season. Flowering is usually in mid-summer but may be somewhat delayed in full shade. Older plants have peeling, cinnamon-colored bark. In winter stems form strong tracery against walls and buildings.

A SIMILAR VINE

Japanese hydrangea vine (Schizo-phragma hydrangeoides) is a climbing hydrangea look-alike. It too is a high-climbing vine but differs from climb-ing hydrangea in flower details and growth habit: it hugs its support more closely, producing a flatter look.

GARDEN COMPANIONS

Climbing hydrangea looks wonderful against brick or stone, especially when in bloom or when the leaves turn crimson in fall. Combine it with other shade-tolerant plants. The white flowers go well with white- or pink-flowered Japanese anemones, astilbe, and the tall white spires of bugbane (Cimicifuga).

OPPOSITE PAGE: *Scrambling over the ground and up a tree are the dense leaves and lacy flower clusters of climbing hydrangea, a shade-tolerant vine that's nearly indestructible once established.* ABOVE: *Climbing hydrangea's tiny flowers form lace-cap clusters several inches wide.*

When The best time to plant climbing hydrangea is early spring. Nursery-grown plants in containers can be planted throughout the growing season if they are watered well. Climbing hydrangea is slow to establish and may take two or three years to settle into a new location. Be patient; if well established it can last for generations.

Where Climbing hydrangea likes rich soil and full sun or light shade. Avoid very dry sites. Aerial roots cling readily to wood, brick, and stone. Plants may survive in protected loca-tions in southern parts of zone 43.

How Loosen soil to a depth of 10 to 12 inches and work in generous amounts of compost or other organic material. Incorporate a controlled-release fertilizer into the soil before planting. Plant at the same depth that the plant was growing in the container. Water immediately after planting. Watering throughout the first two years is essential.

TLC Keep the soil evenly moist from spring until the ground freezes, watering when the top 2 inches of soil has dried out. Consistent watering is especially important during the first 2 years, but even mature plants will wilt at the first sign of drought. Apply 2 to 4 inches of shredded bark, leaf compost, or wood-chip mulch around plants as soon as the ground warms in spring, and replenish as necessary through-out the growing season. Fertilize in spring with a 10-10-10 fertilizer or an organic equivalent sprinkled around the base of plants and watered in well. Plants bloom on old wood, so prune after flowering only as needed. It may take up to 2 years before a vine clings well to a flat surface.

171

Dutchman's Pipe

Aristolochia macrophylla

Dutchman's pipe makes a solid green canopy when grown over an arbor. The vine's big, heart-shaped leaves echo the tropical leaves of the taro relative Xanthosoma 'Chartreuse Giant'.

This is a big, leafy perennial vine that's great for covering a wall or growing on a trellis to screen a porch. Although its name comes from the curious shape of its flowers, the foliage is its most remarkable feature: twining stems 10 to 20 feet long bear kidney-shaped leaves in dense layers, like shingles on a house.

Dutchman's pipe is a woodland native. It belongs to the same family as wild ginger (*Asarum);* both plants have large, broad leaves that obscure the flowers, which are held close to the stems. Finding the flowers is great fun, especially for children. (Be aware that parts of Dutchman's pipe are toxic when ingested.)

Dutchman's pipe is easy to grow from seed, very hardy, and disease resistant. It appreciates a fertile, moist site and full sun but can tolerate dense shade. If it gets too aggressive, it can be cut back in late winter or early spring. The vine doesn't do well in windy areas, so give it some shelter.

PEAK SEASON

Inconspicuous but interesting flowers bloom late spring to early summer; lustrous leaves are deep green all season.

GARDEN COMPANIONS

Dutchman's pipe is attractive with woodland plants like wake robin (*Trillium*), lungwort, bishop's hat, and Japanese painted ferns (*Athyrium nipponicum*); it is also an excellent backdrop for a shady flower border. Given reasonable care, Dutchman's pipe will cover a chain-link fence with elegant foliage, turning a garden liability into a garden asset. Perennials in front of the resulting green wall will stand out strikingly against the handsome foliage.

When The best time to plant Dutchman's pipe is early spring. Nursery-grown plants in containers can be planted all season if they are watered well. Seeds can also be sown directly in the ground in fall, but if you try that, protect the seeds from rodents with chicken wire.

Where Plant in average to rich, well-drained soil. Dutchman's pipe grows best in full sun but tolerates shade, even heavy shade in hottest areas. It does not tolerate dry soils or windy areas. Grow it where you want a dense privacy screen.

How Loosen soil to a depth of 10 to 12 inches and work in 2 to 3 inches of compost or other organic matter. Incorporate a controlled-release fertilizer into the soil before planting. Plant at the same depth that plants were growing in the containers, spacing them 15 to 20 feet apart. Provide a sturdy support. Water immediately after planting.

TLC Keep the soil evenly moist from spring until the ground freezes, watering when the top 2 inches of soil has dried out. Apply 2 to 4 inches of shredded bark, leaf compost, or wood-chip mulch around plants as soon as the ground warms in spring, and replenish as necessary throughout the growing season. Plants will respond well to an annual spring application of 10-10-10 fertilizer or an organic equivalent sprinkled around the base of plants and watered in well. Cut back vines in late winter if they get too heavy.

ABOVE: *Dutchman's pipe leaves grow 6 to 14 inches long and overlap each other to form a dense screen.* LEFT: *Established Dutchman's pipe quickly grows up a porch post.*

Honeysuckle
Lonicera

Honeysuckle is a delightful perennial vine, well behaved and graceful, with clusters of brilliant yellow, orange, or red flowers that bloom sporadically all summer. Its thick, almost serpentine stems wind around their support as they grow upward. Occasionally a branch will drift away from the support and wave about in the air; tie it in place with twine while it's still young and pliant. Honeysuckle vines become gnarled and rigid over time, which adds to the vine's appeal. Their leaves are large, leathery, and round, a fine backdrop for the warm flower color.

Honeysuckle tolerates some shade, but too much shade or poor air circulation will invite fungal problems. The vine also will get ratty looking if it is chronically deprived of adequate moisture or crowded. Given a trellis of its own, an arbored gate, or even a mailbox, it will more than rise to the occasion. Among the most spectacular examples of honeysuckle that I have seen is one that was planted in the 1950s and allowed to conquer about 50 feet of stone and wrought iron fence. Against the dark metal and rustic stone, the handsome foliage and yellow-orange flowers create a striking display in midsummer.

Goldflame honeysuckle vine spilling over a garden wall at peak bloom adds welcome color to the summer garden.

When Plant container-grown honeysuckle vines anytime, spring through late summer.

Where Plant in fertile soil in full sun except where noted.

How Loosen soil to a depth of 10 to 12 inches and work in generous amounts of compost or other organic material. Incorporate a controlled-release fertilizer into the soil before planting. Plant honeysuckle at the same depth that it was growing in the container. Provide a support for the vine's twining stems and give them some guidance regarding what to climb. Water immediately after planting.

TLC Keep the soil evenly moist from spring until the ground freezes, watering when the top 2 inches of the soil has dried out. Consistent watering is especially important during the first 2 years, but even mature plants will wilt at the first sign of drought. Apply 2 to 4 inches of shredded bark, composted leaves or wood-chip mulch around plants as soon as the ground warms in spring and replenish as necessary throughout the growing season. Fertilize in spring with a 10-10-10 fertilizer or an organic equivalent sprinkled around the base of plants and watered in well. Prune after flowering to maintain shape. Next year's flowers will bloom on new wood. Regular washing with the garden hose will help keep aphids from becoming a serious problem.

PEAK SEASON

Tubular orange, red, or yellow flowers bloom from early spring to late summer. Red or purple berries in late summer attract birds.

MY FAVORITES

Trumpet honeysuckle (*L. sempervirens*) is named for the shape of its large red or orange flowers, which grow in clusters of six. 'Sulphurea' (also sold as 'Flava') has yellow unscented flowers in April.

L. brownii 'Dropmore Scarlet', a hybrid of *L. sempervirens* and *L. hirsuta,* is probably the best honeysuckle vine. It is extremely hardy and has red flowers that attract hummingbirds, though the flowers aren't fragrant. 'Hummingbird's Gold' is similar but with bright yellow flowers.

Goldflame honeysuckle (*L. heckrottii*) flowers appear in June and continue to bloom intermittently throughout the summer.

GARDEN COMPANIONS

Honeysuckle is striking on a fence behind small to midsize perennials with blue or lavender flowers, such as veronica, sage, lavender, or catmint. Or plant on a fence with a blue clematis like 'Will Goodwin'. It's also attractive behind low shrub roses and other plants with bright flowers. Just make sure they don't obscure the vine or cut off its air supply.

ABOVE: *Trumpet honeysuckle flowers are nearly 2 inches long.* TOP RIGHT: *'Hummingbird's Gold' is a yellow hybrid.* BOTTOM RIGHT: *Coral pink petals of goldflame honeysuckle reveal golden interior.*

Hop Vine
Humulus lupulus

Although common hop vine is more widely planted as a commercial crop (its flowers are a traditional flavoring for beer), it is an asset in the home garden as well.

Once established, 'Sunbeam' hop vine grows from the perennial roots to 25 feet in one season, here completely covering its supporting wooden fence.

Each year, rough-textured, twining stems spring from perennial roots and grow rapidly to 15 to 25 feet; the young shoots can be cooked and eaten as a vegetable. The hand-size, bright green leaves, usually three lobed and tooth edged, overlap like shingles as the vine gains height. The actual flowers are tiny, but they're enclosed in conspicuous clusters of bracts that resemble pale green, soft, 1- to 2-inch pinecones and even have a pine fragrance.

PEAK SEASON

The fast-growing vines and bright green leaves are attractive all summer. Plants bloom in late summer.

MY FAVORITES

'Aureus' and 'Sunbeam' have chartreuse to golden yellow foliage. Give both afternoon shade if planted in hot, south- or west-facing locations or else the leaves will bleach.

GARDEN COMPANIONS

Looks good with astilbe, hostas, and hydrangeas in shady locations or climbing up an old tree stump.

When Plant dormant roots in early spring.

Where Hop vine does best in good, organically enriched soil, the sort you would use for vegetables or annual flowers.

How Plants are sold as dormant roots. Plant them just beneath the soil surface, with the thick end pointing up. Provide string, wire, or a trellis for support. At the onset of frosty weather in fall or early winter, leaves and stems will turn brown and die. Remove them from their supports before new growth starts in spring.

TLC Throughout the growing season, provide regular moisture during dry periods. You may need to tie young vines in place at first, but in time the stems will begin to attach to the support. Fertilize with an organic or controlled-release fertilizer in fall. Prune only to remove errant growth.

ABOVE: *Fresh new leaves of 'Sunbeam' have the brightest green color.* LEFT: *Pillars of 'Aureus' hop vine are supported by metal posts.*

Kiwi

Actinidia

Kiwis are bold-textured vines that offer varied attractions, especially colorful foliage and delicious fruit. In all species, male and female flowers appear on separate plants—a fact to keep in mind if you want a crop of fruit. The twining vines develop fairly thick trunks and heavy limbs that require sturdy support or attachments.

Hardy kiwi *(Actinidia arguta)* has a fine-textured appearance. Leaves reach 3 to 6 inches long, and fuzzless fruits are just 1½ inches long and come in clusters. Female varieties 'Ananasnaja' and 'Hood River' need a pollinator; 'Issai' (not always easy to locate) is self-fertile.

Flamboyant foliage is the outstanding feature of *A. kolomikta*. The 5-inch leaves, shaped like elongated hearts, may be solid green, white splashed with green, or green strikingly splashed in pink to red. Variegated forms show the best color variety and intensity in cool weather and, in mildest zones, when grown in partial shade. Because male plants are reputed to have better foliage than females, they are generally the kind sold. Reaching as high as 15 feet, the vines bear small, fragrant white flowers in early summer; if plants of both sexes grow near one another, the female vine may later produce inch-long, sweet-tasting yellow fruits.

Actinidia kolomikta 'Arctic Beauty' brightens shady corners, especially in spring, with its white and green variegated leaves.

PEAK SEASON

Spring and summer for attractive foliage. Fall for fruits of hardy kiwi.

MY FAVORITES

I prefer the fruiting female varieties of hardy kiwi *(Actinidia arguta)*, namely 'Ananasnaja', 'Hood River', and 'Issai'. This last one is self-fertile; the first two former ones need a male pollinating variety to produce fruit.

'Arctic Beauty' is a cultivar of *A. kolomikta* that produces fragrant white flowers in spring, but its variegated leaves are the real stars.

The related Chinese gooseberry *(A. deliciosa)* is the kiwi that makes the fuzzy brown, egg-sized fruits with delicious green flesh, but it's too cold-tender to grow in our region. Convince a southern relative to grow it, then visit.

GARDEN COMPANIONS

If planted where it can climb on a fence or trellis, this vine is a useful backdrop for plants such as astilbe, hosta, and Japanese painted fern in shadier locations, and salvias and rudbeckias in sunny locations. *A. kolomikta* looks particularly good with purple cone flower.

ABOVE RIGHT: *'Ananasnaja' is a female fruiting cultivar of hardy kiwi. Plant a male pollinator, such as 'Meader Male', for fruit.*
RIGHT: *Tricolored leaves of 'Arctic Beauty'.*

When Transplants easily at any time, but spring planting of container-grown nursery stock is preferred.

Where Hardy kiwi grows best in good, well-drained soil. Give this plant room. It is rampant when established and it is a sorry gardener who plants kiwi in a too-small place. Figure that 20 to 25 feet of supported climbing space is needed to show off the vine at its best. Or plan on investing in a ladder and pruning shears.

How Kiwis appreciate regular moisture during the growing season, though they can get by with moderate watering.

TLC Train vigorous new stems into place as they lengthen; prune and thin vines in winter while they are leafless. Fruits come on shoots that are at least 1 year old; on dormant stems, fruiting buds appear knoblike, but foliage buds are flat. This vine is accommodating and tolerates a lot of pruning. If it overgrows its space, cut it back to a framework of older wood before growth begins in the spring. Cut away wayward or broken branches anytime during the year.

Trumpet Creeper
Campsis radicans

Big enough to cover an eyesore, trumpet creeper also serves to cloak an arbor. Accents include purple fountain grass, and chartreuse leaves of 'Margarita' ornamental sweet potato.

If you want to cover something like a gazebo with big, brilliant orange flowers and you love hummingbirds, plant trumpet creeper. But keep in mind this vine's single drawback, a tendency to trample everything in its path. The vine puts out aerial shoots, which is how it manages to scale just about any structure to a height of 30 or 40 feet. The dark green, serrated leaves unfurl in late May. Clusters of trumpet-shaped, 3-inch-long, flame-colored flowers bloom from June through September, followed by attractive woody seedpods that may last all winter.

Trumpet creeper is actually a slow-growing vine, but it is determined. Keep it away from the house, as its stems will clog gutters and downspouts, cover up windows, and poke their way through any exposed cracks and crevices. Subzero temperatures will freeze the vine to the ground, forcing it to retrace its steps the following spring.

PEAK SEASON

Trumpet-shaped, orange-scarlet flowers bloom in midsummer. Handsome foliage spring, summer, and fall.

MY FAVORITES

'Flava' has yellow flowers and grows 30 to 40 feet and is among the most outstanding of summer vines.

'Praecox' bears scarlet to orange-scarlet flowers in June. Color varies somewhat from individual to individual, but the overall effect is stunning.

Campsis × *tagliabuana* is showier but less hardy than *C. radicans*. 'Mme Galen' bears orange-red blooms. 'Crimson Trumpet' has deep red flowers.

GARDEN COMPANIONS

Place in front of trumpet creeper plants that will benefit from a solid green background after the vine has finished flowering. Daylilies, lilies, roses, and rudbeckias, and other sun-loving perennials are all good choices.

When Plant nursery-grown plants throughout the growing season, and then water well. Direct-sow seeds in spring or fall.

ABOVE: *'Mme Galen' flowers are larger than common trumpet vine.* BELOW: *'Flava' flowers are variable, yellow to orange.*

Where Plant in well-drained soil in full sun to partial shade. Trumpet creeper tolerates city pollution. It clings to wood, brick, and stucco surfaces with aerial rootlets. Use it for large-scale screening.

How Loosen soil to a depth of 10 to 12 inches and work in 2 to 3 inches of compost or other organic matter. Incorporate a controlled-release fertilizer into the soil before planting. Plant trumpet creeper at the same depth that it was growing in the container. Water immediately after planting.

TLC Keep the soil evenly moist from spring until the ground freezes, watering when the top 2 inches of soil has dried out. Apply 2 to 4 inches of shredded bark or wood-chip mulch around plants as soon as the ground warms in spring and replenish as necessary. The plant will die back to the ground each winter. Pull up suckering roots that invade nearby gardens. Prune in spring to control growth and remove winter-damaged wood. Maintain a framework of branches to keep the plant in a reasonably small space.

Wisteria

Wisteria

This perennial vine's remarkable beauty more than offsets its sometimes aggressive nature. Of several species, Chinese wisteria *(Wisteria sinensis)* blooms first in spring, about a week earlier than Japanese wisteria *(W. floribunda),* and its flowers last longest. But Japanese wisteria has the longest flower clusters and is hardier and better suited to our region. Or, for the far north, gardeners can grow the native Kentucky wisteria *(W. macrostachya)* which is reliably hardy into northern New York. The smooth gray bark and compound leaves of all wisterias combine to give a solid, aged appearance to the structure on which it grows. But it's those long flower clusters that attract the most comment.

Growing wisteria on a house or over an arbor transforms a back-yard into an exotic retreat. The Japanese wisteria shown here bears flower clusters up to 2 feet long that dangle from the vine like elongated bunches of grapes.

When The best time to plant wisteria is early spring. Nursery-grown plants can be planted all season if they are watered well.

Where Plant in full sun. Wisteria will grow in light shade, but you'll have fewer flowers. Plants tolerate a wide range of soils as long as they are well drained. Hot, dry, compacted soils are the exception. Grow wisteria as a focal point in your garden. Draped over an arbor or pergola, it makes a shady refuge. Wisteria can be trained into a form like a small tree if given some support initially. To do so requires patience, a plan, and pruners.

How Loosen soil to a depth of 10 to 12 inches and work in generous amounts of compost or other organic material. Incorporate a controlled-release fertilizer into the soil before planting. This will usually be the last time you need to fertilize a wisteria. Plant at the same depth that the plant grew in the container. Provide a sturdy, well-anchored support to handle the weight of mature vines. Water immediately after planting.

TLC Keep the soil evenly moist from spring until the ground freezes, watering when the top 2 inches of soil has dried out. Consistent watering is especially important during the first 2 years, but even mature plants will wilt in a drought. Apply 2 to 4 inches of shredded bark or wood-chip mulch around plants as soon as the ground warms in spring and replenish as necessary throughout the growing season. Wisterias generally do not need supplemental fertilizer. Prune side branches back after flowering, always leaving at least six leaves per branch. Remove excess branches to improve light penetration and flowering. Wisteria does not have the ability to cling to surfaces. Instead, its stem and side branches twist around supports. If the supports provided are insufficient, wisteria will twine around them and eventually crush them.

Without supports, the vine will crawl along the ground. It may take several years before wisteria has a good bloom, and even after several years the blossom may be slow to begin. Clean up fallen seedpods and seeds, as the seeds themselves are reportedly poisonous.

PEAK SEASON

Fragrant, pendulous flower clusters bloom late spring to early summer. The glossy foliage is attractive all season. Fuzzy fruit pods decorate the vines in fall and into winter.

MY FAVORITES

Japanese wisteria *(Wisteria floribunda)* has the longest flower clusters, and is a fabulous showstopper in full bloom. Flowers are violet or violet-blue and come from buds on last year's growth. 'Rosea' has pale rose flowers tipped in purple with racemes of flowers reaching 18 to 20 inches long. 'Macrobotrys' has reddish violet flowers in clusters that have been measured at 30 inches in length, and is a most spectacular plant, to be sure. *W. macrostachya* 'Aunt Dee' is a Kentucky native wisteria with 8- to 12-inch clusters of bluish purple flowers.

GARDEN COMPANIONS

Plant wisteria on an arbor or a pergola with clumps of shade-tolerant hardy geraniums or a ground cover like ajuga, dwarf periwinkle, or pachysandra at its feet.

The flowers of Japanese wisteria are the most fragrant of all the wisterias. Its leaves turn an attractive golden color in autumn.

Annual Vines

A number of all-time favorite vines are annuals—and no wonder. Starting from seeds planted early in the year, these plants grow quickly to flowering size, giving you both color and bountiful foliage from spring into autumn. They succeed in all zones of our region. Grow them on trellises, posts, walls and fences; the largest growers make a nice display on arbors. A few are even suited to ground cover use. Unless otherwise noted, all do best in a sunny location.

HYACINTH BEAN
(DOLICHOS LABLAB)

This vine offers both colorful blooms and edible beans. Like the familiar vining snap beans, it's a twining climber (to about 10 feet) with leaves composed of three broadly oval, 3- to 6-inch-long leaflets. In spring and summer, loose clusters of purple, sweet pea-like flowers stand out from the vine on long stems; these blossoms are followed by 2½-inch-long beans in velvety magenta purple. A white-flowered form is available.

MORNING GLORY
(IPOMOEA)

Most prominent among the many morning glories is the old-fashioned favorite *Ipomea tricolor,* a vigorous twiner to 15 feet, bearing heart-shaped leaves and the familiar funnel-shaped flowers 3 to 4 inches across. The traditional blue-flowered variety is 'Heavenly Blue', but there are other color choices, such as white 'Flying Saucers', and mixed-color strains, including pink, crimson, purple, and lavender in addition to blue and white. Flowers open in the morning and close by afternoon (though they'll remain open all day when weather is overcast).

PASSION FLOWER
(PASSIFLORA)

Sixteenth-century Spanish missionaries to South America found religious significance in the floral structure of these vines, hence the name "passion flower." You might also see the blooms as a designer's delight, a perfect motif for jewelry or textiles. The flower's virtually identical petals and sepals spread starlike in a flat plane, with a corona of long, threadlike filaments above them. Rising from the flower's center, as though on a pedestal, is an elaborate structure containing the reproductive parts.

Passion flowers are vigorous regardless of soil type. Use them to cover wire fences or provide shade on an arbor or pergola.

There are many different *Passiflora* species that you can experiment with. All are very tender, but they will grow well in our region as annuals.

Maintenance of passion vines amounts to untangling and cleaning up stems killed by cold weather in either winter or early spring. But you can prune excess new growth anytime during the growing season.

CLOCKWISE FROM TOP LEFT: *Hyacinth bean, 'Heavenly Blue' morning glory, passion flower, and black-eyed Susan vine.*

BLACK-EYED SUSAN VINE (*THUNBERGIA ALATA*)

A native of tropical Africa, this twining, 10-foot vine puts on a summer-long show of Halloween-colored flowers. Bright orange flowers with black throats are slender, 1-inch tubes that flare out into five indented lobes. Yellow- and white-flowered varieties are available too, as is solid orange species, orange clock vine *(T. gregorii)*.

In our region, grow normally perennial black-eyed Susan vine as an fast-growing annual, replanting every spring. Plant nursery-grown seedlings or start seeds indoors eight weeks before planting time so plants will be ready to set out when frost danger is past. Provide good, well-drained soil amended with organic matter. Train on strings or a low trellis, or display plants in hanging baskets or window boxes and allow the vining stems to cascade.

185

Roses

Roses are the American flower, and are ingrained in our collective imagination. The image of roses in full bloom, tumbling over arches and trellises, reminds us of the fragrances, the beauty, and the promise of early summer.

Roses are also seen as being difficult, a reputation earned largely because of breeding and our own desire for perfection from this most generous of flowering plants. Wild forms of roses grow throughout the temperate regions of the Northern Hemisphere, not needing our help, blooming freely in early summer, and setting fruit abundantly through the fall. The shapes, leaves, flowers, and hips of the many wild roses remind us of the varied strong and beautiful ancestries of our garden roses.

Old garden roses, primarily European, were notable for their soft, open flowers and the handsome plants that fit well into gardens. Asian roses, both wild kinds and the ones cultivated for centuries in gardens, offered a larger range of colors on repeat-flowering plants. Rose breeders began crossing these Asian and European roses, along with species roses, and in the process created new kinds of roses for generations of home gardeners. These crosses have resulted in our hybrid teas, floribundas, and large-flowered climbers, all of which are valued for their ability to bloom repeatedly through the season and for their amazing array of colors and shadings.

The downside is that many of our modern roses inherited disease susceptibility along with their improved blooms. And some of the grace and romance of the old garden roses was sacri-

ABOVE: *Season-long bloom and good-looking, disease-resistant leaves are hallmarks of modern shrub roses. This one is 'Pink Meidiland'.* OPPOSITE PAGE: *'Queen Elizabeth' is the lovely rose for which the grandiflora class was created.*

ficed. With that in mind, there has been an increasingly successful movement in the last several years to reintroduce older roses into our gardens. There has also been a focus by plant hybridizers on introducing new types of roses that are disease resistant and easy to care for, have better growth habits, flower nearly continuously, and have colorful, fragrant blossoms. We want our roses perfect, and with some help, they do come close.

There are many roses to choose from that are beautiful and easy to grow. You can grow old garden roses and climbers to disguise a small mailbox; climbers that ramble up into a large tree; hybrid teas with showy, exhibition-type blossoms; vigorous grandifloras that are lush with rose fragrance; miniatures that spill over window boxes and the edges of containers on patios; and, to add their own drama to your garden, the standard, or tree, roses. The key to enjoying the queen of flowers is to know what you like and where you want the plants to grow, and then to choose varieties that can do well in our climate and your garden. Growing roses should be easy and fun!

— ANNE O'NEILL

Climbing Roses

Climbing roses are at the heart of many gardens, rambling over fences, mailboxes, pillars, or arches. They disguise boring perimeter walls and fences, and frame entryways.

Climbers may be large or small, and the various kinds assume different shapes and have different habits. However, all of this diversity boils down to two main distinctions. One group, called ramblers, produces long flexible stems from the ground each year. These are the climbing roses that will climb up a tree or cover a beach cottage.

The other group of climbing roses has a more permanent woody framework. They may bloom once or repeatedly, and may have large single flowers or smaller clustered flowers.

Choose a rose that will grow to the height you have available, and then provide suitable support. Choosing a rose that fits well in your garden's color scheme and design is also important, especially given that climbers will be part of your garden and life for many years.

LEFT: 'William Baffin' is one of the most reliable and disease-free roses for our region. OPPOSITE PAGE, TOP: 'Altissimo' flowers are very showy. OPPOSITE PAGE, BOTTOM: 'New Dawn' covers an arbor.

When Plant bare-root roses in early spring or late fall; plant container roses spring through summer. Don't plant roses with leaves if frost threatens.

Where Choose a location with enough space for roots to stretch out, and for branches to reach full size. Plants need at least 5 or 6 hours of full sun daily. Good air circulation will help minimize disease and pest problems.

MY FAVORITES

'Aloha' This rose has fragrant pink blossoms that are large and shapely. It grows 8 to 10 feet high.

'Altissimo' This very popular rose grows 8 to 10 feet high, is hardy, and flowers all summer. Flowers are large, single, and luminously red, with striking yellow stamens.

'Autumn Sunset' Here is a rose that thrives in our summer heat and winter cold, is disease resistant, and produces lovely, fragrant, apricot yellow flowers. Height is 8 to 12 feet.

'Dublin Bay' Flowers of this rose are clear red. Height is 8 to 10 feet. One of the easiest and most effective climbers for the Tri-State region.

'Fourth of July' This exuberant rose produces red and white flowers with yellow stamens. It is disease resistant and grows 8 to 10 feet high.

'New Dawn' This robust rose grows 18 to 20 feet high. This rose is absolutely hardy and probably the best pink rose for our region.

'William Baffin' Absolutely hardy throughout our region, it has large, vibrant, pink blooms, with yellow centers. Grow it as a climber or large shrub.

For more climbing roses, see 'Cécile Brunner' (page 204), 'Jeanne Lajoie' (page 199), and 'Zéphirine Drouhin' (page 203).

How Amend soil with organic matter before planting. Soak the roots of bare-root plants in a bucket of water for a few hours before planting. Space fan-trained climbers about three-fourths of their mature height apart; upright growers about one-fourth of their height. Look for climbing roses that are growing on their own roots, not grafted. If your rose is grafted, plant so that the graft union is 1 to 2 inches below ground level.

TLC When weather is dry, water new roses approximately twice a week and established roses once a week. Water deeply, preferably in the early morning. In spring, place a 1-inch-thick layer of mulch over the soil around plants. In late fall, once weather is reliably cold, cover the base of each plant with 2 inches of mulch to protect it from severe cold. In early spring, remove the mulch, fertilize, and prune. In spring, cut off oldest canes of ramblers at their base; cut back lateral growth of stiff-stemmed roses to 4 or 5 buds.

Floribunda Roses

Floribundas are bush roses, like hybrid teas and grandifloras, and they are equally flowerful and come in an equally wide range of colors. But compared with hybrid teas, floribundas tend to be a little shorter, their flowers a little smaller, more typically arranged in clusters instead of borne singly. Flowers of some floribundas have the classic high-centered flower shape of a hybrid tea. Others are flatter and more informal.

Floribundas were originally bred in Denmark, and gardeners there call them bedding roses because they are so effective in mass plantings. You can grow them as a large-area ground cover, as well as individually in rose beds, or in borders. Some floribundas are well suited to growing in containers.

These roses are very prolific bloomers, and some of the cultivars bloom almost continuously from June until November, with only a relatively short hiatus during the height of summer.

As with hybrid teas, there are climatic and disease challenges for some floribundas in our region. My recommendations are for cultivars that are relatively easy and successful in this area; they also represent the range of what is available from this wonderful group of roses.

When Plant bare-root roses in early spring or late fall; plant container roses spring through summer. In spring, plant as soon as soil is workable, but don't plant roses that have leaves if frost threatens.

Where Choose a location with enough space for roots to stretch out and for branches to reach full size. Plants need at least 5 or 6 hours of full sun daily. Good air circulation will help minimize disease and pest problems.

MY FAVORITES

'Betty Prior' Simple flowers with a single set of pink petals come in large clusters on a hardy, robust plant.

'Chihuly' Variably colored flowers are yellow through orange to red. They're further set off by red new leaves, and later, dark green leaves. Very flowerful.

'Europeana' A great dark red rose proven over many years. Glossy leaves emerge red, then gradually turn dark green.

'Honey Perfume' Golden yellow flowers with ruffled edges have a spicy scent. The bush is nicely shaped and has glossy leaves.

'Hot Cocoa' Dark, smoky orange flowers are fragrant and borne on vigorous and hardy plants.

'Playboy' Orange-red flowers with a single set of petals come on a short, round bush that has very healthy leaves.

'Scentimental' Red and white flowers with multiple petals are strongly fragrant; they look old-fashioned but are much more abundant than old rose varieties.

How Amend soil with organic matter before planting. Soak roots of bare-root plants in a bucket of water for a few hours before planting. Space plants about three-fourths of their

TOP: *'Betty Prior' has an old-fashioned style, but blooms continuously.* BOTTOM: *Clustered 'Europeana' flowers are dark crimson.*

mature height apart. Look for roses that are growing on their own roots, not grafted. If your rose is grafted, make sure to plant the graft union 1 to 2 inches below ground level.

TLC When weather is dry, water new roses approximately twice a week and established roses once a week. Water established roses deeply, preferably in the early morning. In spring, place a 1-inch-thick layer of mulch over the soil around plants. Remove spent blooms to encourage repeat flowering. In late fall, once weather is reliably cold, cover the center of each plant with mulch to protect it from severe cold. In early spring, remove the mulch, fertilize, and prune back to approximately half the normal height of the rose. Cut just above an outward-facing bud. Remove weak and inward-facing canes, as well as any damaged by winter or pests.

OPPOSITE PAGE: *Dazzling orange-red flowers cover 'Playboy' in waves from spring to fall.*

Grandiflora Roses

In the United States, grandiflora roses are recognized as a class similar yet distinct from both hybrid teas and floribundas, in between those two groups in several ways. Some grandifloras have hybrid tea–like individual flowers on long stems, and others have clustered flowers in floribunda style. And in most cases, the flowers are as large as those of hybrid teas.

Some grandifloras are relatively large, but many are not. More important, they are "flower factories" that equal hybrid teas in blossom production.

As with hybrid teas and floribundas, choosing the right plant, putting it in the right place, and providing it with all the basics needed for survival helps ensure that you get many years of pleasure from your plant.

Some grandiflora roses are true garden classics and should be included in any garden where the focus is on fragrance and flowers. And like hybrid teas, grandiflora flowers are excellent for cutting and displaying indoors.

MY FAVORITES

'Cherry Parfait' This rose has white petals with red edges that contrast nicely with dark green leaves.

'Delany Sisters' Pink-blended-with-orange flowers come all season long on a large and vigorous bush. Winter hardy and disease resistant.

'Glowing Peace' Large flowers are a luminous blend of yellow and orange. Leaves are glossy green and resistant to disease.

'Melody Parfumée' Deep plum buds open to fragrant blooms of rich lavender.

'Queen Elizabeth' An outstanding pink flower, this is the rose for which the grandiflora class was created.

'Reba McEntire' Brilliant orange-red flowers have a satinlike quality. Very hardy and easy to grow.

BELOW: 'Cherry Parfait' scent is light and sweet. ABOVE, LEFT: 'Queen Elizabeth' is the classic grandiflora. ABOVE, RIGHT: The scent of 'Delany Sisters' is strong. OPPOSITE PAGE, LEFT: Luminous 'Glowing Peace' has a light tea scent. OPPOSITE PAGE, RIGHT: 'Melody Parfumée' has a rich, spicy scent.

When Plant bare-root roses in early spring or late fall; plant container roses spring through summer. In spring, plant as soon as soil is workable, but don't plant roses with leaves if a frost threatens.

Where Choose a location with enough space for both roots and branches to stretch out and reach full size. Plants need at least 5 to 6 hours of full sun daily. Good air circulation will help minimize disease and pest problems.

How Amend soil with organic matter before planting. Soak roots of bare-root plants in a bucket of water for a few hours before planting. Space plants about three-fourths of their mature height apart. Look for roses that are growing on their own roots, not grafted. If your rose is grafted, make sure to plant the graft union 1 to 2 inches below ground level.

TLC When weather is dry, water new roses approximately twice a week and established roses once a week. Water established roses deeply, preferably in the early morning. In spring, place a 1-inch-thick layer of mulch over the soil around plants. Remove faded flowers to encourage repeat bloom. In late fall, once weather is reliably cold, cover the center of each plant with mulch to protect it from severe cold. In early spring, remove the layer of mulch, fertilize, and prune back to approximately half the normal height of the rose. Cut just above outward-facing buds. Remove weak and inward-facing canes, as well as any damaged by winter or pests.

Ground-Cover Roses

Every bit as glamorous as its cousins, this type of rose simply spreads its canes widely and mounds up to 2 to 4 feet high. Ground-cover roses will blanket sunny slopes, form traffic-proof barriers, and attractively spill out of large containers and over walls. There are several varieties that are totally hardy and reliable in our climate.

Don't assume that ground-cover roses are simply climbers gone wrong. On the contrary, they encompass a distinct group of roses, some of the toughest, in fact. As a group, these varieties are notable for their vigor, disease resistance, and profusion of flowers. They can tolerate conditions that would kill other flowering ground covers. These plants not only survive, they bloom repeatedly through the season.

Ground-cover roses can, once they are established, shade the soil sufficiently to prevent most weeds from starting. Their leaves break the force of rain and irrigation, protecting the soil from washing away, and their roots will form a tight, erosion-resistant mat.

The key to success is choosing plants that are suitable for the space. Be sure to note the ultimate height and width of plants and compare it with your planting space. Always select a ground-cover rose that will fit the space. To do otherwise is to invite a less desirable outcome, not to mention more maintenance.

Spend the time necessary to weed the open spaces between plants until the roses completely cover the soil. Once the ground is covered, the soil is protected and weeds are blocked, and you can sit back and enjoy the show.

MY FAVORITES

Flower Carpet A group of low-growing roses in a range of colors are marketed under this name. All of them are hardy, tough, and very disease resistant. Plants are about 4 feet wide, 2 feet high. Flowers are about 2 inches wide and come continuously through the season.

'Max Graf' The large, 3-inch-wide, pink flowers have white centers and golden stamens. Plants grow 2 to 3 feet high and spread to 8 feet wide. The spring bloom is incredible, as are the hips that follow. Easy, trouble free, and hardy.

'Meidiland Fire' An excellent rose for slopes and banks, it grows 2 feet high and 6 feet wide. The bright red flower is visible from a distance; blooms repeatedly through the season.

'Sea Foam' The sumptuous, white-tinged-pink, 2½-inch flowers cover this plant from June to November. Plants mound about 2 feet high and 6 feet (or more) wide. The plant is vigorous and easy to grow in our region.

TOP: *'Flower Carpet Red'*
ABOVE: *'Flower Carpet White'*
BELOW LEFT: *'Flower Carpet Coral'*
OPPOSITE PAGE: *'Sea Foam'*

When Plant bare-root roses in early spring or late fall; plant container roses spring through summer. Plant as soon as soil is workable in spring, but don't plant roses with leaves if a frost threatens.

Where Choose a location with enough space for roots and branches to reach full size, and where plants will receive at least 5 or 6 hours of full sun daily. Good air circulation will help minimize disease and pest problems.

How Amend soil with organic matter before planting. Soak roots of bare-root plants in a bucket of water for a few hours before planting. Space plants about three-fourths of their mature height apart. Choose roses that are growing on their own roots, not grafted. If your rose is grafted, make sure to plant the graft union 1 to 2 inches below ground level.

TLC When weather is dry, water new roses approximately twice a week and established roses once a week. In spring, place a 1-inch-thick layer of mulch over the soil around plants. In late fall, once weather is reliably cold, cover the center of each plant with a layer of mulch to protect it from severe cold. In early spring, remove this layer, fertilize, and prune. Cut out older canes, and trim or redirect growth back to its allotted space.

Hybrid Tea Roses

If you plant 'Fragrant Cloud', you'll never again complain that modern roses have lost the rose scent. It is one of the most fragrant roses of any type that you can grow and has been internationally recognized for its fragrance.

Hybrid teas are the classic roses of our time. They have long been the most popular type of rose because they do a lot of what most gardeners want: produce large flowers in a range of colors on long, strong, single stems. And they do it repeatedly through the growing season on compact and sturdy bushes.

The first true hybrid teas were bred in the 1860s. By the 1880s they had gained broad recognition, and by the turn of the century, hybrid teas were widely seen to be a huge improvement over most other kinds of roses. They were by far the dominant group of roses to emerge during the early 20th century.

Along with their obvious beauty and other virtues, hybrid teas have also gained a collective reputation for needing attention, and some of this reputation is justified. But for over 100 years, they have dominated the imaginations of most rose gardeners. You can grow many hybrid teas successfully with surprisingly little effort, and other varieties may be worth the extra effort they require for their beauty. All of the hybrid tea roses recommended here are well adapted to our climate, both summer and winter, and will give years of pleasure with minimal effort.

MY FAVORITES

'Alec's Red' A classic hybrid tea form with a very good fragrance.

'Chrysler Imperial' Strongly fragrant, crimson red flowers, introduced in the 1950s and still beautiful.

'Dainty Bess' A wonderful cultivar from 1925, it has single pink flowers and purple stamens. Fragrant.

'Folklore' An orange-flowered, fragrant, disease-resistant rose, it's hardy and very easy to grow.

'Fragrant Cloud' Intensely fragrant, orange-red flowers are produced on short plants. Winter hardiness and disease resistance are superior.

'Mr. Lincoln' This is a true red and a very fragrant rose, with classic, well-formed flowers.

'Mrs. Oakley Fisher' Flowers are buff yellow with a single row of petals. It's a handsome and hardy rose.

'The McCartney Rose' Fragrant, large, pink flowers cover this vigorous plant. Disease resistant and blooms continuously.

'Traviata' Bright red flowers come from this showy plant. Disease resistant and vigorous, it could double as a modern shrub rose (see page 200).

When Plant bare-root roses in early spring or late fall; plant container roses spring through summer. In spring, plant as soon as soil is workable, but don't plant roses with leaves if frost threatens.

Where Choose a location with enough space for both roots and branches to reach full size, and where plants will receive at least 5 or 6 hours of full sun daily. Good air circulation will help minimize disease and pest problems.

'Folklore' is a deliciously fragrant and vigorous garden rose that is also a top exhibition rose.

How Amend soil with organic matter before planting. Soak roots of bare-root plants in a bucket of water for a few hours before planting. Space plants about three-fourths of their mature height apart. Look for roses that are growing on their own roots, not grafted. If your rose is grafted, plant so that the graft union is 1 to 2 inches below ground level.

TLC When weather is dry, water new roses approximately twice a week and established roses once a week. Water established roses deeply, preferably in the early morning. In spring, place a 1-inch-thick layer of mulch over the soil around plants. Remove faded flowers to encourage repeat bloom. In late fall, once weather is reliably cold, cover the center of each plant with mulch to protect it from severe cold. In early spring, remove this layer, fertilize, and prune. Cut back to approximately half the normal height of the rose, always cutting just above an outward-facing bud. Remove weak and inward-facing canes, as well as any damaged by winter or pests.

Miniature Roses

Miniature roses are very similar to modern bush roses, except in size. Few ever exceed 18 inches in height!

These diminutive roses can provide elements of structure and spots of color at the front of borders, as bedding plants and in rock gardens, climbing over small features, spilling over fences, in containers, and even as miniature standard, or tree, roses. These last-mentioned forms are like a garden sculpture, and many gardeners have discovered that they are the perfect finishing touch in their gardens. You can also grow some miniature roses indoors in pots, either adjacent to a bright window or under fluorescent lights.

The original miniatures were raised from a dwarf China rose and were commonly grown on cottage windowsills, especially in Switzerland, where they were rediscovered in 1922 by a plant breeder.

For gardeners with limited outdoor space, the pleasure of enjoying rose colors and forms on a smaller scale is a real bonus.

OPPOSITE PAGE: *One-inch-wide flowers of 'Jeanne Lajoie'.* RIGHT: *Diminutive 'Rainbow's End' looks like a full-size hybrid tea in every way but size.*

MY FAVORITES

'Jeanne Lajoie' This is a lovely climbing miniature rose. Its leaves and flowers are small, but the plant is vigorous enough to cover smaller structures with double pink flowers for many months. Moreover, it is totally hardy and easy to grow.

'Rainbow's End' Golden yellow flowers edged in red cover this rounded bush all season long. Overall, this is a very vigorous plant.

'Red Cascade' A very attractive and free-blooming rose. The plant has small, perfectly formed, dark red flowers and attractive small leaves. Use it to trail over the sides of a container or window box, as a small ground cover, or even as a miniature tree rose.

'Starina' Plants are bushy and rounded. Orange-red flowers emerge from small, pointed, perfectly shaped buds. Leaves are very glossy. Easy to grow, and ideal for containers.

When Plant bare-root roses in early spring, or container roses in spring through summer. In spring, plant as soon as soil is workable, but don't plant roses with leaves if a frost threatens.

Where Choose a location with enough space for roots and branches to reach full size, and where plants will receive at least 5 or 6 hours of full sun daily. Good air circulation will help minimize disease and pest problems.

How Amend soil with organic matter before planting. Soak roots of bare-root plants in a bucket of water for a few hours before planting. Space plants about three-fourths of their mature height apart.

TLC Roots of miniature roses are shallow, so water, fertilizer, and mulch are necessary more often. This is even more true if the plants are growing in containers. Though hardy, miniatures still need some winter protection in our region; cover plants with mulch in late fall. In early spring, prune back to approximately half the normal height of the rose. Cut just above an outward-facing bud. Remove weak and inward-facing canes, as well as any damaged by winter or pests. To grow indoors, use soilless potting mix and a 6-inch or larger container. Place in a cool, bright window, or grow under fluorescent grow lights.

Modern Shrub Roses

Compared with the hybrid teas, which are cultivated for their near-perfect flowers, modern shrub roses are bred to be all-round garden plants. This has happened because rose breeders have listened to gardeners' desires for hardy, good-looking, low-maintenance roses. For the last several years, many of the more exciting breeding breakthroughs have occurred in this large and diverse group of roses, which have many uses in gardens.

Among the most popular shrub roses are those that look and smell like old-fashioned roses, but are much more disease resistant and flower repeatedly through the season. The trademarked David Austin roses are the leading example of these. Others with similar qualities are the Romantica and the Generosa roses.

The ultimate toughness test for any flowering shrub is a median strip, and roses such as 'Carefree Delight' pass the test, blooming all season long.

Many of these newer shrubs are ideal for Tri-State gardeners who desire an easy-care rose. If you can relate to that, roses in this category won't disappoint you.

LEFT: 'Starry Night' is very flowerful all season and is disease free. OPPOSITE PAGE, TOP: Cup-shaped flowers of 'Abraham Darby' have a fruity scent. OPPOSITE PAGE, BOTTOM: Uniquely colored 'Pat Austin' flowers are deeply cupped.

MY FAVORITES

'Abraham Darby' In my experience, this is one of the better David Austin roses for the Tri-State region. Very full flowers are fragrant and have large, pale apricot petals.

'BeBop' This rose has deep red, clustered blooms with yellow centers. Healthy, hardy, easy to grow.

'Carefree Delight' Seemingly never out of bloom, it makes clusters of single pink flowers on a lovely rounded shrub that is totally hardy.

'Golden Wings' Here is one of the few yellow roses that is hardy in this region. The neat, rounded shrub is easy to care for, with the bonus of attractive grayish green leaves.

'Knock Out' Single, cherry red flowers in clusters come nonstop all season long. Very resistant to black spot disease.

'Pat Austin' Bright petals are copper orange inside and pale copper yellow outside. The shrub is hardy and healthy with bright green leaves.

'Sally Holmes' Clusters of large single blooms are amazing both for the effect of the glistening white flowers fading to buff and for their size.

'Starry Night' This relatively short, rounded bush has clusters of single white flowers with yellow stamens.

When Plant bare-root roses in early spring or fall; plant container roses spring through summer. In spring, plant as soon as soil is workable, but don't plant roses with leaves if frost is forecast.

Where Choose a location with enough space for roots and branches to spread out. Plants need at least 5 or 6 hours of full sun daily. Good air circulation will minimize disease problems.

How Amend soil with organic matter before planting. Soak roots of bare-root plants in a bucket of water for a few hours before planting. Space plants about three-fourths of their mature height apart. Choose roses that are growing on their own roots, not grafted. If your rose is grafted, make sure to plant the graft union 1 to 2 inches below ground level.

TLC When weather is dry, water new roses approximately twice a week and established roses once a week. Water deeply, preferably in the early morning. In spring, place a 1-inch-thick layer of mulch over the soil around plants. In late fall, once weather is reliably cold, cover the center of each bush with mulch to protect it from severe cold. In early spring, remove this layer of mulch and fertilize. Little pruning is needed. Remove some of the oldest canes, along with weak growth. Prune repeat-flowering kinds in early spring; prune plants that bloom only in late spring after blooms fade.

Old Garden Roses

The old garden roses are primarily those that were grown in Europe before the hybrid teas came along. Typically, these roses have gentle flower and plant shapes, very fragrant blossoms, and a kind of nostalgic charm that provides a perfect counterpoint in modern rose gardens.

Some old garden roses bloom only once a year, in spring, but others are repeat bloomers. The bushes are handsome, and many offer showy hips in fall.

Several of these roses earn a place in the garden just for their heady fragrance. With one of these roses nearby, the long days of June signal not just the beginning of summer, but the onset of a particular sort of olfactory pleasure, one that can evoke memories and feelings outside of our normal range of perceptions. Perhaps that is why rose attar, the distilled oil of rose fragrance, was once nearly priceless.

Old garden roses are all-round garden plants with many qualities to charm you and enhance your garden.

OPPOSITE PAGE: *Thornless 'Zéphirine Drouhin' is a good choice for planting near walks.* RIGHT: *Delicately colored 'Mme. Hardy' is intensely fragrant.* FAR RIGHT: *'Jacques Cartier' has outstanding fragrance.*

MY FAVORITES

'Ispahan' Pink blossoms and an outstanding rich rose scent are more than enough to endear this rose to gardeners. Easy to care for and hardy.

'Jacques Cartier' This sweet-scented, light pink rose blooms abundantly in June and repeats late in the season. Healthy, easy-to-grow shrub.

'Königin von Dänemark' This rose bears large, light pink, and very fragrant flowers in such abundance that it may need a little support to hold flowers aloft.

'Mme. Alfred Carriere' Hard to beat if you want lovely white, double, very fragrant flowers. It's hardy for its type but still needs some winter protection in our region.

'Mme. Hardy' Well-formed, true white, very fragrant green-centered flowers are held above soft green leaves. Blooms in spring and fall.

'Zéphirine Drouhin' An almost thornless 8- to 10-foot-tall large shrub or climber with sweetly scented, soft, full pink blooms.

When Plant bare-root roses in early spring or late fall; plant container roses spring through summer. In spring, plant as soon as soil is workable, but don't plant roses with leaves if frost threatens.

Where Choose a location with enough space for both roots and branches to reach full size, and where plants will receive at least 5 or 6 hours of full sun daily. Good air circulation will help minimize disease and pest problems.

How Amend soil with organic matter before planting. Soak roots of bare-root plants in a bucket of water for a few hours before planting. Space plants about three-fourths of their mature height apart. Choose roses that are growing on their own roots, not grafted. If your rose is grafted, make sure to plant the graft union 1 to 2 inches below ground level.

TLC When weather is dry, water new roses approximately twice a week and established roses once a week. Water established roses deeply, preferably in the early morning. In spring, place a 1-inch-thick layer of mulch over the soil around plants. In late fall, once weather is reliably cold, cover the bases of each plant with mulch to protect them from severe cold. In early spring, remove this mulch and fertilize. Prune to remove older canes and weak growth. Prune repeat-flowering kinds in early spring, spring-blooming kinds after bloom.

203

Polyantha Roses

Polyantha roses are generally considered the precursors of the floribundas and have many characteristics in common with them.

Individual polyantha flowers are small, even insignificant, and they are usually not fragrant. But the overall effect from the masses of blooms can be amazing. For long periods beginning in June, continuing through peak season and well into fall, these small plants are covered with blossoms.

These roses are usually small, bushy plants ideally suited for borders and bedding. Many are also good in containers—even indoors—and provide a casual but colorful look not offered by many other garden plants. They bloom nonstop in clusters and are among the most beloved of smaller flowered roses. 'Cécile Brunner', the Sweetheart Rose, is probably the best known, and no other rose makes a more perfect boutonniere.

Polyanthas are easy to grow, relatively disease resistant, and hardy. Most are small, so need to be in front of other plants if they are in mixed borders, but some larger forms are available that can make large shrubs. Give a polyantha a spot in your garden with good soil, nutrition, light, and water, and it can be an incredibly rewarding plant.

When Plant bare-root roses in early spring or late fall; plant container roses spring through summer. In spring, plant as soon as soil is workable, but don't plant roses with leaves if a frost threatens.

Where Choose a location that includes enough space for roots and branches to spread out and reach full size. Plants need at least 5 or 6 hours of full sun daily and good air circulation.

How Amend soil with organic matter before planting. Soak bare-root plants in a bucket of water for a few hours before planting. Space plants about three-fourths of their mature height apart. Look for roses that are growing on their own roots, not grafted. If your rose is grafted, make sure to plant the graft union 1 to 2 inches below ground level.

TLC When weather is dry, water new roses approximately twice a week and established roses once a week. Water established roses deeply, ideally in the early morning. In spring, place a 1-inch-thick layer of mulch over the soil around plants. In late fall, once weather is reliably cold, cover the center of each bush with mulch to protect crowns from severe cold. In early spring, remove the layer of mulch, fertilize, and prune. Reduce the size of the plant by approximately half, cutting just above an outward-facing bud. Remove weak and inward-facing canes, as well as any damaged by winter or pests.

MY FAVORITES

'Cécile Brunner' Perfectly formed, thimble-sized light pink flowers are held in open sprays. The 3-foot-high plants are very easy to grow, though winter protection is required. A larger climbing form is also available.

'Marie Pavié' Thornless stems are profuse producers of white blooms. The compact plant is very easy to grow, as it's both disease resistant and winter hardy.

'The Fairy' Profuse blooms from June through November are a charming blush pink. Excellent border or container plant; disease resistant and winter hardy.

'White Pet' Tiny pompomlike flowers in dense clusters cover this small mound of a plant thickly enough to make an impression from a distance. Very easy to grow, it is disease resistant and winter hardy.

OPPOSITE PAGE: *'The Fairy' spills casually over the edge of a path.* RIGHT: *'The Fairy' flowers up close.* FAR RIGHT: *'White Pet' produces masses of white flowers in large clusters.*

Species Roses and Their Hybrids

I f "honor thy parents" were a truism among roses as it is among people, the species roses would be the most honored type. Various individuals among these roses have been crossed and then recrossed hundreds or thousands of times in order to produce the vast array of roses that we have today. Moreover, rose breeders go back to the species all the time, crossing them into hybrids, hoping to add their vigor, disease resistance, and hardiness to new offspring (and sometimes succeeding).

But most important to know is that the species roses (including their cultivars and hybrids) are outstanding roses in their own right. They are often more beautiful than almost any other kind of shrub when used appropriately. The red-ripening rose hips are frequently spectacular, and because they last for months, are more than enough incentive to add these roses to your garden. Also use species roses as specimen or foundation plants, or in mixed plantings where roses can take center stage during their peak seasons and retire to the chorus during the rest of the year.

When Plant bare-root roses in early spring or late fall; plant container roses spring through summer. In spring, plant as soon as soil is workable, but don't plant roses with leaves if a frost threatens.

Where Choose a location with enough space for both roots and branches to reach full size, and where plants will receive at least 5 or 6 hours of full sun daily. Good air circulation will help minimize disease and pest problems.

How Amend soil with organic matter before planting. Soak roots of bare-root plants in a bucket of water for a few hours before planting. Space plants about three-fourths of their mature height apart. Look for roses that are growing on their own roots. If your rose is grafted, make sure the graft union is 1 to 2 inches below ground level.

TOP: *'Buff Beauty' flowers are 4 inches wide and fragrant.* BOTTOM: *Small red flowers of 'F. J. Grootendorst' come in large clusters.* OPPOSITE PAGE: *Dainty 'Ballerina' flowers come in large sprays.*

MY FAVORITES

'Ballerina' Here's a truly great garden plant that covers itself in hydrangea-like masses of single pink blossoms all season.

'Buff Beauty' Full, ruffled yellow flowers bloom in June and in fall. Medium-sized shrub with arching canes and dark green leaves.

'F. J. Grootendorst' Fringed red flowers cover this vigorous and tall rose. It's one of the best hedge plants.

Rosa glauca Prized for its distinctive blue-green leaves and round, red hips. The small pink flowers are charming, and stems are nearly thornless.

R. × *harisonii* (Harison's yellow) A favorite in mixed shrub borders, this rose covers itself in yellow, licorice-scented blossoms from May into June.

R. moyesii 'Geranium' This is an elegant plant with long canes that produces bright red flowers with red stamens. Handsome hips follow in autumn.

R. xanthina hugonis (Father Hugo's rose) The yellow flowers of this rose appear early in the season. The shrub is very attractive.

'Stanwell Perpetual' Lovely, fragrant, blush pink blooms appear all season on this compact shrub. It's very hardy, reliable, and vigorous.

TLC When weather is dry, water new roses approximately twice a week and established roses once a week. Water established roses deeply, preferably in the early morning. In spring, place a 1-inch-thick layer of mulch over the soil around plants. In late fall, once weather is reliably cold, cover the center of each bush with mulch to protect them from severe cold. In spring, remove this mulch and fertilize. Cut out older and spindly canes, and remove suckers to restrain spreading.

Bulbs

Mention "bulbs" and most of us think of tulips and daffodils blooming in April or May. Perhaps you know that hyacinths are also spring bulbs, but do colchicum or Siberian squill ring a bell? And there are wonderful bulbs for summertime bloom, such as lilies and ornamental onions.

Bulbs offer a burst of color, often just when our gardens need it most. In this chapter you'll learn about bulbs that bloom in spring, summer, and fall. In addition, you'll discover that according to botanists, not all the plants we call bulbs are technically bulbs.

Crocuses and gladiolus are corms, for example; caladiums are tuberous roots, and tulips are true bulbs. These technical terms refer to the underground parts of the plants. True bulbs, such as tulips, contain the minute beginnings of stems, roots, leaves, and flowers—compact packages that lie dormant underground until spring when they realize their full potential. Corms, tubers, and rhizomes are thickened stems; tuberous roots are swollen roots.

A BULB'S LIFE

For the most part, all bulbous plants are grown the same way: you dig holes, plant the bulbs, and then wait several months for green growth to appear aboveground. Much the same as most perennials, the flowers of bulbous plants typically last about 2 weeks, longer in cool spring weather, and, depending upon the bulb, not as long in hot weather. Choose the right ones, and bulbs can supply color when your garden is desperate for it. Daffodils and Siberian squills are especially lovely in spring when carpeting a woodsy area before the trees have leafed out. Gladiolus bloom in mid- to late July, when most gardens are in the doldrums, and caladiums add summer color to shady places.

Bulbous plants use their leaves to send nutrients down to their underground storage components, so don't remove leaves after plants have bloomed until they're at least beginning to yellow and wither. This is where companion planting really helps. In spring, clumps of forget-me-nots, unrolling fern fronds, emerging hostas, and astilbe easily hide the fading bulb leaves. Crocuses are small enough that their leaves wither away inconspicuously. Tulip leaves are more troublesome because their large size makes them difficult to disguise, but larger perennials such as daylilies are helpful in camouflaging the fading leaves. Alliums and lilies bloom in early to midsummer, when the garden has filled out and withering bulb leaves aren't as obvious.

ABOVE: *Dogwoods shelter tulips, fritillarias, and hyacinths.*
OPPOSITE PAGE: *Tulips and daffodils herald spring's arrival.*

AFTER-BLOOM CARE

After flowering, many bulbous plants can be left in the ground indefinitely. Daffodils, crocuses, some alliums, and Siberian squill are enthusiastic "naturalizers." That means they come back more plentifully each year. Some bulbous plants, such as caladiums, must be dug up for winter storage and replanted the following season.

Bulbs may seem like push-button plants, programmed to perform on schedule, but designing with them takes planning. Choose carefully and time their planting right, and bulbs will add another layer of life and color to your garden.

—JUDY GLATTSTEIN

209

Allium

Allium

Alliums are ornamental onions that show their family resemblance in many ways, except they don't have that pungent onion smell. They bloom in mid- to late summer, depending on the variety, and may spread by reseeding. Their ball of flowers balanced on a narrow, blue-gray stem reminds me of a soap bubble. Straplike leaves grow at the base of the plant. The leaves are bright green to grayish green to blue-gray. Alliums are pest resistant, and they make great cut flowers. And after they fade in the garden, the dry flower heads are also attractive for bouquets. Small alliums are short and dainty, so they are more effective when used in groups. The large alliums top out at about 2 feet tall, with leaves that begin withering at the tips as soon as the flowers start to open. With their strong architecture and perfect symmetry, these taller ornamental onions are beautiful in a formal garden. Large ones are quite striking when planted in groups of three or five; smaller ones look great in groups of ten.

Allium 'Globemaster', with its distinctive spherical flowers on tall stems, adds color and drama to an otherwise serene, mostly green garden.

When Plant dormant allium bulbs in early fall. Potted, nursery-grown plants are best planted in spring.

Where Alliums grow well in full sun and prefer well-drained soil. Choose a site where the dying foliage will be hidden by neighboring plants. One of the smaller alliums, yellow-flowered, spring-blooming *A. moly,* is suitable for naturalizing in lightly shaded woodland gardens.

How Amend the soil with organic matter and plant each bulb at a depth two to three times its diameter. Space bulbs 4 to 18 inches apart, depending on the variety. Plant smaller alliums in several clustered groups of three to five. Plant the larger alliums also in threes, but space them more widely.

TLC Keep alliums well watered during the growing season, but stop watering once the foliage begins to turn yellow; most are tolerant of dry conditions once established. Do not remove foliage until it is withered and brown. Fertilize with a controlled-release 10-10-10 or an organic equivalent in spring just after shoots emerge. A light summer mulch will help suppress weeds. To prevent alliums from reseeding throughout the garden, remove flower heads as soon as blooms fade. Allium bulbs are rodent proof.

Alliums come in a variety of sizes, colors, and shapes. TOP TO BOTTOM: *A dry flower head of Star of Persia; drumstick allium; 'Purple Sensation'; and Turkestan allium.*

PEAK SEASON

Late spring into early summer

MY FAVORITES

Allium giganteum grows 3 to 3½ feet tall and produces 6-inch purple globes in June or early July.

'Globemaster' produces softball-size clusters on 2½- to 3-foot-tall stems. It blooms in late May or early June.

Turkestan allium (*A. karataviense*) has 4-inch-wide flower clusters, and is one of the few ornamental onions with leaves that look good during bloom. Plant it with hardy geraniums.

Drumstick allium (*A. sphaerocephalum*) has tight, 1-inch-wide, wine purple flower clusters; the flower head and long stem resemble a drumstick.

'Purple Sensation' has rich purple flowers that look good with other purple or blue flowers, and adds vivid contrast to yellow flowers.

Star of Persia (*A. christophii*) grows 15 to 18 inches tall and has lavender, starlike flowers that form a 10-inch ball in late spring or early summer.

GARDEN COMPANIONS

Plant large alliums with yellow daylilies, yarrow, ornamental grasses, and Siberian irises.

Seed heads are attractive, but plant lady's-mantle or taller sun-loving perennials to hide fading foliage.

Fancy-leafed Caladium
Caladium bicolor

I love caladiums for the way their colorful leaves light up shady areas where so few other plants are willing to bloom. They create a real tropical look in the garden, are pest free, and even provide attractive foliage for summer bouquets. Caladiums are one of the few bulbous plants that appreciate a constantly damp site. And they are true summer-loving plants, finicky about cool soil and chilly nights. Wait to plant them in the garden until it is shorts-and-iced-tea kind of weather. They need a long lead time, so planting dormant tubers into the garden usually results in a disappointing performance. Give them a head start indoors, using a heat mat to provide bottom warmth. Remember to keep them constantly moist, even while starting up.

Caladiums are great container plants too, especially useful for that shady nook. I like to use a large container, then mix and match caladiums with summer annuals that also prefer shade and damp soil, such as impatiens and fibrous-rooted begonias. A fern adds just the right finishing touch.

Bringing season-long color to a shady patio is 'Postman Joyner' caladium combined with 'Red Deco' impatiens. 'Blackie' ornamental sweet potato provides contrast.

PEAK SEASON

Summer until frost

MY FAVORITES

'Candidum' has elegant green-veined white leaves 10 to 18 inches long; they show up nicely in low light conditions.

'Gingerland' is a modestly sized caladium with 6- to 12-inch-long leaves. Leaves have many red speckles on an off-white background.

'Pink Beauty' has pink marbling in the center of its green leaves, which are further accented with red ribs.

'Postman Joyner' has pale red, rather translucent leaves with dark red veins and a wide green margin.

'White Queen' has large white leaves set off by a pencil-thin green edge, showy red veins, and a central blotch.

GARDEN COMPANIONS

Plants that prefer shade and damp soil, such as ferns and astilbe, make good companions for caladiums. Consider pairing white-leaved caladiums with white flowering *Astilbe* 'Bridal Veil'; pink caladiums with pink flowering *Astilbe* 'Bressingham Beauty'; or red caladiums with crimson red *Astilbe* 'Fanal'.

Annuals such as impatiens, fibrous-rooted begonias, and shiso (*Perilla frutescens*) also add a bright and colorful accent.

When Start tubers indoors, then plant outside once days are reliably warm.

Where Caladiums need rich soil, high humidity, warm days and nights, and plenty of water.

How Set them knobby side up so that tops are even with the soil surface.

ABOVE: *'Pink Beauty' grows about 18 inches high.* BELOW: *'Gingerland' caladium in front of purple-foliaged shiso.*

TLC Keep plants well watered, and fertilize them lightly throughout the growing season. Dig tubers in the fall after leaves die, but definitely before frosts arrive. Remove most of the soil and dry them in light shade for a week or so. Then pack them in dry peat moss or vermiculite and store at 50° to 60°F/10° to 16°C for the winter. If you were growing caladiums in a pot, just bring the entire pot indoors, allow it to dry out, and then store in moderately cool conditions. Dormant tubers planted outdoors will normally produce only a few large leaves. But if you scoop away the tiny shoots—I use something like a melon baller or grapefruit knife—the tuber will respond by producing more leaves, though they will be smaller.

Colchicum

Colchicum

Colchicum autumnale *'Album' blooming through a low ground cover in October.*

Colchicums look like oversize crocuses that flower at the wrong end of the gardening season. It is because they are blooming in fall when other bulbs are being planted, and because they are pest resistant that these plants are so appealing to me. Some have been in cultivation since the 17th century—now that's enduring popularity!

Different species of colchicum come from western or central Europe, northern Turkey, Iran, or the Caucasus region of Russia. In autumn up come clusters of long-tubed, flaring, 4-inch-wide flowers in lavender pink, rose purple, or white. Leaves do not appear until the following spring. Colchicum are so eager to flower that they'll do it right in the bag. But the flowers have a richer color and sturdier appearance if the corms are planted in the ground. Besides, there they'll grow roots and replenish moisture and nutrients used up in flower production.

Colchicums are not cheap, but even three make a great display and an unusual addition to your garden.

PEAK SEASON

September and October

MY FAVORITES

Colchicum autumnale is more modest in size than other species. It has lavender, cuplike flowers that are wonderful when they pop up through lamb's ear *(Stachys byzantina)*. 'Album' has white flowers.

C. speciosum has larger flowers and needs a sturdier companion. I use it in a mix-and-match fashion in front of shrubs such as dwarf barberries or beauty berry *(Calicarpa americana)*, or one of the deciduous azaleas.

C. 'Waterlily' is a double form. It can fall over when the flowers fill with rain, so plant it with a sturdy supporting framework of dwarf perennials or a vigorous ground cover.

GARDEN COMPANIONS

Think of two different sets of garden companions for colchicums: one when they're flowering in the fall, and the other when the leaves appear, then age and collapse. Pair them with sturdy plant neighbors that won't be smothered when the yellowing colchicum leaves die in late June. Vigorous, hard-to-discourage plants like lamb's ear work well, as do fall-blooming asters such as 'Purple Dome' and 'Autumn Joy' sedum. In lightly shaded areas, try smaller hostas to distract attention from colchicum's leaves.

When Plant when the corms become available in July and August.

Where Colchicums grow in sun or partial shade in fertile soil. They can naturalize in lawns, but you'll have to mow around their leaves in May and June.

How Plant 3 to 4 inches deep and 6 to 8 inches apart. Colchicums require water during prolonged dry periods, especially in late summer just before they will flower. Fertilize with a bulb fertilizer or an organic equivalent in early spring just as leaf tips poke above the soil.

ABOVE: Colchicum autumnale *growing up through sweet alyssum.* BELOW: *Large, 4-inch-wide flowers of 'Waterlily' often need support to remain upright.*

TLC Leaves show for about 2 months in spring to early summer, then die out, long before their flower clusters appear in fall. Colchicums are completely pest resistant, untroubled by deer, rabbits, mice, or voles.

Crocus
Crocus

Purple and yellow is a classic color combination for Dutch crocuses. They also come in white, blue, and lavender.

The large Dutch hybrid crocuses ("large" compared with other crocuses, that is) are a forecast of spring, flowering in March in a range of bright Easter-egg colors. They're so modest in price that it's easy to scatter them around the garden in quantity, plugging them into a lawn where the grasslike leaves are not a problem as they wither and fade away.

I look forward to seeing their grassy dark leaves poking up through the snow in February or March, followed by the fat buds and the vivid purple, yellow, and white flowers in April.

Crocuses prefer full sun and well-drained, gritty soil. Some gravel dug into the ground improves drainage and also makes things difficult for the voles that tunnel around and eat crocus corms.

PEAK SEASON
Spring

MY FAVORITES
Dutch crocus *(C. vernus)* is most common; many hybrids are available.

'Jeanne d'Arc' has pure white flowers with a purple flush at the base, accented with bright orange stamens.

'King of the Striped' has grayish white flowers striped in lilac blue.

'Pickwick' is grayish white with handsome purple stripes.

RELATED SPECIES
Snow crocus *(C. chrysanthus)* flowers early, often getting coated with winter's last white hurrah. Colors range from white to pale or deep yellow through several shades of blue. 'Princess Beatrix' is sky blue, with a yellow base.

C. flavus 'Golden Yellow' has big (for a crocus) golden yellow flowers that appear earlier than the Dutch crocus.

C. tomasiniannus tolerates some shade, doing fine under trees. 'Ruby Giant' has rich, reddish purple flowers; 'Barr's Purple' is deep purple.

GARDEN COMPANIONS
Crocuses look best when grouped together and grown in masses. They want full sun, so combine them with ground covers such as creeping thyme. They're also sweet with violas.

When Plant spring-blooming crocus corms as early in fall as possible.

'Princess Beatrix' is a particularly charming variety of the very early-blooming C. chrysanthus.

Where Crocuses prefer full sun and well-drained, sandy loam with abundant organic matter. Plant where the inconspicuous leaves can be left to die throughout summer. Crocuses thrive in lawns and can be naturalized there. Scatter a drift of the small corms across the grass, then make a slit in the turf with a spade and tuck the corms into it. You'll get to enjoy the flowers in spring well before the lawn needs mowing, and afterwards the grasslike crocus leaves will hardly be noticeable.

How Dig a bed or individual holes to a minimum depth of 8 inches, setting the soil aside. Sprinkle a bulb fertilizer in the bottom, and space corms about 4 inches apart. Plant crocus corms root end down (the small flat place is the bottom), and 3 inches deep. Mix enough organic matter with the loosened soil to make it light and fluffy, and fill the bed or holes about half-full with the amended soil. Cover with the remaining soil and water well. Squirrels, chipmunks, and mice love to feast on crocuses. Deter them by lining the bottom, sides, and top of the planting bed with hardware cloth. Remove the top lining in spring before growth starts.

TLC Water established crocuses in the spring only if the season is dry, and avoid excessive watering in summer, when plants are dormant. Fertilize with a bulb fertilizer or an organic equivalent in early spring just as tips poke above the soil.

217

Daffodil

Narcissus

Daffodils are the bulb everyone knows and loves. What's not to like about a plant that's not only good-looking in gardens and indoors as a cut flower, but is also pest resistant and comes back year after year?

Their bright colors and perky shapes make daffodils the most ebullient of plants, the perfect antidote to winter doldrums. In addition to yellow, daffodils come in orange, pale pink, peach, white, and combinations thereof, and in many shapes, sizes, and bloom times. The classic flower form has a cuplike center surrounded by petals, but there are also double-flowering daffodils as well as varieties with multiple flowers on each stem. The slender, strappy leaves are more attractive than tulip foliage and are thus more palatable to gardeners who hate to look at withering leaves.

Daffodils are quite fragrant and amazingly tough and reliable. They come back every year without fail. One year some daffodils in my garden swallowed their pride and came back even after being dug up and tossed on the compost heap—accidentally dug up, of course. If that's not enough to win our hearts, many varieties naturalize, expanding their spread and number of flowers significantly every year.

White 'Ice Follies' contrasts with yellow 'Carlton' and echoes the white bark of birch.

PEAK SEASON

Early to midspring

MY FAVORITES

'Actaea' has been around for centuries. It blooms late so extends the daffodil season in my garden.

'Barrett Browning' has a showy orange-red cup, set off by white petals. It is tough enough to stand up to spring rain and wind.

'Carlton' is a very popular large-cup daffodil, and for good reason. The two-tone yellow flowers make even a rainy gray day seem sunny.

'February Gold' blooms late in the Tri-State region, in March. Still, this small charmer brings reliable cheer to the last days of winter.

'Geranium' has a cluster of several small, fragrant white flowers, each with a pumpkin orange center.

'Ice Follies' is my favorite daffodil. I appreciate its super perennial nature, which insures that the creamy white petals and large yellow cup appear in my garden every spring.

GARDEN COMPANIONS

Plant early daffodils with other early bloomers like Siberian squill. Daffodils planted with blue forget-me-nots have a more practical attribute: the forget-me-nots mask the daffodils' foliage as it withers.

When Plant bulbs in fall as early as you can get them. Daffodils need 10 to 12 weeks of growing time to form roots properly.

LEFT: *'Geranium'*; CENTER: *'Carlton'*; RIGHT: *'Barrett Browning'*.

Where Daffodils do best in full sun, although they tolerate light shade. They require loamy, well-drained soil (soggy soil leads to rot). Daffodils can be naturalized in lawns.

How Dig a bed to a minimum depth of 1 foot, or dig individual holes spaced 5 to 8 inches apart, setting the soil aside. Sprinkle a bulb fertilizer or an organic equivalent in the bottom. Mix organic matter with the loosened soil and fill the bed or holes to about 8 inches from the surface. Plant each bulb with the fat end down at a depth three times its diameter (bulbs planted too shallowly may not survive cold winters). Cover with the remaining soil and water well.

TLC Water bulbs frequently the fall they are planted. Bulbs planted late in the season should be protected with a 6-inch layer of winter mulch. As soon as the weather begins to warm in spring, start watering generously again. Fertilize with a bulb fertilizer or an organic equivalent before growth appears. An organic mulch such as shredded leaves or bark can be placed around plants when they are 3 to 4 inches tall, but keep it away from the leaves. Cut back on watering as foliage dies down after blooming. Do not remove daffodil foliage until it begins to turn yellow and becomes unsightly. If you have naturalized daffodils in the lawn, do not mow until the leaves have died back, at least 7 weeks after the last flowering. Begin regular watering again in late summer, when flower buds form below ground for next year. A fall application of bulb fertilizer is also beneficial.

Gladiolus

Gladiolus

The somewhat stiff flower spikes of gladiolus can be difficult to work into the garden. But they're such great cut flowers that I like to grow them simply in a row, in some out-of-the-way corner or in the vegetable garden, not for show but just to have them available for bringing inside. Also, they're one of the few bulbs that can provide an extended bloom season by planting in sequence once a week over a month or so.

Gladiolus are sun lovers, and need a moist but well-drained situation. Their tall flower spikes and stiff, sword-shaped leaves mean gladiolus usually need to be staked if they're not to fall over. For strong stems, plant the corms in an 8-inch-deep furrow and backfill as the shoots grow, making sure that the corm is covered with an inch or two of soil to start. Then, as the leaves grow, fill in the rest of the hole.

LEFT: *Gladiolus make the most extraordinary and long-lasting cut flowers, keeping 2 to 3 weeks in a vase.* OPPOSITE PAGE, TOP TO BOTTOM: *Abyssinian sword lily (G. callianthus 'Murielae'); 'Plum Tart'; a large-flowered pink hybrid from a mix; and 'Great River'.*

PEAK SEASON
Summer to fall

MY FAVORITES
There are so many it's difficult to pick favorites. But here's a selection of some of the more notable hybrids.

'Green Star' has soft lime green flowers, with a hint of lemon at edges.

'Mon Amour' is indeed one to love, with delicious soft shades of cream, yellow, and pink all in the same flower.

'Theresa' has warm orange flowers with sunny yellow hearts.

'Violetta' has deep violet, almost wine purple flowers, accentuated with some white veining in the throat of each flower.

RELATED SPECIES
Abyssinian sword lily is the common name of Gladiolus callianthus 'Murielae'. It also has swordlike leaves, and fragrant, pure white flowers with a central maroon blotch on the lower petals. It sparkles when planted in front of burgundy foliage, either a dark-leafed canna such as 'Red King Humbert' or a purple-leafed barberry.

GARDEN COMPANIONS
Plant a group of 5 or 6 corms (one in the center, the rest around it) in combination with cannas, tall zinnias, or midsize ornamental grasses.

When Plant corms in spring after soil has warmed. Grandiflora hybrids will flower about 100 days after planting; the smaller hybrids and species will bloom in about 80 days.

Where Choose a sunny but sheltered site, such as near a house foundation, and where soil drains well.

How Gladiolus are corms, just like crocus. Examine the corm for the flat place—the bottom—and face it down. Plant 4 to 6 inches apart and 3 or 4 inches deep. Sometimes gladiolus are so eager to get growing that the leaf bud starts to grow before the corms are even planted. If you are staggering their planting (some now, others a week or so later), choose any that show signs of growth to plant first.

TLC Cut flower spikes for indoor display as soon as lowest buds open. Gladiolus can be surprisingly hardy, surviving average winter conditions. Where they are protected, such as next to a house foundation that provides more sheltered conditions, you can leave the corms in the ground for next year's bloom. If you are keeping corms for next season, cut the stalk off below the lowest flower before flowers go to seed to maximize energy stored in the bulb.

*May overwinter in zones 32 and 34, but usually replanted each season.

Hyacinth
Hyacinthus orientalis

'Blue Giant' hyacinths look great planted in masses, as their penetrating color is their best feature.

Hyacinths are a favorite of mine for their fragrance. The first year they're often bloated and overblown, but in the second and subsequent years they have a looser, more graceful appearance.

Hyacinths strike me as quintessentially Dutch. Of course, Holland is the home of the bulb industry and most famous for its tulips. But something about the hyacinth's tidy, upright domesticity makes me imagine them in every window box in Amsterdam.

Hyacinths are extremely fragrant and come in blue, purple, pink, yellow, and white. They are well suited to containers and among the best bulbs for forcing (that is, coaxed out of dormancy early to bloom as indoor houseplants). Their rigid shape and waxy blooms have an almost plastic primness that makes them a bit challenging to design with in the landscape; they benefit from the softening influence of ground covers like dwarf periwinkle *(Vinca minor)* and pachysandra. They should be planted in groups of three or more, but don't expect them to naturalize as well as the grape hyacinth *(Muscari)* or wood hyacinth *(Hyacinthoides hispanica),* two bulbs that are often mistaken for common hyacinth.

PEAK SEASON
Early to midspring

MY FAVORITES
'Anna Marie' has pale pink flowers for a soft springtime appeal that works well with early dwarf tulips.

'Blue Giant', 'Blue Jacket', and 'Delft Blue' all have lovely blue flowers.

'Carnegie' has creamy white flowers and is very sweet scented.

'City of Harlem' is a rich, creamy yellow that blends well with just about any color, and is charming with deeper yellow and blue pansies. I paired it up with *Narcissus* 'Ice Follies' in my garden and they look great together.

'Gypsy Queen' has flowers of a most uncommon salmon orange color.

'Lord Balfour' is an heirloom variety dating back to 1883, with wine-colored flowers shading to a paler margin.

GARDEN COMPANIONS
Hyacinths look good in groups of three, five, or more, and combined with other bulbs in pots and window boxes. In the garden, soften their rigid formality with clumps of forget-me-nots or ground covers like dwarf periwinkle (*Vinca minor*).

When Plant bulbs in fall as early as you can.

Where Hyacinths require full sun or partial shade and well-drained, average garden soil. Plant them in pots, in a flower bed, or within a ground cover near a doorway or sitting area, where you can enjoy their heady fragrance.

How Dig a bed to a minimum depth of 1 foot, or dig individual holes 4 to 6 inches apart, setting the soil aside. Sprinkle a bulb fertilizer in the bottom. Mix enough organic matter with the loosened soil to make it light and fluffy, and fill the bed or holes about half full with soil. Plant bulbs 5 to 6 inches deep with the root end down. Cover with the remaining soil and water well.

Very fragrant 'Carnegie' hyacinth with its creamy white flower is a late-spring bloomer.

TLC Water bulbs frequently the fall they are planted. Cover the bed with 6 inches of winter mulch when the top 2 inches of the ground has frozen. Remove mulch as soon as the weather begins to warm in spring, before the bulb foliage is up. Begin watering generously again. Fertilize with a bulb fertilizer or an organic equivalent just as tips poke above the soil. An organic mulch such as shredded leaves or bark can be placed around plants when they are 3 to 4 inches tall, but keep it away from the leaves. Cut back on watering as foliage dies down after blooming. You may remove spent flower stalks, but do not remove foliage until it is completely withered and brown. Begin regular watering again in late summer, when flower buds form underground for the next year. Rodents are not attracted to hyacinth bulbs.

Lily
Lilium

ilies are grown for their large, showy, and fragrant flowers. The most common lilies for gardens are the early-blooming (June) Asiatic varieties and the later (July and August) oriental lilies. All are elegant flowers that add panache to the garden and beauty to a bouquet. Whether I plant one or a handful, visitors always notice them.

ABOVE: *'Connecticut Star' is hardy and pest free, and quickly spreads to fill a large space with brilliant color.*
OPPOSITE PAGE: *One of the most popular lilies is the 'Stargazer', an Oriental type.*

Asiatic lilies have slightly smaller blooms ranging from white to vivid shades of yellow, pink, red, and orange. The flowers grow on stems that rise out of attractive clumps of slender leaves. Oriental lilies have large white or pink flowers often spotted with gold or banded with red. They are so aromatic and painterly, they always remind me of prom night. They are the perfect corsage flower. The oriental types grow on tall stems whose leaves fan out from top to bottom; they sometimes need staking. These lilies are best in the back of the border, where their flowers have no trouble attracting attention and their less-appealing features are kept in the background. Newer hybrids of both types have much-improved hardiness and disease resistance, making lilies among the easiest garden plants.

PEAK SEASON

Early summer to early fall

MY FAVORITES

Any of the Asiatic hybrid lilies: All are easy to grow and are available both as dormant bulbs in early spring and as potted, about-to-bloom plants in early summer. 'Connecticut Star' is a good example of this type.

'African Queen' is a wonderful lily with golden yellow flowers that are overlaid with a hint of reddish brown. Stake to support the top-heavy flower stem.

'Casablanca' is a pure white Oriental lily. Its fragrant white flowers make it a top choice for the moonlight garden.

'Stargazer' is also an Oriental type. It has many fans, for its cranberry flush over white petals accented with ruby red spots.

GARDEN COMPANIONS

Plant Asiatic lilies in the middle of a border behind bushy plants like catmint and cranesbill (Geranium). Oriental lilies need their leaves masked and other plants to lean on; they do well in the back of a border. White lilies are exquisite in an all-white garden with other white-flowered plants. All summer-blooming lilies go well with purple coneflower, liatris, and phlox.

When Plant bulbs in fall as early as you can get them. Some lily bulbs are available in spring; plant these as soon as you get them home. Nursery-grown lilies can be planted anytime if they are given ample water.

Where Most lilies do best in full sun in well-drained, slightly acidic to acidic soil. Heavy or compacted soils can lead to rot. Lilies will tolerate partial shade. They look best planted in groups of three or more and are excellent in a perennial border, where other plants can soften their leaves and stems.

How Loosen the soil to a depth of 1 to 1½ feet. Mix in peat moss. For each bulb, dig a hole to a depth that is three times the bulb's diameter. Space the holes at least 8 inches apart. Add bulb fertilizer to the bottom of each hole, then fill halfway with soil. Plant the bulbs with the fat end down. If your variety will need staking, install the supports now to avoid damaging the bulbs. Cover with the remaining soil and water well. Nursery-grown lilies should be planted at the same depth that they were growing in the pots; remove all blooms and buds to help plants become established. Stake taller varieties.

TLC Water regularly to keep the soil evenly moist. In cold climates, cover bulbs planted in late fall with a thick layer of organic mulch after planting to keep the soil warmer and to delay warming of the bed in spring. (After the first year, only Oriental lilies require winter protection in cold climates.) Place an organic mulch such as shredded leaves or bark around plants when they are 3 to 4 inches tall, and protect plants from browsing deer. Every spring after planting, fertilize with 10-10-10 or an organic equivalent. Avoid getting chemical fertilizer on the leaves, as it may burn them. After the flowers fade, cut the main stem just below the lowest bloom.

Siberian Squill
Scilla siberica

Scilla siberica 'Spring Beauty' spreads quickly to turn the spring-time landscape a glorious shade of blue. The nodding, bell-shaped flowers cluster at the tops of the 3- to 6-inch stems.

Easy to grow and pest proof, this sturdy little bulb with its bright blue flowers is one of those carefree, plant-and-forget bulbs that comes back year after year as a herald of spring. Bulbs of Siberian squill don't cost much, meaning it's easy to justify planting lots of them. Come next spring you'll be glad you did.

Siberian squill have electric blue flowers and are obliging about growing in a sunny lawn or, because they bloom before the trees leaf out in spring, in light shade. I appreciate their vivid color and the fact that once they settle down, they start to propagate themselves, making more and more of a show every year. I toss them around the garden by the hundreds; some under a star magnolia, others with a forsythia, more next to lungwort *(Pulmonaria)* and other early perennials. They're successful in combination with just about everything.

Blooms come early compared with most other bulbs, early March where I live in New Jersey. Siberian squill naturalizes in lawns as eagerly as any bulb I know and can convert a yard into a virtual sea of blue.

PEAK SEASON
Early spring

MY FAVORITES
'Spring Beauty' is a somewhat larger-flowered variety of this small bulb, with the same strong blue color.

Scilla tubergeniana is a paler, earlier-blooming version, with translucent white flowers, each petal accented with a thin blue line down the center.

GARDEN COMPANIONS
Siberian squill are excellent with dwarf early tulips, as well as *Tulipa kaufmanniana* and *T. greigii* cultivars.

BELOW: *White* S. tubergeniana

When Plant bulbs as early in fall as possible.

ABOVE: *Siberian squill naturalizes readily, and its ultramarine blue is a welcome herald of spring.*

Where Siberian squill prefers full sun to partial shade and well-drained soil. It is ideal planted in drifts among shrubs or perennials or under deciduous trees. Scilla is the best bulb for naturalizing in lawns.

How Dig a bed to a depth of 6 inches, or dig individual holes about 3 inches apart, setting the soil aside. Mix enough organic matter with the loosened soil to make it light and fluffy, and fill the bed or holes about half-full with the soil. Plant the bulbs 2 to 3 inches deep with the root end down. Cover with the remaining soil.

TLC Water bulbs right after planting. Water in spring only if the season is dry, and avoid excessive watering in summer, when plants are dormant. You may remove spent flower stalks to help prevent the plants from self-sowing, but do not remove foliage until it is completely withered and brown. You can dig and divide after the foliage has died in summer, but the small bulbs are so inexpensive, it's easier to just plant new ones in fall. Rodents are not attracted to Siberian squill bulbs.

Tulip

Tulipa

Tulips bloom in a rainbow of colors. If only they were more reliable about flowering year after year, and if deer didn't eat them!

Tulips bloom early and late in spring, depending on the variety, marking that wonderfully heady transition from winter to summer. The earliest tulips are the species types, with short stems and flowers that open in sunshine and close at night or in cloudy weather. Later come the aristocrats, like the Darwins and the Darwin hybrids, with their elegant simplicity, and the Parrot tulips, which are just the opposite, all ruffles and cacophonous color. Later still, 'Angélique' makes her entrance; this feminine tulip has a soft pink, ruffled, peony-like flower.

I think of the May-flowering, tall-growing Darwin, Triumph, Parrot, and Lily-flowered tulips as an odd assortment of annuals that I plant in the fall, enjoy in the spring, then discard when their flowers fade. The earlier, lower-growing species types are much more reliable about repeating their performance annually.

Lily-flowered 'Moonshine' contrasts with fringed 'Blue Heron' in both form and color.

'Douglas Bader' tulip blooms in late May, so it combines well with mahogany-colored 'Black Diamond'.

PEAK SEASON

Early to late spring

MY FAVORITES

Darwin and Triumph tulips are the big, popular, May-flowering tulips. They're showy, but only bloom once, so I treat them as annuals. Yellow-mauve 'Fritz Kreisler' and creamy 'Ivory Floradale' are current favorites.

Lily-flowered tulips have pointed petals that bend backwards. I like bright yellow 'Moonshine' and the old favorite 'White Triumphator'.

Parrot tulips have a blowsy form, and big snip-edged petals. Red and white 'Estella Rijnveld' makes a superb cut flower.

'Red Riding Hood', a Greigii hybrid, is carmine red with mottled leaves. It's vivid enough to be a standout in the garden, small enough to tuck into a window box.

'Heart's Delight' is a rose red and creamy yellow Kaufmanniana hybrid that blends with everything.

GARDEN COMPANIONS

Tulips' big, strappy, gray-green leaves can be lovely when the flower is blooming, but they quickly get floppy and tattered as they turn yellow. Plant tulips behind perennials such as hostas that will fill out just as the spring bulbs are fading, and with annuals such as forget-me-nots.

When Plant bulbs late in fall, even as late as Thanksgiving if the ground is not already frozen (I've planted as late as Christmas with good results). Early planting sometimes confuses tulips, and they waste energy sending up leaves, only to have them freeze with the onset of cold weather.

Where Tulips do best in full sun, but they tolerate late-day shade. They require well-drained soil. Choose a site with good overhead light to prevent stems from leaning toward the light source. They look best massed in beds or pots.

How Dig a bed to a minimum depth of 12 inches, or dig individual holes 4 to 6 inches apart, setting the soil aside. Sprinkle a bulb fertilizer in the bottom. Mix enough organic matter with the loosened soil to make it light and fluffy, and fill the bed or holes to about 8 inches from the surface. Plant each bulb at a depth three to five times its diameter, with the pointed end up. Cover with the remaining soil and water well. To deter rodents, line the bottom, sides, and top of the planting bed with hardware cloth. Remove the top lining in spring before growth starts.

TLC Water bulbs frequently the fall they are planted. Cover the bed with 6 inches of winter mulch when the top 2 inches of the ground has frozen. Remove mulch as soon as the weather begins to warm in spring, before the bulb foliage comes up. Begin watering generously again. An application of bulb fertilizer just as the tiny tips poke through the soil is beneficial, but do not fertilize during or right after bloom, as this can lead to disease problems. An organic mulch such as shredded leaves or bark can be placed around plants to retain moisture and reduce weed growth. Cut back on watering as foliage dies down after blooming. Do not remove tulip foliage until it dies completely. Begin regular watering again in late summer when next year's flower buds are forming underground. Fertilize again in fall.

Once upon a time, American vegetable gardens were laid out in straight rows and fenced to keep out livestock or wild animals. Plants were grown from seeds harvested the previous year, and produced bumper crops that were tasty and fragrant but short-lived once harvested, so much was dried or canned.

As the interests of agribusiness took precedence over those of backyard growers, new vegetable hybrids were developed that had tougher skin to survive the rigors of shipping and a longer shelf life in the supermarkets. Seed catalogs featured these new, improved hybrids, and traits such as disease resistance often helped gardeners overcome problems that long plagued crops such as cucumbers or melons. Sometimes, though, home gardeners found that newer wasn't always better. An "improved" tomato, for example, might have tougher skin but inferior flavor, fragrance, or color. Home gardeners began mixing and matching, using hybrid seed when it offered disease resistance, and saving and trading the seeds of plants they called heirlooms. As the word suggests, heirlooms are old-fashioned varieties that retain the flavor, juiciness, fragrance, color, or whimsical shape that inspired a gardener long ago to save their seeds. Often, these are the varieties that make "homegrown" mean something special.

AESTHETIC INFLUENCES

As appreciation for distinctive flavors and colors has grown, so has the interest in food crops as garden plants. The form of the vegetable garden itself has changed, becoming more eclectic, imaginative, and pleasing to the eye. Just as flower gardeners combine annuals with perennials, flowering shrubs, ornamental trees and conifers, grasses, and native plants,

ABOVE: *This raised-bed garden features vegetables but includes daylilies, nasturtiums, and other flowers.* OPPOSITE PAGE: *Rosemary trained as a tree becomes showy as well as useful.*

food gardeners combine parsley, fennel, leaf lettuce, cabbage, beans, and dill for their looks as well as their taste. And herbs are often grouped together in pots by the back door, handy for cooking and lovely to look at.

Gardening knowledge is flowing in both directions. Flower gardeners learn from food gardeners about the effects of toxic chemicals and the benefits of organic gardening methods, even for nonedible crops. Composting is now a routine practice among all gardeners, and garden experts always recommend amending garden soil with organic matter to encourage microorganisms and earthworms, and to do some of the soil-building work chemical fertilizers used to do. Crop rotation and the use of cover crops like buckwheat have become standard practices.

THE KITCHEN GARDEN

These changes in the content and form of the food garden are embodied in what we call the modern kitchen garden. Besides herbs and vegetables, kitchen gardens often include dwarf fruit trees, clipped shrubs, and flowers, along with design elements such as geometric patterns that impose a sense of order on abundant plant growth, and artfully designed functional structures (fences, trellises, benches) that add to the beauty of the garden. Birdhouses, sculpture, and homemade garden decorations are the icing on the cake.

In choosing the best herbs and vegetables for the Tri-State region, I looked for plants that possess the traits most prized by modern American kitchen gardeners. Whether a hybrid or an heirloom, it should taste good, be disease resistant, and be decorative. I hope the following Top 10 gets you out into the garden. As your garden expands, you'll want to look for the same qualities in whatever herbs and vegetables you grow.

— MARCIA EAMES-SHEAVLY

231

Asparagus

After a winter of slush, wet boots, and sniffles, the first tender harvest of asparagus—lightly steamed and drizzled with butter—can renew your springtime determination to plant a veritable Eden of vegetables.

Asparagus is a perennial. Its bright green spears reach up to the spring sun year after year—possibly for decades—so you'll want to plan a permanent location for your patch.

Growing asparagus takes 3 years from seed to harvest, so most people choose to buy 1-year-old crowns—food-storage stems with scraggly dry roots growing downward and nubbly growth buds sticking up. Give the roots a soft, rich bed, and they'll reward you with years of plentiful spears.

In late spring or early summer, when emerging spears are less than ½ inch wide, stop harvesting, and let those spears develop ferny foliage, which will build food reserves for next year's crop. Remove the ferny growth when it turns brown in autumn, or alternatively, leave the dried growth over winter so it can catch insulating snow, and then remove the foliage early in spring.

PEAK SEASON

Harvest in spring when shoots appear the second year after planting (harvest sparingly). Third-year harvest will be fuller. Snap or cut off all spears 5 to 10 inches long, leaving white stubs on the plants. Stop harvesting established plantings once pencil-thin spears begin emerge.

MY FAVORITES

Varieties that produce mostly male spears are most productive (they don't waste energy producing seed). The all-male Jersey series tends to do very well, and is your best bet. 'Jersey Giant' and 'Jersey Knight' are noted for their disease resistance; 'Jersey Prince' has thick spears and high yields.

GARDEN COMPANIONS

Many gardeners find that keeping asparagus in a separate location from the annual vegetables makes care a little easier. Locate your asparagus planting near your other perennial favorites, such as strawberries and rhubarb.

OPPOSITE PAGE: *Allowing the fernlike asparagus leaves to grow recharges the roots for next year's harvest.*
RIGHT: *Ready-to-harvest spears of 'Jersey Knight' emerge in spring.*

When Sow seeds in flats 12 to 14 weeks before you intend to set out plants. Set out plants in spring (when danger of frost has passed). Set out crowns (clumps of roots and dormant buds) in winter or early spring.

Where Fertile, well-drained, sandy to clay loam, pH 6.0–6.7.

How The older method of planting in trenches is no longer viewed as necessary by most gardeners. About five weeks before date of last spring frost, simply space crowns 15 inches apart on loose soil, and spread out roots. Don't crowd crowns. Cover with several inches of soil, and apply a 1-inch layer of compost to the surface in spring and fall. Water through the growing season, especially during dry spells. Cut stems back to 4 or 5 inches after they turn brown in the winter.

TLC Fertilize with a high-nitrogen fertilizer (such as 16-4-8) at planting, and in the first year, in spring before spears emerge and again after harvest. Mulch in winter. In spring, keep the bed weeded and watch for asparagus beetles. Remove and compost dead foliage in fall to reduce their numbers. The first year after planting, let all the spears shoot up and leaf out; the feathery foliage nourishes the growing roots, which in turn supply nutrients to feed the plant through the winter and give the next season's spears strength for growth. The second spring you can harvest the first few spears. When spears begin to look spindly (about $\frac{1}{4}$ inch in diameter), let them grow up and leaf out. By the third spring, the asparagus will produce spears in full force over a long season (four to eight weeks).

Beans

'Royal Burgundy' snap beans have attractive red-pink flowers and dark purple pods that change to dark green after cooking.

Hundreds of bean varieties are sold for the home garden. Don't know beans about them? No matter. All are grown similarly, and fall into one of three groups—snap, shell (or shelly or shelling), or dry—signifying the growth stage at which they taste best.

Snap beans, my favorites, are grown for their edible pods, which are tastiest when young. Most snap beans (also called string or green beans) are stringless and so tender you can eat the stem end. Filet beans, harvested daily when no bigger than the width of a small pencil, are becoming very popular. Romano beans are flattened snap beans.

Shell and dry beans are grown for the edible seeds inside the pods. Shell beans are best when the seeds have just matured. Dry beans taste best after the seeds have completely dried out in the pods. Lima, navy, pinto, and kidney beans are dry beans.

Each of the three types is available in bush and vine (pole) forms. Pole beans are slower to mature but picking beans off the vines stimulates the plants to produce more, so you get two to three times as many beans in the same space. Pods come in colors ranging from yellow to green to purple, but they all turn green when cooked.

When Sow seeds outdoors a week or two after the threat of frost has passed, when soil temperature is 55°F/13°C or higher. Seeds rot in cold, wet soil. To extend the harvest of bush beans, sow successive crops every 2 weeks up to 12 weeks before the first expected fall frost.

Where Beans need a warm, sunny location and light soil that is well drained and rich in organic matter. Avoid saline soils. Place pole beans along the north side of the garden where they won't shade other sun-loving vegetables.

How Sow seeds 1 inch deep, 2 to 3 inches apart. Plant bush types in rows 3 feet apart. Pole beans need some sort of support, such as a trellis, string, or tepee-style poles, which should be set in place before planting seeds. To make a tepee, lash together five tall bamboo stakes at the top with twine.

PEAK SEASON

Midsummer to first frost

MY FAVORITES

There are several types of beans and hundreds of varieties. My personal favorite is 'Jacob's Cattle'. I harvest some as snap beans, and then let the rest go as dry beans, which are absolutely beautiful!

Snap or green beans are the most popular among home gardeners. Top varieties include: 'Bush Blue Lake'; French filet types 'Nickel' and 'Verandon'; 'Royal Burgundy', which sports a lovely purple color; and 'Improved Tendergreen'.

Pole beans include: 'Blue Lake'; 'Fortex'; and 'Kentucky Wonder'.

Wax bean (yellow) favorites include: 'Goldkist' and 'Goldmarie'.

Edible soybeans are harvested before they mature and dry. Best varieties for our region include: 'Besweet 2020'; 'Beer Friend'; 'Butterbeans'; 'Early Hakucho'; and 'Green Pearls'.

GARDEN COMPANIONS

Plant beans with other vegetables and herbs or surrounded by annuals such as verbena, zinnias, and marigolds. Pole beans grown on tepee-style supports look good in the center of a round kitchen garden or along the back row of a rectangular gardens.

TOP: *Pole beans twine up stakes.*
BOTTOM: *The classic 'Kentucky Wonder'.*

TLC Beans need an even supply of water—about 1 inch a week. Thin seedlings of bush types to 5 to 6 inches apart, pole beans 6 to 8 inches apart. After plants have their second set of true leaves, mulch with 2 inches of chopped leaves, grass clippings, or other fine-textured organic material to conserve moisture and control weeds. Beans have the ability to "fix" nitrogen, so avoid adding fertilizers high in nitrogen or plants will produce too much leaf growth at the expense of beans. Harvest snap beans when the pods are about ⅛-inch-thick, before seeds begin to swell. Harvest shell beans when pods are plump and bright green. Harvest dry beans after pods have dried on the plant. To avoid spreading diseases, never work around beans when the foliage is wet.

Highbush Blueberries
Vaccinium corymbosum

Two plants per person will produce all the fresh blueberries the average gardener can enjoy, with enough left over for a wealth of blueberry cobblers, muffins, pies, and pancakes.

Highbush blueberries are native to our region so are obviously well adapted and easy to grow. They require only what we have plenty of: sun plus cool, moist, acidic, and well-drained soil.

Beyond the delicious and healthful fruits, highbush blueberries are handsome plants. Use them for hedges or in shrub borders. Most varieties are tall (to 6 feet or more), but there are varieties that are lower growing. Dark green or blue-green leaves change to red, orange, or yellow in fall. Spring flowers are tiny, white or pinkish, and urn shaped. Interestingly, you'll get fruit with one variety, but you need to plant more than one variety for large berry size.

When Plant rooted cuttings of highbush blueberries in early spring; container plants anytime.

Where Blueberries are finicky about site requirements, but once you meet them, they're a low-maintenance plant. They need moist, well-drained, acid soil (pH of 4.5 to 5.5) that is rich in organic matter. This is the same kind of soil that suits rhododendrons and azaleas; if either of these plants are thriving in your garden or neighborhood, blueberries likely will as well.

How If you're in doubt about your soil, test its pH and amend as necessary the fall before you plan to plant.

A standard variety because of its hardiness and versatility, 'Bluecrop' grows 4 to 6 feet high and bears generously.

PEAK SEASON

By choosing a range of varieties from early to late, you can stretch the harvest from July through August.

MY FAVORITES

'Bluecrop' is somewhat drought resistant; 'Blueray' grows upright, and is productive; 'Darrow' is vigorous and very productive; 'Duke' is excellent in the early season and has good size and flavor; 'Elliot' comes in very late in the season; 'Jersey' is vigorous, hardy, and widely grown; 'Lateblue' is very productive and ripens over a short period.

At 3 feet high, the "half-high hybrids" are literally half as tall, and have been bred for cold hardiness. Top varieties: 'Northblue' has large, dark blue, good quality berry; 'Northsky' and 'North Country' are both early and sweet; and 'St. Cloud' has light blue berries and good flavor, but is more susceptible to winter injury.

GARDEN COMPANIONS

Grow at least two different varieties for larger fruits. Plant blueberries near other perennials, or plant in rows as a border.

OPPOSITE PAGE: *In full bloom, highbush blueberries prove their ornamental value. At harvest, the fruits prove delicious.*

TLC Unlike many fruit plants that send their roots deep in search of sustenance, blueberries are dependent on a network of fine roots growing near the soil surface to satisfy all their moisture and nutrient needs. As a result, they need a particularly consistent degree of both soil moisture and air, and they cannot compete with weeds. Soggy, waterlogged soil will prove as deadly as dry soil, and cultivating with a rake or hoe will damage roots. Cover soil around plants with a thick mulch of composted sawdust or bark. Insect pests of the typical sort are rarely a problem, but birds will compete for the fruits. Covering plants with plastic netting is the best defense. Prune in early spring. Select two of the new canes each year, removing all other new growth. Repeat each year, keeping the strongest new canes, from the time the bushes are planted until they are about 8 years old and oldest canes are about an inch thick. Early in the ninth year, remove the two largest canes, and all but two of the largest 1-year-old canes. Repeat annually, taking out any broken, winter-damaged, or diseased wood first. No "haircuts" or you'll remove fruiting wood!

Herbs (Annual)
Basil, cilantro, and parsley

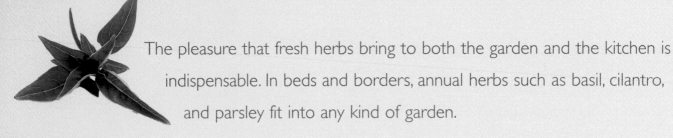

The pleasure that fresh herbs bring to both the garden and the kitchen is indispensable. In beds and borders, annual herbs such as basil, cilantro, and parsley fit into any kind of garden.

BASIL

Basil, a tender perennial grown as an annual, loves hot, sunny weather. If you can give it that, along with plenty of water and elbow room, it will grow from a spindly seedling to a knee-high bush in no time. Even in a spot that gets only 4 hours of full sun, you'll still have enough basil to enjoy pesto a few times a week—your plants just won't be huge.

• Basil *(Ocimum basilicum)*. Fragrant, bright green leaves grow on 6-inch- to 2-foot-tall plants. *Best culinary varieties:* 'Italian Pesto', 'Lettuce Leaf', 'Mammoth Sweet', 'Mrs. Burns', 'Napoletano', 'Genovese', 'Profuma di Genova', 'Red Rubin', and 'Sweet Basil'. 'Purple Ruffles' and 'Opal Basil' have good quality, deep purple foliage. *Growing tip:* Plant after soil warms and nighttime temperatures are above 60°F/16°C. To encourage branching

The rich green leaves of 'Crispum' parsley are an attractive foil for flowers as well as a useful kitchen herb.

on young seedlings, cut back stems to just above the first set of leaves when plants have developed three pairs of leaves. *Harvest tip:* Prune often to avoid flower formation. When a stem has developed four pairs of leaves, cut each stem down to just above the first set. Continue cutting plants back throughout the season, or set out new seedlings in succession a month or so apart and harvest an entire plant for pesto.

CILANTRO

Cilantro looks like flat-leaf parsley, but the flavor couldn't be more different. It's often responsible for the distinctive flavor of Mexican or Asian dishes. If you're unfamiliar with it, try it before planting: people seem to either absolutely love it, or not.

• Cilantro *(Coriandrum sativum)*. Bright green leaves on foot-tall stems look similar to flat-leafed parsley. "Cilantro" refers to the leaves (great garnish for guacamole); the seeds are called coriander. *Best culinary varieties:* Grow types that are slow to bolt (go to seed); these are labeled as such or sold as a variety called 'Slo-Bolt' and 'Santo'. *Growing tip:* Cilantro grows best in cool weather. Plant in early spring after the last frost. Start from seed; cilantro transplants poorly. Plant in succession every few weeks through summer. Once it goes to seed, leaf flavor changes, but you can harvest the seeds for use later. *Harvest tip:* Cut off leaves as needed, or harvest the entire plant before it starts to flower.

PARSLEY

Parsley is one of the prettiest plants for the kitchen garden—or any garden, for that matter. The deep green foliage naturally falls into perfectly sculpted waves, and the plant fills out quickly when its leaves and stems are regularly snipped for cooking. Italian parsley, also called flat-leafed or broadleaf parsley, has larger, flatter leaves than the more common curly parsley. Both are used in cooking. Curly parsley is identified with American dishes; it is chopped and sprinkled over everything from soups to mashed potatoes and is an essential ingredient in buttery sauces. Italian parsley, a bit more assertive in flavor, is a staple of Italian cooking.

- Parsley *(Petroselinum crispum)*. Flat or curly green leaves grow in clumps. Flat-leafed types grow 1 to 2 feet tall; curly types to 1 foot. Biennial often grown as an annual. *Best culinary varieties:* 'Giant Italian' (or 'Gigante D'Italia') is best for cooking; the curly type, such as 'Crispum', is a common garnish. 'Forest Green' is a tasty and productive curly cultivar. 'Frisca' is very curly and attractive, with high-quality leaves. *Growing tip:* Start new plants each year from seeds or transplants. Seeds are slow to germinate;

soak them in warm water overnight before sowing in place, in early spring. Allow several weeks for germination. Or set out nursery transplants once soil is workable. *Harvest tip:* Pick outside leaves so the center of the plant continues to develop new ones.

HOW TO GROW ANNUAL HERBS

SUN Plant herbs where they'll get at least 6 hours of full midday sun (4 hours is minimum for adequate growth).

SOIL Slightly acid to nearly neutral soil (pH 6.3 to 6.8) is best. Provide loose, well-drained, moderately fertile soil. Dig in compost before planting. In pots, be sure to use a high-quality potting mix.

FERTILIZER Fertilize with fish emulsion every time you cut plants back. I also like to use dried blood as a fertilizer, and I'm convinced it discourages deers from browsing.

GARDEN COMPANIONS

If you're the kind of gardener that dashes to the garden often for a little of this or that, you may want to locate these plants based on use. Cilantro, parsley, and basil are often paired with tomatoes, for example, and if you're likely to whip up the occasional salsa or pasta sauce, having these together in the garden will promote your using them often!

Herbs (Perennial)
Oregano, rosemary, sage, and thyme

Perennial herbs are good-looking and tough landscape plants, in addition to their culinary utility. In kitchen gardens, use perennial herbs such as thyme or sage as long-lived perennials. Rosemary can live outdoors in only our mildest regions, but will thrive for years if moved indoors for winter. All herbs need sun and well-drained soil of average fertility.

OREGANO

Oregano is a zesty mint relative that thrives in well-drained soil and full sun. Spaghetti or pizza sauce couldn't exist without it.

- Oregano *(Oreganum vulgare)*. 'Aureum' oregano has gold leaves and pink flowers; 'Aureum Crispum' has curly golden leaves and a spreading habit; 'Compactum' is a few inches tall, spreads widely, and seldom flowers; and 'Erfo' has large numbers of fragrant leaves. All zones.

'Aureum' golden oregano is just as flavorful as the green form.

ROSEMARY

A Mediterranean native, rosemary looks as if it might be related to sage or lavender, but don't let that fool you into thinking that rosemary acts like those herbs—which love nothing more than baking in the sun with nothing to drink for days on end. I found this out when I noticed the leaves of my rosemary were falling off. I thought some sort of bug had infested the plant, until a gardening friend tipped me off to the real problem. Rosemary needs regular watering. Mine was dying of thirst. I watered it twice a day for a week and it rebounded nicely. This requirement extends to overwintering it; don't let yours succumb to the dry heat and low humidity that is common in homes during the winter.

- Rosemary *(Rosmarinus officinalis)*. 'Albus' rosemary has white flowers; 'Benenden Blue' ("pine-scented" rosemary) has blue flowers and the strong scent of pine; 'Hilltop Hardy' is cold hardy; 'Majorca Pink' has pink flowers; and 'Miss Jessup's Upright' is very hardy and has an erect habit. Zone 32; all zones if indoors in winter.

RIGHT: *Yellow-edged leaves of 'Aurea' golden sage.* FAR RIGHT: *A few rosemary stems add flavor to barbecues.* BOTTOM: *Tiny lilac flowers adorn common thyme in late spring and summer. Strip leaves from stems and use them fresh or dry, and store them for use later.*

SAGE

The typical sage is a 2-foot-tall plant with grayish green leaves, but there are variegated kinds with golden and purplish leaves too. But whatever the leaf color, sage lends lots of flavor to food. If you grow your own, you'll find the flavor subtly milder and sweeter too.

• Sage *(Salvia officinalis).* 'Aurea' sage leaves are golden; 'Berggarten' never flowers and has large silvery leaves; 'Icterina' has yellow and green leaves; 'Nana' is dwarf; 'Purpurascens' ('Red Sage') leaves have a purplish tint; 'Tricolor' leaves are gray, white and purplish. All zones.

THYME

Common thyme grows about 1 foot tall and has tiny, $\frac{1}{4}$-inch green leaves. In the kitchen its delicate flavor is appreciated for blending other flavors together.

• Thyme *(Thymus vulgaris).* 'Argenteus' thyme has silver variegated leaves, and 'Aureus' has golden leaves. All zones.

HOW TO GROW PERENNIAL HERBS

SUN Perennial herbs need 6 hours of full midday sun (4 hours is minimum for adequate growth). Shelter rosemary from winter winds, or bring plants indoors to a sunny window.

SOIL Slightly acid soil (pH 6.3 to 6.8) is best. Provide loose, well-drained, moderately fertile soil. Incorporate compost into the soil before planting. In pots, use a high-quality potting mix.

FERTILIZER Mix an organic fertilizer or compost into the soil in early spring.

241

Peppers
Sweet, spicy, and hot

'Sweet Banana' is a slender Italian frying pepper.

What a variety of sizes, shapes, colors, and flavors of peppers are available to home gardeners! Choose from short and blocky, long and skinny, cone shaped, round, or crumpled—in nearly all shades of the rainbow. Select flavors from mild and sweet to sizzling hot and pungent. Use peppers cooked by themselves and with other foods, or raw in salads and appetizers.

Best known are the bell peppers. Usually harvested while green to maximize production, they'll turn red, yellow, or orange if left to fully mature. A quartet of non-bell sweet peppers—pimientos, Italian frying peppers, sweet Hungarian, and cherries—is worth seeking out and growing. These specimens have thinner flesh, are less watery, and have a more concentrated sweet-pepper flavor than big bell peppers.

Pimientos are relatively small peppers with thick, sweet flesh. They're used for flavoring sauces and dips and in salads and appetizers.

Pointed Italian frying peppers are yellow-green to red when mature. As the name implies, they are used for frying or for cooking with various meats.

Sweet Hungarian yellow peppers are slender, pointed, and 4 to 6 inches long. Often, these peppers will produce more reliably in hot weather than bell peppers. They are usually harvested when yellow, but they turn red when mature. Only use fully red, ripe peppers for drying, either in the sun or in a dehydrator.

Cherry peppers are globe shaped, about 1½ inches wide, and sweet. They are harvested for pickling whole, either when green or when they turn red at maturity.

Hot peppers range in size from 1½-inch-long 'Tabasco' to 7-inch-long 'Pasilla'. Colors include green, red, and shades of brown. They're used for making sauces, pickling, and dried seasonings.

Some hot peppers, such as 'Hungarian Wax Hot' and hot cherry peppers, look just like their sweet counterparts.

Mature red 'Cayenne' peppers.   Purple 'Secret' sweet bell pepper.

PEAK SEASON
Summer to fall

MY FAVORITES
Bell peppers
'Gourmet'—an orange bell with thick walls and fruity sweet flavor; 'Jingle Bells'—small fruits that turn to red; 'Secret'—an eggplant purple bell.

Sweet peppers
'Cubanelle'—smooth frying pepper that ripens to red; 'Gypsy'—a high-yielding, disease-resistant, yellow-orange pepper; 'Sweet Banana'—waxy with 6-inch-long, thin-walled cylindrical fruit, yellow ripening to red; crisp and tasty.

Hot peppers
'Ajo Amarillo'—4- to 5-inch-long fruits that mature to a deep orange color; 'Cayenne'—extra hot, tapered dark green to red; 'Habanero'—green to a pinkish orange, and extra hot; eat them if you dare; 'Hungarian Wax'—conical three-lobed yellow pepper, a good hot one for our region; and 'Jalapeño'—short, rounded, dark green with a reddish tinge and an excellent smoky heat, easily my favorite hot pepper.

GARDEN COMPANIONS
Try interplanting with lettuce or mesclun. After the greens have matured and are harvested, the peppers will fill in the area.

When Set out plants in spring (1 week or more after last frost date, or once temperature has warmed to at least 65°F/18°C). Sow seeds in flats indoors 6 to 8 weeks before you intend to set out plants in garden.

Where Full sun and rich, well-drained soil.

How Set out plants 18 to 24 inches apart in rows spaced 2½ to 3 feet apart.

TLC Sweet peppers grow on stiff, rather compact, large-leafed bushes, and mature in 60 to 80 days. They grow well almost everywhere and the Tri-State region is no exception. Taller, more spreading hot pepper plants have smaller and narrower leaves than sweet pepper varieties. Hot peppers ripen later and are best suited to areas with long, warm growing seasons, but they can be grown here; other than preferring slightly warmer weather, they require the same care as sweet peppers. Sweet peppers grow best when daytime temperatures range between 70° and 75°F/21° and 24°C. Hot peppers prefer slightly warmer temperatures. They thrive when daytime temperatures are between 70° and 85°F/21° and 29°C. For sweet and hot peppers, if night temperatures fall below 60°F/15°C or stay above 75°F/24°C, blossoms often fall off and fruit set is poor. Harvest peppers by cutting them off with hand shears.

Salad Greens
Lettuce and more

What goes into the salad bowl ceased being a simple matter of iceberg lettuce and Thousand Island dressing years ago. One of the most popular salad options adapts the French practice of snipping tender leaves of young lettuces and other greens to make a "mesclun mix." It's easy to do and has been widely embraced in this country. Why not grow your own? Salad greens are pretty in the garden and not difficult as long as you start early, expect little through midsummer (lettuce will bolt in hot weather), and resume as temperatures cool.

'Red Salad Bowl' is an oak-leaf lettuce with especially bright red color.

The most flavorful and attractive lettuces are loose-leaf, butterhead, and romaine. Once you're hooked on these, you'll want to spice up your salads with other leafy greens such as arugula, claytonia, red orach, mustard, chicory, spinach, mâche, cress, endive, nasturtiums, and radicchio.

PEAK SEASON

Midspring to first frost

MY FAVORITES

Mesclun seed mixes are very easy and handy. And now there are a range of them, from mild to spicy, as well as lettuce-only.

Butterhead

'Bibb'—crisp, delicate flavor; 'Buttercrunch'—compact, fan-shaped head and resists bolting; 'Nancy'—large Boston type for spring and fall; 'Red Cross'—very red butterhead; and 'Summer Bibb'—early and resists bolting.

Leaf

'Black-Seeded Simpson'—early, with large, crinkled, light green leaves; 'Oakleaf'—mild and has lobed green leaves; and 'Red Salad Bowl'—has red leaves, resists bolting.

Romaine

'Balloon'—large, pale green, heat tolerant; 'Jericho'—tall, heavy heads that stay sweet in hot weather; 'Little Caesar'—small but flavorful; and 'Parris Island Cos'—the old-fashioned classic, and still one of the best.

GARDEN COMPANIONS

Use lettuces to edge your herb or kitchen garden. They can help contain spreading herbs. Seed with late-season crops to save space; then harvest well before those crops reach maturity.

When Salad greens like the cool, sunny conditions of late spring and early summer. Sow seeds as soon as the soil can be worked, as early as a month before the last frost date, and again in mid- to late summer for a fall crop. Make successive sowings every 10 days to extend your harvest.

Where Plant salad greens where they'll get lots of sun. They are tolerant of most soil types, although they prefer fertile, slightly acidic soil that drains well. Many salad greens are very ornamental and great additions to a flower border or containers.

How Add plenty of organic matter to the soil and rake it smooth before sowing seeds or setting out plants. (If slugs are a problem in your area however, a great deal of organic matter will encourage them.) The small seeds should be scattered on the surface and pressed lightly into the soil. They need light to germinate.

TLC Salad greens require an even supply of water. Weed carefully around plants to avoid damaging the shallow roots. Plants will benefit from regular applications of nitrogen fertilizer. Begin harvesting leaves from loose-leaf lettuce as soon as they're large enough to be used, cutting from the outside of the plant first. Once the hot weather of summer arrives, most lettuces will go to seed (bolt), and you'll probably want to remove them to make room for another type of crop. Salad greens' short lives mean they're safe from most insects and diseases, but overly moist soil can lead to rot. Rabbits and birds are especially attracted to salad greens and are hard to deter. Consider planting an extra row to accommodate them. Blood meal scattered around plants after every rain is sometimes effective at repelling rabbits and deer.

'Jericho' is a romaine lettuce that is notably more tolerant of hot weather than other varieties.

Squashes
Winter and summer squash, pumpkins

As one butternut squash ripens on the vine, a flower promises another one to come.

Some strange law of nature decreed that these particular vegetables must resemble oversize acorns, turbans, alien spaceships, or elongated balloons. Most squashes are large, flamboyant plants, with lovely blossoms in creamy yellow or brilliant orange from which the fruits emerge and swell into those amazing shapes. The bush types are more manageable, but vining types produce more fruit and can be quite beautiful when trained to grow on a fence or trellis.

Squashes are divided into two groups. Summer squashes—like the long, slender zucchini and the round, flat pattypan with scalloped edges—are harvested early and eaten while still tender (though some pattypans can be stored and eaten later like winter squash). Winter squashes are harvested late, and their thick, shell-like skins have to be removed before eating.

Pumpkins, the largest and most famous of the winter squashes, are really in a class by themselves—grown as much for ornamental as for culinary uses.

PEAK SEASON

Midsummer to first frost

MY FAVORITES

Winter squashes

Acorn 'Heart of Gold' has green and white skin with pale orange flesh.

Buttercup/Kabocha 'Ambercup' produces very flavorful 3-pound fruits.

Butternut 'Long Island Cheese' has deep orange flesh; 'Waltham' has large, tan fruits, and stores well.

Hubbard 'Red Kuri' has beautiful scarlet, teardrop shaped fruits, and smooth-textured, moist flesh.

Miscellaneous 'Bush Delicata' is a must for gardeners short on space.

Pumpkins 'Small Sugar' for pies.

Summer squashes

Crookneck 'Early Golden Summer' is tender if eaten while small; 'Multipik' has glossy yellow fruit.

Hybrids 'Gold Rush' has bright yellow skin; 'Spacemaster' is small but very productive.

Pattypan or scallop 'Sunburst' has golden fruit.

Straightneck 'Goldbar' is light yellow with smooth skin; and 'Saffron' fruits are clear yellow.

GARDEN COMPANIONS

Train vining squashes to a fence or trellis to save space. Try pairing squashes with beans and corn for a traditional native American planting.

TOP: 'Red Kuri' squash tastes as good as it looks. BOTTOM: 'Ambercup' is a very flavorful variety of squash.

When Plant seedlings or sow seeds directly in the ground after all danger of frost has passed. Start seeds indoors in individual pots two to three weeks before you plan to plant them outside. Acclimatize seedlings to outdoor temperatures over a period of 7 to 10 days before planting them outdoors.

Where Squashes need all-day sun and plenty of water. Soil should be rich in organic matter to retain moisture. Grow the bigger squashes and pumpkins in a large patch where there's no competition for sun or nutrients. Grow bush types in large containers or garden beds. Small-fruited vining types can be grown on trellises.

How Loosen the soil to a depth of 10 to 12 inches and work in 2 to 3 inches of compost or other organic matter. Incorporate a controlled-release fertilizer before planting. Space plants 3 to 5 feet apart in rows 4 to 6 feet apart.

TLC Squashes need an even supply of water—about 1 inch a week. Once plants are established, mulch soil with 2 inches of chopped leaves, grass clippings, or other fine-textured organic material, or cover soil with black plastic to retain moisture and control weeds. Squashes are heavy feeders, requiring regular applications of fertilizer throughout the growing season. Harvest summer squashes while they're still young and tender. Winter squashes and pumpkins must be fully mature before harvesting. Watch for squash bugs and vine borers.

Strawberries

Fresh-picked strawberries have a fragrance comparable to perfume, and are sweet and tart with an intense "berry-ness" superior to those sold in supermarkets. New Jersey and New York are leading producers of strawberries, so you likely will find them easy to grow.

Strawberries are well suited for small gardens. If you don't have room to grow them in mounded rows as farmers do, plant them in raised beds, tubs on a sunny patio, window boxes, hanging baskets, or decorative strawberry pots; you can even grow them as a ground cover (strawberry runners will form a mat).

Strawberry plants are pretty too, with dark green leaves and glossy red fruit. Their dime-size white blossoms resemble single-petaled roses, which is no coincidence; strawberries are in the Rosaceae family, which includes roses and many fruit trees.

Plants classified as June bearers produce their crop from June to July, or during the summer's first heat wave. These are the best type for Tri-State gardeners and the kind I recommend. Day neutrals have largely replaced the old everbearers, but they require much more intensive care. With the exception of trying them in containers, day neutrals are a crop for those gardeners ready for a greater challenge.

PEAK SEASON

June and July

MY FAVORITES

'Allstar'—produces large, orange-red (almost peachy-colored) fruits abundantly and late in the season; 'Cabot'—ripens berries late; 'Cavendish'—ripens berries early in the season, and produces tremendous yields; 'Earliglow'—is an early-season variety with outstanding flavor; 'Honeoye'—ripens in the early part of the season, is very productive, and has a slightly tart flavor; 'Jewel'—ripens late in the season, has good flavor and an attractive rich red appearance; 'Lateglow'—is the standard late-season variety for good quality; and 'Northeaster'—ripens early and usually with higher quality berries than 'Earliglow', the standard of early strawberries.

GARDEN COMPANIONS

Consider locating your strawberries in the same part of the garden as other perennial crops, such as rhubarb and asparagus.

OPPOSITE PAGE: *Remind yourself what real strawberry flavor is by growing your own.* ABOVE RIGHT: *A summer mulch of straw keeps berries clean. It also helps maintain soil moisture and reduce weeds.*

When Plant in spring, after the ground can be worked.

Where Day neutrals are a good choice for strawberry pots, because you'll reap the visual reward of red berries over many months. June bearers do well planted in the matted-row system, in garden rows, and in raised beds. Give plants full sun. If your garden terrain slopes, that's a bonus, as it will enhance drainage. Don't plant strawberries in areas where water settles.

How Soak roots for half an hour or until rehydrated. Dig a hole to accommodate the roots just to the crown, positioning each plant so its crown is slightly above ground level. Plant as a "matted row," spacing 15 to 18 inches apart, in rows about 4 feet apart. Remove flower blossoms the first year, allowing plants to freely form runners.

TLC Strawberries prefer fast-draining, humus-rich soil (slightly acid rather than alkaline). Most soils need generous amounts of compost. Around Thanksgiving, mulch berries with straw or lightweight floating row covers to provide winter protection. Remove straw mulch as soon as you can in March, and remove floating row covers before flowering begins. Keep a straw mulch between the rows to conserve moisture, discourage weeds and pests, and keep fruit from getting splashed with soil. At the end of the strawberry harvest, renovate the planting by setting your lawn mower at its highest setting, and mowing off leaves (really!). Till under plants to re-establish 12- to 18-inch-wide rows. Fertilize lightly at renovation; reddish leaves at this time indicate a nitrogen deficiency. Water if it hasn't rained within the week. Feed potted strawberries monthly with a liquid fertilizer. If birds tend to find the fruit before you do, cover plants with netting. Watch for botrytis gray mold and tarnished plant bugs.

Tomatoes

The cherry tomato 'Sungold' is noted for its excellent flavor. This one is twining up a spiral support.

Every fall after the last of the tomatoes has been harvested, I announce that next year I'm going to plant fewer tomatoes. They're such a rewarding crop, and I simply forget how productive they are. Yet, each gardening season arrives, and there are the early tomatoes and cherry tomatoes, tomatoes for canning and cooking, big beefsteaks for sandwiches, and luscious heirlooms. The choices are dizzying, and all very tempting.

Tomatoes are easy to maintain and care for if you grow what you need, and plant in moderation. The bush (determinate) types get to a certain size and stop growing, then produce tomatoes for a 10-day period. The vining (indeterminate) types are a little more rampant, as they continue to grow and produce until the frost kills them. They need staking and a lot of space, but many gardeners feel that the varieties are worth it.

Tomatoes are quite attractive, especially when you include a range of multi-colored ones. Colors range from white to yellow to red to purple to almost black, and tomatoes may be even variegated and striped.

PEAK SEASON
Midsummer to first frost

MY FAVORITES
Cherry 'Sungold'—considered by many to be the best-tasting cherry tomato.

Grape 'Red Grape'—oblong, firm, and meaty with great taste.

Heirlooms 'Brandywine'—an indeterminate with very large pinkish fruit, moderate yields, and excellent flavor.

'Green Zebra'—early-maturing, green-and-chartreuse-striped heirloom tomato with a zingy flavor.

Main crop 'Better Boy'—midseason indeterminate with large fruit.

'Celebrity'—deep red, medium-sized, globe-shaped fruit; plants are disease resistant and vigorous.

'Northern Exposure'—excellent flavor, determinate, and does well in cooler areas with short seasons.

Paste 'Amish Paste'—tasty fresh or in sauce.

'San Remo'—vigorous plant with large, excellent fruit with few seeds.

GARDEN COMPANIONS
Plant multicolored cherry tomatoes in pots with ornamental peppers. Plant your favorite kitchen companions, such as basil, cilantro, and peppers, nearby.

When Plant tomato plants outside after all danger of frost has passed, on a cloudy day if possible to reduce transplant shock. Sow seeds indoors 6 to 8 weeks before the last frost date.

Where Tomatoes need all-day sun and consistently moist soil. Soil should be fertile and rich in organic matter. Compact bush types can be grown in large containers.

How Harden off seedlings before planting them outside by gradually exposing them to outdoor conditions. Loosen the soil to a depth of 10 to 12 inches and work in 2 to 3 inches of compost or other organic matter. Incorporate a controlled-release fertilizer before planting. Space plants 6 feet apart if allowed to sprawl, 3 feet apart if staked (stake at planting time). Water well, and give each plant a half-cup of starter fertilizer solution.

TLC Tomatoes need an even supply of water—about 1 inch a week. Cracked and deformed fruits with a corky blossom end (called blossom-end rot) are the result of an uneven water supply. Once plants are established, mulch beds with 2 inches of chopped leaves, grass clippings, or other fine-textured organic material, or cover soil with black plastic to retain moisture and control weeds. Tomatoes are moderate feeders, benefiting from light applications of fertilizer or compost throughout the growing season. Don't overdo the nitrogen, however, or you will have all vines and no fruit. All tomatoes grow best if they're staked or caged; it keeps fruits off the ground, increases air circulation around plants, and reduces the chance of infection from soilborne diseases. Harvest fruits when they are evenly colored and slightly soft. Store at room temperature. To ripen green tomatoes, place them in a warm place away from sunlight. Rotate crops each year to avoid pest problems. Plant disease-resistant varieties when you can; watch for leaf spots; they are likely signs of disease. Keep your eyes open for tomato hornworm, whiteflies, aphids, and Colorado potato beetles.

Tomatoes come in many shapes, colors, sizes, and flavors.

Seasonal Chores

You don't have to be an obsessive planner to recognize the virtue of a checklist of seasonal chores. In gardens, what happened last year is very likely to happen again, which is why I've logged the questions that come into the New York cooperative extension office where I work. This list addresses what I've learned to expect each season.

—DAVID CHINERY

Spring

PLANTING

PLANT BARE-ROOT AND CONTAINER PLANTS. Plant bare-root plants, such as cane berries, fruit trees, grapes, roses, and strawberries, as soon as soil is workable. Plants that don't tolerate bare-root transplanting, such as rhododendrons, azaleas, and some conifers, are sold in containers. For tips on planting both kinds of plants, see pages 254 and 255.

OPPOSITE: *'Kwanzan' Japanese flowering cherry blooms in April, after the earliest flowering cherries.*

PLANT SEEDS OR SEEDLINGS of annual herbs, such as basil, cilantro, and dill. Later, deadhead them regularly so they keep producing fresh foliage and don't go to seed.

PLANT SUMMER-FLOWERING PERENNIALS AND ANNUALS in the garden as soon as the soil is warm and workable and there's no danger of a late frost. Pinch leggy plants to encourage bushier growth.

PLANTING A ROSE OR OTHER BARE-ROOT SHRUB

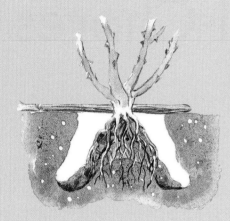

1 Make a firm cone of soil in a planting hole wide enough to fit roots. Spread the roots over the cone, positioning the plant at the same depth that (or slightly higher than) it was in the growing field. Use a shovel handle or yardstick to check the depth.

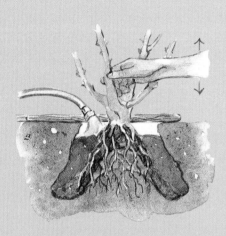

2 Hold the plant upright as you firm soil around its roots. When backfilling is almost complete, add water. This settles the soil around the roots, eliminating any air pockets. If the plant settles below the level of the surrounding soil, pull it up gently while the soil is saturated to raise the plant to the proper level.

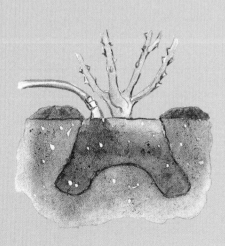

3 Finish filling the hole with soil, then water again. Take care not to overwater while the plant is still dormant, because soggy soil may inhibit the formation of new roots. When the growing season begins, build up a ridge of soil around the planting site to form a basin that will keep water from running off; water the plant whenever the top 2 inches of soil are dry.

SOW SEEDS of lettuces and other cool-weather crops, such as peas, spinach, and cabbage, in early spring. Plant beans, corn, pumpkins, and squash later once soil is thoroughly warmed.

START SEEDS of slower-growing vegetables indoors under fluorescent lights by early April, 6 to 8 weeks before outdoor planting time. Choose both early-maturing varieties, such as 'Early Girl' tomato, and later-ripening types, like 'Brandywine', to extend harvest from weeks to months.

MAINTENANCE

BEGIN LAWN CARE. To thwart crabgrass and other germinating weeds, apply a pre-emergent herbicide, such as corn gluten meal, to your lawn by the time forsythia is in full bloom. Wait until Memorial Day to fertilize. You can start a new lawn or repair an existing one now, but late summer is a better time.

DIVIDE PERENNIALS when new shoots have poked up through

the soil. Early spring (or fall) is a good time to divide mid- to late-summer bloomers, such as daylilies, delphiniums, phlox, daisies, irises, asters, and rudbeckia. Wait to divide early-spring bloomers until they've finished flowering. Peonies, Siberian irises, and other plants with fleshy roots should be divided in fall.

FERTILIZE PERENNIALS with a controlled-release fertilizer. Or try this organic formulation: 1 tablespoon fish emulsion and ½ teaspoon seaweed or kelp in a gallon of water. Water with this mixture every few weeks during growing season.

GIVE PLANTS TIME. Don't be too hasty to pronounce a bare plant dead. Some plants, in-cluding rose of Sharon, butter-fly bush, and some ornamental grasses, are very slow to devel-op new foliage in the spring. If in doubt, scratch the bark and bend a twig; healthy twigs are pliable and green inside.

LOOK FOR FREEZE-THAW DAMAGE. Young plants may have been heaved out of the soil. Push the uprooted plants

PLANTING A CONTAINER PLANT

Place the container on its side and roll it on the ground while tapping it to loosen the roots. Up-end the container and slide the plant out. Cut off any badly coiled roots.

1 Dig a planting hole at least twice as wide as the rootball and slightly shallower, and spread the roots out over the central plateau of firm soil. Adjust the plant until it sits an inch or so above the surrounding soil.

2 Backfill the hole with the unamended soil that you dug from the hole. (Amending the soil will only encourage the roots to circle around the plant instead of probing outward in search of nutrients.)

3 Mound the soil to create a ridge around the plant to direct water to the roots. The trunk should not be directly exposed to water or it may rot. Irrigate gently.

back into the ground, tamp the soil lightly with your foot, and add a layer of mulch.

PRUNE ROSES by cutting out dead or crossing canes and weak growth.

PRUNE EARLY-FLOWERING SHRUBS like forsythia after they've finished blooming. For light shaping, simply cut back the longest shoots. To rejuvenate large, old shrubs, cut one-third of each shrub's oldest branches to the ground, then cut the remaining branches to a third of their previous height.

FERTILIZE TREES AND SHRUBS that grew poorly last year or suffered winter injury. Use an acidic fertilizer for rhododendrons, azaleas, and blueberries.

GROOM SPENT BULBS. Snap off spent flowers of spring bulbs, but allow the leaves to wither naturally before cutting them off. This gives bulbs time to store energy for next year's blooms.

USE CAGES OR RINGS TO STAKE BUSHY PERENNIALS, such as peonies, before they bloom. Hollyhocks, lilies, delphiniums,

and other tall plants with heavy blooms can be tied to bamboo stakes. Plant tall, skinny plants next to sturdier ones that they can lean on for support.

PREPARE VEGETABLE BEDS by removing weeds and spreading 2 to 4 inches of compost over the surface. When the soil is dry, rototill it to a depth of 6 inches, or turn it over by hand.

PRUNE FLOWERING CHERRY, PLUM, AND PEACH TREES after they have bloomed. To discourage canker diseases, prune when weather is predicted to be dry and over 60°F/16°C for several days.

PRUNE PINES. Prune new shoots on pines (called "candles") by shortening them one-third to one-half their length. This helps to shape the trees and creates denser growth.

PRUNE APPLE AND PEAR TREES in late winter or very early spring before the buds begin

OPPOSITE: *Flashy orange and yellow tulips are backed by a tulip-themed fence. Cool-colored pansies and forget-me-nots are lower-growing color complements.*

HOW TO STAKE VARIOUS PLANTS

Support thin-stemmed, bushy perennials with a grid (upper left) or stakes and string (bottom left). Tie tall plants to a bamboo stake (right).

to swell. Avoid making many small cuts, which encourages excessive leaf growth, when taking off a larger branch will do.

SPRAY FRUIT TREES. Before buds swell, apply horticultural oil to fruit trees and ornamentals with previous insect problems to kill pests before the growing season starts.

THIN SEEDLINGS that you started indoors, and gradually acclimate them to outdoors by placing them in a sheltered location for a few hours a day before transplanting outdoors.

Summer

PLANTING

SOW SEEDS of warm-season crops, such as corn and beans, directly into the garden.

START A NEW LAWN. August and September are the best months to start a new lawn. After a soil pH test, spread the required lime or sulfur, a starter fertilizer high in phosphorus, and 2 to 4 inches of compost. Rototill to a depth of 6 inches, firm the soil lightly by rolling, and spread the seed. Cover the area with weed-free straw or other mulch and keep the soil slightly moist, checking daily. Be patient! Perennial ryegrass germinates in about a week, fescues in two, and Kentucky bluegrass in three weeks or more.

MAINTENANCE

CHECK RHODODENDRONS, blueberries, and pin oaks for signs of iron deficiency (chlorosis). Yellow leaves with deep green veins are an indicator. Spraying leaves with a foliar spray containing iron is a temporary solution. Testing soil pH, and correcting it if necessary, provides long-term results.

CUT BACK EARLY-BLOOMING PERENNIALS. After flowers are spent, cut back by one-third perennials such as catmint, dianthus, foxglove, and hardy geraniums, to promote growth of fresh leaves and flowers. Later in summer, shear perennials such as purple coneflower,

Foxglove flower spikes grow to 5 feet high or more. Cut off the main flowering stem after flowers fade to encourage flowering side shoots.

rudbeckia, and phlox after they've finished flowering. This will keep your garden looking tidy and encourage plants to put on fresh growth. Discontinue shearing in early fall.

DEADHEAD ANNUAL FLOWERS. Remove the spent flowers of annuals to promote re-blooming.

PRUNE ROSES. Climbing and pillar roses can be thinned again in midsummer after the flowers have faded by cutting out the flowering canes close to the roots. After blooms have died on a hybrid tea or floribunda rose, cut the stem just above a leaf with five leaflets, which will encourage the development of a new flowering shoot.

PRUNE SUMMER-BLOOMING SHRUBS, like potentillas and hydrangeas, for shape after they've flowered.

PINCH PERENNIALS. Some perennials, such as chrysan-themums, border phlox, bee

Close planting, mulch, and frequent, light cultivation will keep you ahead of weeds in early summer. Here, white Siberian iris, snapdragons, and lamb's ears show off.

balm, and 'Autumn Joy' sedum can be pinched or sheared to delay their bloom period and create a denser plant. Try it with a few to test your results!

STAY AHEAD OF WEEDS. Keep bare spots between plants weeded until plants fill in. Dig out deep-rooted weeds like dandelions with a hand weeder or trowel. Use a hoe to pull up weeds with shallow roots.

259

STOP FERTILIZING TREES AND SHRUBS so that new growth has time to develop hardiness before winter.

STRATEGIZE TO STOP SLUGS. Place a board or rock on the ground; squash or drown in soapy water the slugs that congregate underneath. Bands of diatomaceous earth will discourage their travel. Slugs are also attracted to saucers of beer; they fall in and drown.

TREAT POWDERY MILDEW on zinnias, phlox, and bee balm when temperatures are below 85°F/29°C by spraying the leaves with this home remedy: 1 tablespoon *each* of baking soda and horticultural oil in 1 gallon of water.

WATCH FOR PESTS. Look for drooping, twisted, chewed, or discolored foliage, which may indicate an insect problem.

Check the undersides of leaves and use a hand lens if the culprit is not readily apparent. Low-toxicity products, such as insecticidal soap, horticultural oil, and neem, control many pests with little environmental impact. Read the label to make sure that the product will control the pest and that it is safe to use on the infested plant.

WATER CONTAINER PLANTS. Keep container plants well watered and fertilized. You may need to water plants

daily in dry weather. Watering leaches nutrients from the soil, so fertilize at least once a week unless you've applied a controlled-release fertilizer.

WATER DURING DROUGHTS. Most plants need at least 1 inch of water per week to flourish in hot summer conditions. If rainfall provides less, irrigate as needed. Conserve water by using soaker hoses and collected rainwater. Water in early morning; evening sprinkling can cause fungal problems.

OPPOSITE PAGE: *By late summer, shrubs such as oak-leaf hydrangea (rear) take center stage along with 'Sunny Border Blue' speedwell (Veronica).* RIGHT: *On a shady patio, coleus and tuberous begonia thrive in containers.*

Fall

PLANTING

PLANT COLD-HARDY ANNUALS.
Pansies, chrysanthemums, and flowering cabbages are excellent for late-season color. Also, cover hardy perennial mums with mulch by late fall.

PLANT SPRING BULBS such as tulips, daffodils, anemones, hyacinths, and Siberian squill in mid-October. If you're planting bulbs in masses, an auger greatly speeds the process of digging holes. Or plant bulbs by excavating the entire bed to the proper depth. Add bulb fertilizer when planting. Mark the locations of your bulbs so you don't mistakenly dig them up, and so you'll know if any are missing come spring. Complete most planting by late October, but tulips can go in as late as November.

PLANT TREES AND SHRUBS. Fall planting encourages root development and lets plants get established before spring. Roots will grow as long as the soil temperature is above 40°F/4°C. Keep new plantings well watered until winter.

TRANSPLANT DECIDUOUS TREES AND SHRUBS after they've gone dormant but before the ground freezes hard. Dormant plants are less likely to suffer from transplant shock. Dig as wide a rootball as possible, and stake large trees and shrubs.

MAINTENANCE

CHECK FOR GRUBS. Cut out a 1-square-foot section of lawn and examine the roots and soil. Grubs are white and **C**-shaped, and have six legs. More than five grubs per section examined indicates a population large enough to warrant control. If action is necessary, treat your entire lawn with predatory nematodes, a non-toxic and effective control. After application, keep lawn moist to aid control.

CLEAN UP PLANT DEBRIS. Put most dead and dying plants on the compost heap, but put weeds that have seeds attached and plants that are diseased in the trash.

COLLECT AND COMPOST LEAVES. Compost fallen leaves that aren't used to mulch beds. Or shred them with a lawn mower and leave them to decompose on the grass.

DIG UP TENDER BULBS. Bring dahlia, gladiolus, and tuberous begonia bulbs indoors after the first frost kills leaves. Let dahlia roots dry in the sun for several hours, then divide multiple roots with a sharp knife, cutting through the stem base. Allow begonia tubers to dry for several weeks before dividing them. Store in plastic bags filled with peat moss in a cool place (40° to 50°F/4° to 10°C) until spring, checking periodically to make sure they don't dry out.

DIVIDE PERENNIALS WITH FLESHY ROOTS, such as peonies, Oriental poppies, and Siberian irises, if they show signs of overcrowding. Divide other perennials now, as long as there's a month before the first killing frost so that roots have time to establish before plants go dormant.

Exploding into fiery color in fall, the sugar maple is one of the most dominant native trees of northeastern forests and gardens.

Spidery seed heads of flowering alliums combine with 'Autumn Joy' sedum and coleus.

KEEP WATERING your garden as needed as long as it's warm enough to keep a garden hose outside. When temperatures dip to freezing, drain the hoses, store them inside, and turn off outdoor spigots.

LABEL PERENNIALS. Mark the positions of perennials with durable tags so you won't disturb their roots when you plant bulbs in late fall or work in the garden in spring.

LOOK FOR GYPSY MOTH. Check tree trunks and limbs, buildings, and fences for tan gypsy moth egg cases. Scrape off and destroy if possible.

MOVE HOUSEPLANTS INDOORS. In the evening bring in houseplants and tender container plants such as geraniums, tuberous begonias, and fuchsias, as nighttime temperatures may drop precipitously at this time of year.

FERTILIZE LAWNS. If you only want to fertilize once a year, this is the time to do it! The best time is right around Labor Day. If you can, apply fertilizer again, about the time you mow for the last time of the season in November. At that time, use a "winterizer" type fertilizer.

GROOM PERENNIALS. Cut down ratty-looking perennials. Leave those with good fall color and attractive seed heads until spring if you wish. Many ornamental grasses look beautiful in winter as well.

MULCH FOR WINTER. Once the ground is frozen, add a thick layer of mulch over marginally hardy perennials such as butterfly bush and blood grass. This helps keep soil temperatures even, which helps prevent plants from being uprooted in a freeze-thaw cycle.

PROTECT EVERGREENS from drying out in winter through a combination of sun, wind, and too little snow cover. Spray them with an antidessicant to reduce transpiration. Use burlap screens in windy places, and wooden "tepees" below roofs where snow and ice fall.

PROTECT ROSES. Tender hybrid tea and floribunda roses planted in exposed areas are susceptible to frost. Protect them with one of three barriers: A mound of soil over the crown of the bush; a tar-paper or wire-mesh collar around the plant and filled with peat moss, pine bark mulch, or straw; or a plastic rose cone purchased from a garden center placed over the plant.

SHOP FOR BARGAINS. Shop at nurseries now to get some of the best bargains on trees, shrubs, and perennials that still need a home. If you don't have a place to plant them, completely sink the containers in the vegetable garden or other open space and the plants will survive winter.

In fall, reds and golds fill gardens. Here, red-leaved flowering dogwood trees complement asters and chrysanthemums.

Winter

PLANNING AND PLANTING

PLACE ORDERS FOR SEEDS AND PLANTS. When the seeds arrive, mark packets with optimum sowing dates for your area. Calculate these dates by using the number of days from germination to maturity—usually printed on the packets—and factoring in the average spring and fall frost dates in your area. Prepare for indoor seed-starting by collecting peat pots and other necessary equipment.

PLAN NEXT SEASON'S PROJECTS. Draw a diagram and write up a plant list. Winter is a good time for reflection on successes and failures as well as future projects. Use a garden journal to record your ideas and thoughts for next spring.

PLANT INDOOR AMARYLLIS. For a cheerful winter display, pot up amaryllis bulbs and place them on a sunny windowsill.

MAINTENANCE

CHECK STORED BULBS AND ROOTS. Check up on stored tubers and tuberous roots to make sure they are not drying out. Sprinkle water over them to keep them moist (but not wet) if necessary.

CHECK MULCH. If there is no snow cover, check on your winter mulch, adding more as necessary.

Winter weather brings a different kind of beauty into gardens. Even freezing rain can be an asset, such as when it coats fruits of tea crabapple (Malus hupehensis).

CLEAN AND OIL GARDEN TOOLS. Slide shovels and forks up and down in a large bucket of sand with a little oil to clean them, or use steel wool and a wire brush. Sharpen shovels, hoes, and pruning tools with a file or sharpening stone.

PRUNE FRUIT TREES in late February or March, before buds begin to swell.

SERVICE LAWN MOWER. Now's a convenient time of year to give your lawn mower a tune-up. Change the oil, air filter, and spark plug. Have the blade sharpened at the hardware store or mower repair shop, or replace the blade with a new one.

STORE BIRD SEED in steel or plastic garbage cans with tight-fitting lids to foil mice and insect pests.

WASH OFF HOUSEPLANTS. Put your houseplants in the bathtub and give them a shower periodically to remove dust.

In winter, when annuals and perennials are gone or invisible, permanent plants are welcome. 'Heritage' river birch offers the rich texture of peeling bark. The evergreens include rhododendrons and dwarf conifers.

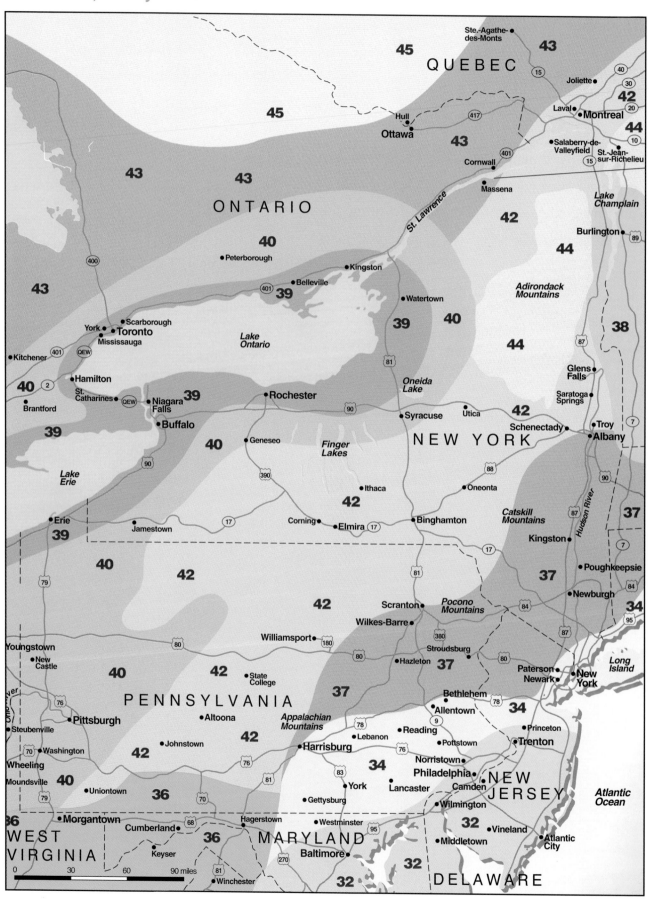

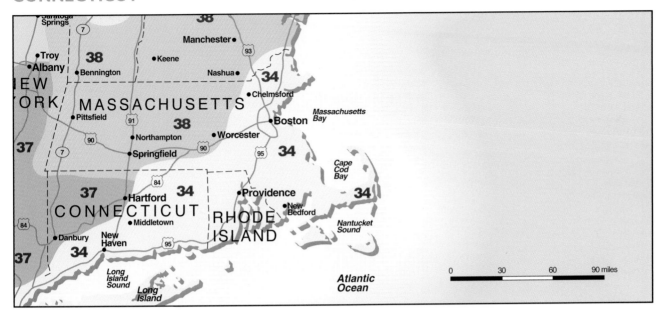

SUNSET'S GARDEN CLIMATE ZONES

A plant's performance is governed by the total climate: length of growing season, timing and amount of rainfall, winter lows, summer highs, humidity. Sunset's climate zone maps take all these factors into account—unlike the familiar hardiness zone maps devised by the U.S. Department of Agriculture, which divide the U.S. and Canada into zones based strictly on winter lows. The USDA zones tell you only where a plant may survive the winter; our climate zone maps let you see where that plant will thrive year-round. Below are brief descriptions of the nine zones found in New York, New Jersey, and Connecticut.

Zone 32, Southern New Jersey. *Growing season:* late March to early November. Rain falls year-round (40" to 50" annually); winter lows are 30° to 20°F/–1° to –7°C.

Zone 34, Lowlands and Coast, Long Island. *Growing season:* late April to late October. Ample rainfall and humid summers are the norm. Winters are variable—typically fairly mild (around 20°F/–7°C), but with lows down to –3° to –22°F/–19° to –30°C if arctic air swoops in.

Zone 37, Hudson Valley and Appalachian Plateau. *Growing season:* May to mid-October, with rainfall throughout. Lower in elevation than neighboring zone 42, with warmer winters: lows are 0° to –5°F/–18° to –21°C, unless arctic air moves in. Summer is humid and warm to hot.

Zone 38, New England Interior. *Growing season:* May to early October. Summers feature reliable rainfall and lack oppressive humidity of lower-elevation, more southerly areas. Winter lows dip to –10° to –20°F/–23° to –29°C, with periodic colder temperatures due to influxes of arctic air.

Zone 39, Shoreline Regions of the Great Lakes. *Growing season:* early May to early October. Springs and summers are cooler, autumns milder than in areas farther from the lakes. Lows reach 0° to –10°F/–18° to –23°C.

Zone 40, Inland Plains of Lake Erie and Lake Ontario. *Growing season:* mid-May to mid-September, with rainy, warm, variably humid weather. The lakes help moderate winter lows; temperatures typically range from –10° to –20°F/–23° to –29°C, with occasional colder readings.

Zone 42, Interior New York and St. Lawrence Valley. *Growing season:* late May to late September. This zone's elevation gives it colder winters than surrounding zones: lows range from –20° to –40°F/–29° to –40°C. Summers are humid and rainy.

Zone 43, Northernmost New York and Southern Ontario. *Growing season:* late May to mid-September. The climate is humid from spring through early fall; summer rains are usually dependable. Arctic air dominates in winter, with lows typically from –20° to –30°F/–29° to –34°C.

Zone 44, Northeastern New York. *Growing season:* June to mid-September. Latitude and elevation give fairly cool, rainy summers, cold winters with lows of –20° to –40°F/–29° to –40°C.

Index Pages listed in *italics* include photographs.